Contents

Treading Lightly in the Wild **6-7**
Regional Map **8-9**
An Invitation to Explore **10-13**
Big and Beautiful **14-15**

Southeast 16

Map **18** Inside Passage **22** Misty Fiords
National Monument **28** Anan Wildlife
Observatory **32** Creek Street **33**
Deer Mountain Trail **36** Alaska Raptor
Center **37** Admirality Island National
Monument-Kootznoowoo Wilderness **38**
Tracy Arm-Fords Terror Wilderness **46**
Mendenhall Glacier **48** Mount Roberts **50**
Point Adolphus **50** Glacier Bay National
Park and Preserve **52** Alaska Chilkat Bald
Eagle Preserve **59** Chilkat State Park **61**
Klondike Gold Rush National Historical Park
62 Chilkoot Trail **65** Russell Fiord Wilder-
ness **68** Lituya Bay **73**

South Central 74

Map **76** Wrangell-St. Elias National Park and
Preserve **80** Nabesna Road **87** Prince
William Sound **88** Thompson Pass **94**
Chugach National Forest **96** Kayak
Island **100** Chugach State Park **102**
Alaska Native Heritage Center **108** Tony
Knowles Coastal Trail **110** Kincaid Park **112**
Potter Marsh **113** Seward Highway **114**
Kenai Fjords National Park **119** Mount
Marathon **125** Alaska SeaLife Center **125**
Caines Head State Recreation Area **127** Fox
Island **128** Kenai River **129** Kenai National
Wildlife Refuge **130** Kachemak Bay State
Park and Wilderness Park **134** Iditarod
National Historic Trail **139** Nancy Lake
State Recreation Area **144** Independence
Mine State Historical Park **146** Denali State
Park **148** Denali Highway Scenic Drive **154**
Delta Wild and Scenic River **158**

The Interior 160

Map **162** Denali National Park and
Preserve **166** Nenana to Fairbanks Scenic
Drive **181** Creamer's Field Migratory
Waterfowl Refuge **182** Chena River State
Recreation Area **185** Chatanika River
Recreation Site and Area **187** White
Mountains National Recreation Area **188**
Steese National Conservation Area **192**
Tetlin National Wildlife Refuge **195**
Yukon-Charley Rivers National Preserve **196**

Southwest 200

Map **202** Lake Clark National Park and
Preserve **206** McNeil River State Game
Sanctuary **211** Katmai National Park and
Preserve **214** Kodiak Island Archipelago **220**
Walrus Islands State Game Sanctuary **225**
Wood-Tikchik State Park **230** Alaska
Maritime National Wildlife Refuge **233**

The Arctic 238

Map **240** James Dalton Highway **244**
Arctic National Wildlife Refuge **252** Gates
of the Arctic National Park and Preserve **260**
Noatak National Preserve **266** Kobuk Valley
National Park **268** Cape Krusenstern
National Monument **272** Seward
Peninsula **273** Bering Land Bridge National
Preserve **275**

Other Sites **280**
Resources **281-283**
Index **284-287**
About the Author and Photographer **287**
Illustrations Credits **287**
Credits **288**

Cover: Kayaking on Byers Lake, Denali State Park
Page 1: A brace of grizzly bear cubs in Katmai National Park
Pages 2-3: Sunset on Punchbowl Lake, Misty Fiords National Monument
Opposite: Backcountry snowboarder scaling Worthington Glacier

Treading Lightly in the Wild

Sitka spruce, Point Adolphus

NATIONAL GEOGRAPHIC GUIDE TO AMERICA'S OUTDOORS: ALASKA takes you from the watery wonderland of the Inside Passage and Prince William Sound over the skyscraping Alaska and Brooks Ranges to the wide-open spaces of the Arctic. Packed with parks, forests, wilderness areas, lakes, and wildlife refuges, Alaska is a sparsely populated immensity tailored to the outdoors enthusiast.

Visitors who care about this region know they must tread lightly on the land. Ecosystems can be damaged, even destroyed, by thoughtless misuse. Many have already suffered from the impact of tourism. The marks are clear: litter-strewn acres, polluted waters, trampled vegetation, and disturbed wildlife. You can do your part to preserve these places for yourself, your children, and all other nature travelers. Before embarking on a backcountry visit or a camping adventure, learn some basic conservation dos and don'ts. Leave No Trace, a national educational program, recommends the following:

Plan ahead and prepare for your trip. If you know what to expect in terms of climate, conditions, and hazards, you can pack for general needs, extreme weather, and emergencies. Do yourself and the land a favor by visiting if possible during off-peak months and limiting your group to no more than four to six people. To keep trash or litter to a minimum, repackage food into reusable containers or bags. And rather than using cairns, flags, or paint cues that mar the environment to mark your way, bring a map and compass.

Travel and camp on solid surfaces. In popular areas, stay within established trails and campsites. Travel single file in the middle of the trail, even when it's wet or muddy, to avoid trampling vegetation. Be particularly sensitive in boggy or coastal areas, and avoid stepping on mussels, sea stars, and the like. When exploring off the trail in pristine, lightly traveled areas, have your group spread out to lessen impact. Good campsites are found, not made. Travel and camp on sand, gravel, or rock, or on dry grasses, pine needles, or snow. Remember to stay at least 200 feet from waterways. After you've broken camp, leave the site as you found it.

Pack out what you pack in—and that means *everything* except human waste, which should be deposited in a hole dug away from water, camp, or trail, then covered and concealed. When washing dishes, clothes, or yourself, use small amounts of biodegradable soap and scatter the water away from lakes and streams.

Be sure to leave all items—plants, rocks, artifacts—as you find them. Avoid potential disaster by neither introducing nor transporting non-native species. Also, don't build or carve out structures that will alter the environment. A don't-touch policy not only preserves resources for future generations; it also gives the next guy a crack at the discovery experience.

Keep fires to a minimum. It may be unthinkable to camp without a campfire, but depletion of firewood harms the backcountry. When you can, try a gas-fueled camp stove and a candle lantern. If you choose to build a fire, first consider regulations, weather, skill, and firewood availability. At the beach, build your fire below the next high-tide line, where the traces will be washed away. Where possible, employ existing fire rings; elsewhere, use fire pans or mound fires. Keep your fire small, use only sticks from the ground, burn the fire down to ash, and don't leave the site until it's cold.

Respect wildlife. Watch animals from a distance (bring binoculars or a telephoto lens for close-ups), but never approach, feed, or follow them. Feeding weakens an animal's ability to fend for itself in the wild. If you can't keep your pets under control, leave them at home.

Finally, be mindful of other visitors. Yield to fellow travelers on the trail, and keep noise levels low so that all the sounds of nature can be heard.

With these points in mind, you have only to chart your course. Enjoy your explorations. Let natural places quiet your mind, refresh your spirit, and remain as you found them. Just remember, leave behind no trace. ■

MAP KEY and ABBREVIATIONS

National Park	N.P.
National Historical Park	N.H.P.
National Historic Site	N.H.S.
National Monument	NAT. MON.
National Park & Preserve	N.P. & PRES.
National Recreation Area	N.R.A.
National Forest	N.F.
State Forest	S.F.
National Wildlife Refuge	N.W.R.
Bald Eagle Preserve	
Game Sanctuary	
National Conservation Area	N.C.A.
State Game Refuge	S.G.R.
State Wildlife Sanctuary	S.W.S.
Wildlife Refuge	
State Park	S.P.
Provincial Park	P.P.
State Historical Park	S.H.P.
State Recreation Area	S.R.A.
State Recreation Site	S.R.S.
Indian Reservation	I.R.
National Wild & Scenic River	N.W. & S.R.

U.S. Interstate or Trans-Canada Highway — State or Provincial Highway — Other Road

(5) (16)   (1) (37)

Ferry   Inside Passage   Canoe Trail

Trail   Railroad   Pipeline

Continental Divide

BOUNDARIES
STATE, PROVINCIAL, or NATIONAL

FOREST   N.P.   WILD.

POPULATION

● SEATTLE	above 500,000
● Anchorage	50,000 to 500,000
● Juneau	10,000 to 50,000
• Haines	under 10,000

ADDITIONAL ABBREVIATIONS

Cr.	Creek
Fk.	Fork
Gl.	Glacier
HWY.	Highway
I.-s.	Island-s
L.	Lake
M.	Middle
M.A.	Management Area
MEM.	Memorial
Mt.-s.	Mount-ain-s
N.H.L.	National Historic Landmark
N.H.T.	National Historic Trail
Pen.	Peninsula
PKWY.	Parkway
Pt.	Point
R.	River
RD.	Road
R.R.	Railroad
Sanc.	Sanctuary
Terr.	Territory
TR.	Trail
WILD.	Wilderness

▢ Point of Interest	╫ Falls		
✹ State capital	Intermittent Lake		
+ Elevation	Glacier		
⟩⟨ Pass	Swamp or wetland		
△ Campground	}-{ Tunnel		

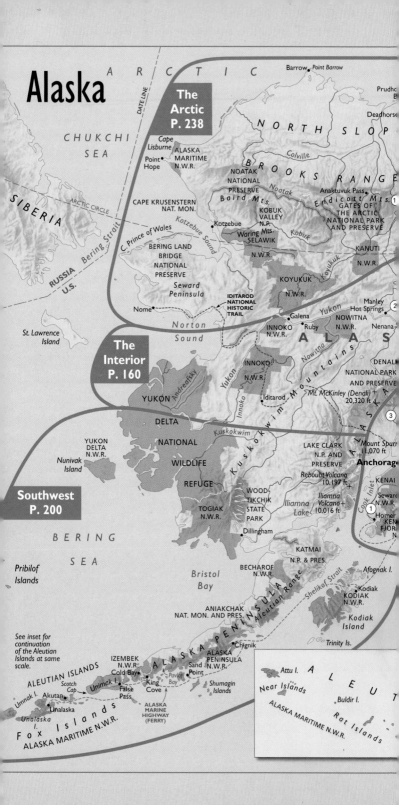

Alaska

The Arctic P. 238

The Interior P. 160

Southwest P. 200

A R C T I C

Barrow • Point Barrow

Prudh Ba

Deadhorse

N O R T H   S L O P

CHUKCHI SEA

DATE LINE

SIBERIA

Cape Lisburne

Point Hope

ALASKA MARITIME N.W.R.

Colville

B R O O K S   R A N G E

Baird Mts.

Noatak

NOATAK NATIONAL PRESERVE

Anaktuvuk Pass

Endicott Mts.

GATES OF THE ARCTIC NATIONAL PARK AND PRESERVE

CAPE KRUSENSTERN NAT. MON.

ARCTIC CIRCLE

C. Prince of Wales

Kotzebue Sound

Kotzebue

KOBUK VALLEY N.P.

Waring Mts. SELAWIK N.W.R.

Kobuk

KANUTI N.W.R.

RUSSIA
U.S.

Bering Strait

BERING LAND BRIDGE NATIONAL PRESERVE

Seward Peninsula

KOYUKUK N.W.R.

Koyukuk

Manley Hot Springs

St. Lawrence Island

Nome

IDITAROD NATIONAL HISTORIC TRAIL

Norton Sound

Galena

Ruby

Yukon

INNOKO N.W.R.

A L A S

NOWITNA N.W.R.

Nenana

Nowitna

DENALI NATIONAL PARK AND PRESERVE

YUKON

Andreafsky

Yukon

INNOKO N.W.R.

Innoko

Iditarod

Kuskokwim Mountains

Mt. McKinley (Denali) 20,320 ft

DELTA

NATIONAL

WILDLIFE

REFUGE

Kuskokwim

Mount Spurr 11,070 ft

YUKON DELTA N.W.R.

Nunivak Island

LAKE CLARK N.P. AND PRESERVE

Redoubt Volcano 10,197 ft

Anchorage

WOOD-TIKCHIK STATE PARK

TOGIAK N.W.R.

Iliamna Lake

Iliamna Volcano 10,016 ft

KENAI N.W.R.

Seward

KENAI FJOR

Dillingham

Cook Inlet

Homer

B E R I N G   S E A

Pribilof Islands

Bristol Bay

KATMAI N.P. & PRES.

BECHAROF N.W.R.

Aleutian Range

Shelikof Strait

Afognak I.

Kodiak

KODIAK N.W.R.

Kodiak Island

Trinity Is.

ANIAKCHAK NAT. MON. AND PRES.

A L A S K A   P E N I N S U L A

Chignik

See inset for continuation of the Aleutian Islands at same scale.

IZEMBEK N.W.R.
Cold Bay

ALEUTIAN ISLANDS

Scotch Cap

Umnak I.

Akutan

Unalaska

Unalaska I.

Unimak I.

False Pass

King Cove

Sand Point

ALASKA PENINSULA N.W.R.

Pavlof Bay

Shumagin Islands

ALASKA MARINE HIGHWAY (FERRY)

F o x   I s l a n d s

ALASKA MARITIME N.W.R.

Attu I.

Near Islands

A L E U T

Buldir I.

Rat Islands

ALASKA MARITIME N.W.R.

NUNAVUT

O C E A N

B E A U F O R T   S E A

• Kaktovik

Mackenzie Bay

ARCTIC

NATIONAL

WILDLIFE

REFUGE

IVVAVIK NATIONAL PARK

VUNTUT N.P.

• Inuvik

N O R T H W E S T

Phillip Smith Mts.

Wind

Sheenjek

Old Crow •

T E R R I T O R I E S

Mackenzie

ARCTIC CIRCLE

Great Bear Lake

Bell

Porcupine

Chandalar

8

• Fort Yukon

YUKON FLATS N.W.R.

Circle •

WHITE MTS. N.R.A.

STEESE

6

N.C.A.

• Fairbanks

YUKON-CHARLEY RIVERS NAT. PRES.

Charley

Ogilvie Mts.

Eagle •

5

M a c k e n z i e   M o u n t a i n s

S e l w y n   M t s.

K A

R A N G E

Delta Junction •

2

Tanana

• Tok

5

Dawson
9

Klondike

Yukon

2

Y U K O N

4

U.S.

C A N A D A

4

1

TETLIN N.W.R.

T E R R I T O R Y

Susitna R.

1

Wrangell Mts.

WRANGELL-ST. ELIAS N.P. & PRES.

ALASKA HIGHWAY

1

• Whitehorse

1

C h u g a c h

4

Mts.

Mt. Logan 19,551 ft +

KLUANE N.P & RESERVE

2

B R I T I S H

Valdez •

CHUGACH N.F.

ST. ELIAS

Bering

3

C O L U M B I A

• Cordova

Mt. St. Elias 18,008 ft

M O U N T A I N S

Skagway •

A
L
A
S
K
A

Prince William Sound

Montague I.

Yakutat Bay

TONGASS

• Haines

GLACIER BAY N.P. & PRES.

Juneau ✪

ALASKA MARINE HIGHWAY (FERRY)

C O A S T   M O U N T A I N S

South Central P. 74

G u l f   o f   A l a s k a

N

NATIONAL

Chichagof I.

ADMIRALTY ISLAND NAT. MON.

37

Southeast P. 16

Sitka •

ALEXANDER

Kupreanof I.

INSIDE PASSAGE

37A

• Stewart

MISTY FIORDS NAT. MON.

0   miles   200

0   kilometers   300

Baranof Island

ARCHIPELAGO

FOREST

Maurelle Is.

Revillagigedo I.

Ketchikan •

Prince of Wales I.

U.S.

P A C I F I C   O C E A N

Forrester I.

CANADA

QUEEN

CHARLOTTE

ISLANDS

Umnak I.

B E R I N G   S E A

Islands of Four Mountains

I A N   I S L A N D S

ALASKA MARITIME N.W.R.

Andreanof Islands

P A C I F I C   O C E A N

An Invitation to Explore

I'VE HAD A LOVE AFFAIR with Alaska for 25 years.

As with most love affairs, this one has had a few roller-coaster rides. Like the time I traveled the Iditarod Sled Dog Race trail from Ruby to Galena; it was –55°F, I couldn't feel my hands, my feet stung with cold, and the wind blew in my face for hours. Or the time an old hand near the Wrangell Mountains promised me I could get a chocolate milkshake once I got to Nabesna, which entailed a ten-day slog through wet tus-socks and the worst mosquitoes I've ever seen; Nabesna turned out to be a ghost town. Or the time I went on assignment to cover combat fishing in the seining fleet in the Southeast; a storm blew up, I got deathly seasick, and two kindly fishermen from Petersburg had to hold me by my knees over the side of theirfishing boat.

Or, finally, there was the time I went to the Brooks Range on a romantic

Chena River State Recreation Area

notion to ski after the migration of the caribou. The herd went down a different valley that year. I was camping outside Anaktuvuk Pass. The villagers were so eager to spot any caribou that one morning as I went to chip ice off the stream to boil for tea, a bullet zinged by my ear. Someone thought—at least from a distance—I looked good enough to eat.

But even the worst times in Alaska have been grand adventures. In the main, it's been a glorious ride.

Although this is a book about the many jewels of Alaska—the small twinkling emeralds and the big impressive diamonds—it is also a window into the magic that is Alaska. Part of that magic is the people who live here and the people like yourself who come to explore.

For many, the classic image of the rugged Alaskan is a huge, Paul Bunyanesque character with Popeye muscles, striding the landscape. For me, however, the man who best personifies this place was short and slight, with an elfin grin and twinkling eyes—a man known affectionately (and not just a little bit reverently) as the Father of the Iditarod Sled Dog Race, the late Joe Redington, Sr. And, I wager, most Alaskans would agree with me.

"Alaska," a friend told me many years ago, "is so awesome, so much more extreme than anywhere else—higher, deeper, colder, lighter longer—yet instead of making you feel puny, it encourages you to be more of who you are." In many ways, you have to live up to the landscape here. You have to respect it. If you don't, you'll either be lucky or you'll die.

This introduction, then, is really an invitation to come and be more of who you are—to revel in the beauty, to feel the magic. It's also a thank-you to my two teammates on the project, who kept me laughing throughout. What greater pleasure could one experience than to be in a beautiful place with magnificent creatures and share in wonderful camaraderie?

An important first rule of the wilderness is "Always know your guides or be prepared to fend for yourself," so let me introduce my fellow guides. My coauthor, Tom Walker—nicknamed "Wilderness Walker" by an admiring newspaper reporter—is a tall, spare woodsman who lives in a cabin on the outskirts of Denali National Park. Sometimes stern and forbidding to the uninitiated, Tom commands an impressive array of talents. He has an encyclopedic knowledge of Alaska. A former big-game guide, he is now known in the north as a superb wildlife photographer. Tom is also a master artist who has built more than 30 exquisite log cabins and written the definitive book on the craft. As the deadline for this book approached, Tom's e-mails and phone calls to me got funnier and funnier. Often they contained his proposed solution to any problem in life: chocolate milkshakes.

Photographer Michael Melford, who lives on an island in Mystic, Connecticut, arrived in Alaska with a tall order: Shoot the state in four months. We all had a good laugh at that notion, for this is a country where storms can maroon you on the Walrus Islands for days or weather can pin you down in the Aleutians for weeks. Here winter comes early and breakup is late. Yet Michael darted about this huge state like Peter Pan on speed, covering thousands of miles with minutes to spare. With a little finesse and a lot of collusion by the Fates, he kept on schedule. His eyes were never still—always taking in the light, the color, the movement, the promise—as he looked for the perfect picture. His mantra: "Every day, a miracle!"

Because Michael has photographed all over the world, I asked him if he ever got jaded watching animals he'd seen many times before. At this, he grew uncharacteristically serious. "Never," he said. "To see an animal in the wild is a gift." For the most part, though, when taxed with too many questions about the essence of life too early in the day, Michael's solution was the same as Tom's: chocolate—an extra dose in his morning coffee!

So you see, it is clearly the chocolate and the beauty that bind us all together on these adventures. We wish you the same happy combination.

Nan Elliot

Don't try this at home: Dog paddling in Prince William Sound

Floatplane on Lake Hood

Big and Beautiful

Scale and diversity foil all who try to simplify Alaska. Its immense and ceaseless grandeur numbs the mind, glazes the eye, and plagues the writer who would describe it. The intellect cannot close the suitcase on this subcontinent. Always a spare peninsula or archipelago or coastal plain dangles out after the sweaty struggle to buckle the straps.

—William E. Brown, *This Last Treasure: Alaska's National Parklands*

ALASKA IS SUCH A VAST TREASURE CHEST that choosing the gems tucked into the pages of this book was a jeweler's fantasy—and dilemma. A few of the sites we've chosen to profile are easy to get to; most are not. The journey there, however, will surely be as compelling as the route to the summit or the path through the forest to the edge of a turquoise lake.

Have we done every place justice? Hardly. This is but a sneak preview. Each jewel in Alaska's crown—be it a single peak, a lone trail, a 1000-mile stretch of coast, a roaring glacier, or a river of salmon patrolled by hungry brown bears—is a gift to be unwrapped, layer by layer. Each of us brings to the experience of this land his or her own curiosity, wildness, sense of adventure, and delight.

What we can tell you is that Alaska is big—really big. There are 365 million acres here. As one state resident points out, "If you were to explore 1,000 acres a day, 365 days of the year, it would take you 1,000 years to uncover all of Alaska."

An Italian geographer once visited the University of Alaska to observe the design of the state's regional atlases. The diversity of the state amazed him. "Alaska," he declared, "is like six different countries in Europe all under the same flag." He was correct—and then some. From the treeless tundra in the north, where the Arctic Ocean freezes in winter, Alaska stretches 1,500 miles south to a temperate coastal rain forest whose mountains rise sheer from the sea. From the Coast Mountains to Attu Island, Alaska is nearly as wide as the lower 48. And with the tip of its Aleutian chain crossing the International Date Line, Alaska is at once the most northern, the most western, and the most eastern state in the Union.

We've divided this grand drama into five regions. Southeast stretches 600 miles along a narrow mainland from Dixon Entrance in the south to Icy Bay in the north. A flight over the southeast would reveal an intricate network of fjords, waterways, snowcapped peaks, ancient ice, and dense forests. Off the coast are hundreds of mountainous islands; some are the largest in the United States, while others are just rocky pinnacles rising out of crashing surf. These shelter an inland waterway that is the main transportation corridor to the north country. With no roads to southeast Alaska except the ones at its northern edge that lead into Alaska's interior, access is by plane or boat.

South Central is the product of Alaska's grand and tumultuous nature. Tectonic activity is high here, causing frequent earthquakes, tsunamis, and volcanoes. Active volcanoes—part of the Ring of Fire stretching toward the heart of Siberia—rise out of Cook Inlet and dominate the Wrangell Mountains. The land is laced with mountain ranges, glacier systems, and wide river valleys. Two of the state's largest rivers—the Susitna and Copper—course down the region's western and eastern boundaries.

Crowning the Interior is the highest mountain in North America, Mount McKinley, which the Athapaskans call Denali ("the high one"). Bounded by the mystical white Alaska Range to the south and the primeval Brooks Range to the north, the interior is famous for its its winter darkness and cold—two powerful forces to be reckoned with. Temperatures in the interior routinely plunge far below zero; the coldest temperature ever recorded in Alaska (−80° F) was at Prospect Creek.

Remote, lonely, and awe-inspiring is the Southwest, with its mountains, river deltas, rolling treeless tundra, and chain of volcanic islands curving out through the Gulf of Alaska and into the Bering Sea. Wildlife refuges, national parks, and wild and scenic rivers abound here. Storms are ferocious, the wind never ceasing.

Far to the north, the Arctic is breathtaking in regal style. From the Brooks Range—the "range of blue light"—the land sweeps flat to the Arctic Ocean. Sky dominates. The light of the midnight sun has an unearthly quality. In summer at Point Barrow, the sun does not set for 84 days; in winter it does not rise for 67 days. Vast herds of caribou roam the tundra. Mosquitoes swarm in legions. And in a land where the sea is frozen most of the year, the polar bear is king.

Amid so much spectacular country, where to begin? A good strategy is to pick one place to explore in depth, knowing that you are experiencing one of the planet's last great wilderness treasures. The majesty, peace, and solitude you find will almost certainly inspire you to help protect the wild places of the north. ■

Southeast

Cruise ship near Ketchikan

IN 1879, THAT RUGGED SCOT and renowned preservationist
John Muir came north to explore southeast Alaska. He
was astonished by what he saw. The grandeur of the forests and islands, the majesty of the glacier-clad mountains
and ice-filled fjords—all seemed to live "still in the morning of creation." For Muir, this was "the very paradise of
poets." He wrote so eloquently about Glacier Bay, one of
the region's most spectacular locations, that within ten
years steamships were hauling in the first visitors. Today,

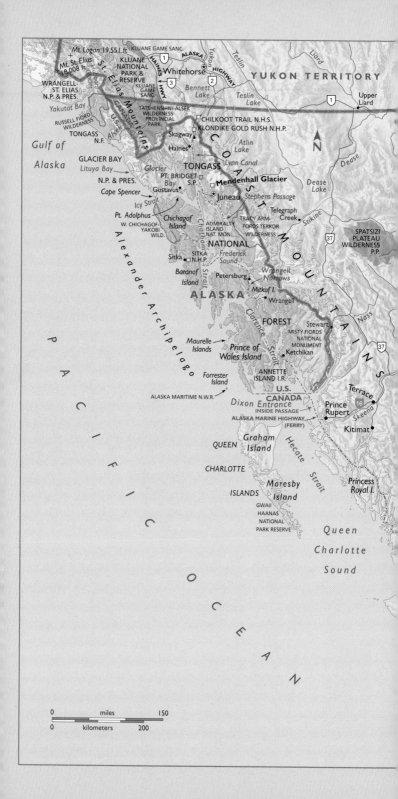

Mt. Logan 19,551 ft
KLUANE GAME SANC.
Mt. St. Elias
18,008 ft
WRANGELL-
ST. ELIAS
N.P. & PRES.
KLUANE
NATIONAL
PARK &
RESERVE
HAINES HWY.
ALASKA HWY.
Whitehorse
Yukon River
Teslin
YUKON TERRITORY
Liard
KLUANE GAME
SANC.
Bennett
Lake
Teslin
Lake
Upper
Liard
Yakutat Bay
RUSSELL FIORD
WILDERNESS
TONGASS
N.F.
TATSHENSHINI-ALSEK
WILDERNESS
PROVINCIAL
PARK
St. Elias Mountains
Alsek
Tatshenshini
CANADA
CHILKOOT TRAIL N.H.S.
KLONDIKE GOLD RUSH N.H.P.
Skagway
Haines
Atlin
Lake
Lynn Canal
Dease
Lake
Dease
Gulf of
Alaska
GLACIER BAY
Lituya Bay
N.P. & PRES.
Cape Spencer
Pt. Adolphus
Glacier
Glacier
PT. BRIDGET
S.P.
Gustavus
Icy Strait
TONGASS
Mendenhall Glacier
Juneau
Stephens Passage
Telegraph
Creek
Stikine
SPATSIZI
PLATEAU
WILDERNESS
P.P.
W. CHICHAGOF-
YAKOBI
WILD.
Chichagof
Island
ADMIRALTY
ISLAND
NAT. MON.
Chatham Strait
TRACY ARM
FORDS TERROR
WILDERNESS
NATIONAL
Frederick
Sound
Wrangell
Narrows
37
Sitka
SITKA
N.H.P.
Baranof
Island
Petersburg
Mitkof I.
Wrangell
ALASKA
FOREST
Stewart
MISTY FIORDS
NATIONAL
MONUMENT
Ketchikan
Nass
37
Alexander Archipelago
Maurelle
Islands
Prince of
Wales Island
Forrester
Island
ANNETTE
ISLAND I.R.
U.S.
ALASKA MARITIME N.W.R.
Dixon Entrance
CANADA
INSIDE PASSAGE
ALASKA MARINE HIGHWAY
(FERRY)
Prince
Rupert
Terrace
Skeena
Kitimat
P A C I F I C
QUEEN
CHARLOTTE
ISLANDS
Graham
Island
Moresby
Island
GWAII
HAANAS
NATIONAL
PARK RESERVE
Hecate
Strait
Clarence Strait
Princess
Royal I.
Queen
Charlotte
Sound
O C E A N

N

0   miles   150
0   kilometers   200

Glacier Bay is a national park. But the rest of southeast Alaska—that narrow strip of shoreline bounded on the east by the steep Coast Mountains and on the west by the stormy North Pacific Ocean—is almost completely encompassed within the boundaries of Tongass National Forest. Tongass—an old-growth, temperate rain forest of Sitka spruce, western hemlock, and cedar—is the largest national forest in the United States. Stretching about 600 miles north from Dixon Entrance to Yakutat Bay, Tongass covers nearly 17 million acres, more than a third of it designated as wilderness.

"Wilderness," as defined by the Wilderness Act of 1964, is land that retains "its primeval character"—a place where humans are only visitors. Of the 19 wilderness areas in Alaska's national forests, Misty Fiords National Monument (more than two million acres) is the largest, while Maurelle Islands Wilderness (just under 5,000 acres) is the smallest. This chapter introduces you to four of these unique wilderness areas: Misty Fiords in southern Alaska on the border of Canada, Kootznoowoo on Admiralty Island, Russell Fiord in the northeastern Gulf of Alaska, and Tracy Arm-Fords Terror south of the state's capital, Juneau.

The water between the islands and the mainland is known as the Inside Passage. The following pages invite you to take a guided "virtual cruise" of this waterway. Unlike other parts of coastal Alaska, the sea here does not freeze in winter. Instead, it is warmed by the strong Kuroshio current from Japan. The ice is never far away, however. Tucked up at the head of many of the fjords are massive glaciers that seem to tumble out of the mountains and into the sea. These glaciers calve the occasional icebergs that float out into the Inside Passage.

Bergs are not the only objects that break the surface of the water. Every summer, to the delight of residents and tourists alike, hundreds of humpback whales return from their breeding grounds off Hawaii to bulk up on the tiny marine creatures that proliferate in these cold, northern waters. To watch one of these 35-ton creatures breach the surface and then throw itself backward into the water with a crash is an unforgettable sight. Be on the lookout for humpbacks diving and feeding in all the popular waterways of the Southeast, whether your vessel of choice is a cruise ship, a ferry, or a kayak. In particular, watch for the leviathans in Chatham Strait and Sitka Sound, in Icy Strait around Point Adolphus, and in Glacier Bay, Frederick Sound, and Stephens Passage, as well as off-shore in the open ocean.

Swimming in from the ocean every year, all five species of Pacific salmon fight the currents to make their way upriver to spawn. Awaiting their annual return are the world's densest concentrations of brown bears, bald eagles, and anglers. On Admiralty Island—where you can visit Pack Creek, paddle Seymour Canal, or simply walk the beaches—there's about one brown bear, or grizzly, per square mile and one bald eagle's nest per mile of coast. If you miss the eagles here, head to the Alaska Chilkat Bald Eagle Preserve outside Haines. There you'll find the world's largest gathering of bald eagles, which fly in each November to feed on a salmon banquet.

The product of thousands of years of tectonic activity, the Coast Mountains march northward parallel to the Gulf of Alaska, rising ever higher until they reach the St. Elias Mountains, the world's tallest coastal mountain chain. Mount St. Elias (18,008 feet) is the second highest peak in Alaska. (The tallest, Mount McKinley—Denali—at 20,320 feet, is also the highest summit on the continent .) Here you will find the magnifi-cent Hubbard Glacier, the longest valley glacier in North America. Also on the gulf coast is Lituya Bay, an enchanting microcosm of nearly every all geologic hazard the North Pacific Ocean can muster.

Most visitors experience the Coast Mountains by flight-seeing. For a more immediate experience of just how imposing—and steep—these mountains are, strike out on foot along the Chilkoot Trail, part of Klon-dike Gold Rush National Historical Park.

Recreational opportunities in the Southeast are boundless. In addition to the whale-watching mentioned above, there's luxury cruising, glacier and wildlife viewing, ice climbing, mountaineering, helicopter-hiking, kayaking, sailing, backpacking, camping, fishing, parasailing, and beach-combing. So pick a spot on the map, and pack an adventurous spirit. Be sure to bring your fleece and rain jacket, too: Southeast weather is cool at best, even in summer. More often, it's damp and downright bone chilling. After all, there's a reason this forested area is so green: It receives 50 to 200 inches of rain a year. ■

Sitkoh Bay and Chichagof Island

Inside Passage

■ 900 nautical miles ■ From Vancouver, British Columbia, to Skagway, Alaska
■ Best months May-Aug. ■ Sailing, kayaking, sportfishing, whale-watching, glaciers ■ Fishing license required ■ Contact Southeast Alaska Discovery Center,
Ketchikan, AK, phone 907-228-6220; or Alaska Department of Fish and Game,
phone 907-486-4791; or Forest Service Information Center, Juneau, AK, phone
907-586-8751. www.fs.fed.us/r10/tongass

BY WAR CANOE, BRIGANTINE, FISHING BOAT, ferry, cruise ship, sailboat, kayak,
wooden dory, oceangoing rowing shell, and even floating bicycle, people
have explored the protected waterways of the Inside Passage of Canada
and Alaska for hundreds of years. Twenty-five years ago, for example,
two adventurous souls unwittingly pioneered a new way to navigate these
waters. Rowing a Grand Banks dory from Seattle, Washington, to Glacier
Bay, Alaska, the young men put in to shore late one night and pitched

Bow of the *M.V. Observer*, Inside Passage

their tent on the British Columbia coast. Little did they know that they had set up camp on a beach lying below the high-tide line of a coast with some of the highest tides in the world. By midnight the sea was lapping at their seam-sealed, watertight tent. As the waters continued to rise—and with the two adventurers still fast asleep inside—the tent gently floated out toward the shipping lanes of the North Pacific Ocean.

Most visitors who sail the Inside Passage today choose a slightly more seaworthy vessel: a cruise ship from Vancouver, British Columbia, to the head of the inland waterway at Skagway, Alaska. Hundreds of islands buffer these inside waters from the storms and swells of the Pacific. Slipping through straits, sounds, and passages, oceangoing cruise ships press on into smaller canals and arms, and from there into even tighter inlets and narrows, to linger in the region's bays and harbors. Sailing these waters can be tricky. Summer fog and passing vessels, swift currents and tidal rips, whirlpools and icebergs, sandbars and suckholes—these are just some of the navigational challenges of the Inside Passage.

What to See and Do

The first day out of port, cruise ships sail through the **Strait of Georgia,** passing over the infamous **Ripple Rock** and on up the east coast of **Vancouver Island.** Now 47 feet below the water's surface at low tide, Ripple Rock used to be one of the deadliest marine hazards on the Pacific coast. This underwater mountain ripped into the hulls of more than a hundred ships and claimed 114 lives before its demolition by the Canadian government in 1958.

Dangerous waters, indeed: Sailors once called the western coast of Vancouver Island the Graveyard of the Pacific—testament to the sunken ships that litter the ocean floor there. In response to the demands of mariners, the first lighthouse in the region was built in 1873 at Cape Beale, at the southern entrance to Barkley Sound. Today, dozens of lighthouses dot the coastlines of the Inside Passage. Though most are automated, some of the Canadian ones still have lighthouse keepers.

Sailing up **Johnstone Strait** in July and August, cruise ship passengers may see pods of orcas (killer whales), which return each summer to massage themselves on the beach rocks at **Robson Bight.** Wander the beaches anywhere along this coast at low tide and you'll understand the local saying, "When the tide is out, the table is set." The sea here is rich with salmon, cod, crab, and halibut, and at low tide the exposed shores abound with all manner of edible sea life, including mussels, clams, and seaweed.

In the more open waters of **Queen Charlotte Sound,** hundreds of Dall's porpoises and Pacific white-sided dolphins may swim alongside your ship. To tell them apart, look for the creatures that gracefully leap clear of the water; these are apt to be dolphins. Gregarious and fast, dolphins often ride the bow waves of the ship. Dall's porpoises, though also fast swimmers, are rarely so acrobatic; they almost never show their flukes. From a distance, the black-and-white markings of the porpoises are often mistaken for those of orcas. There the similarity ends, however; the porpoise weighs in at 300 pounds, whereas the orca can top 8 tons.

Alaska waters begin at **Dixon Entrance.** From here, ships sail along the east side of **Prince of Wales Island,** the largest island in Alaska after Kodiak. If you are on a small cruise ship or a ferry, your vessel may be able to skinny its way through the **Wrangell Narrows,** a slice of water about 21 miles long that flows into Frederick Sound. Although this route cuts about 65 miles off your journey, it may well take you longer: The shallow water and the tide ebbing and flooding from both ends of the narrows set up dangerous riptides. Navigators carefully choose their times between high and low tide; if there's fog, they'll often wait for the next tide. More than 70 navigational markers guide ships through, their red, green, and white blinking lights earning the waterway the nickname Christmas Tree Lane.

Sitka spruce, Baranof Island

Any time you're sailing through narrow passages, you may hear the ship's naturalist urging the passengers to "Look for the golf balls high up in the trees!" It's an old and effective trick that helps passengers spot the white heads of bald eagles among the branches. A threatened species elsewhere in North America, these magnificent birds thrive in Canada and Alaska, where their population is estimated at 30,000 to 40,000. Ravens are plentiful, too. There's little need to "look for the hockey pucks high up in the trees"; these birds are everywhere. Renowned for their intelligence, ravens are the pranksters of the mythological realm. In the traditional stories of the Tlingit, Haida, and Tsimshian peoples of southeast Alaska, Raven is a very special character. Known as the Creator, he stole the sun, moon, and stars—and so brought light to a dark world.

While strolling or jogging around the decks of your cruise ship, scan the surface of the ocean for humpback whales. The 15-foot-high vapor plume, or spout, of the humpback is far more visible than the plume of most other whales. The humpback almost always shows its tail flukes before it dives, the markings on the underside of which are as distinctive as human fingerprints. (Indeed, they are the means by which scientists track these enormous endangered creatures through the oceans of the world.) **Frederick Sound** and **Stephens Passage** are both good whale-watching venues.

On the eastern side of **Admiralty Island** (see pp. 38-41 and 44-46), be sure to scan the beaches for another spectacular mammal: bears. The Tlingit people call the island Kootznoohoo, or "fortress of the bears." Early Russian explorers called it the Island of Fear. More brown bears live here per square mile than anywhere else in the world, with the possible exception of the Alaska Peninsula—the finger of land in southwestern Alaska that extends out to the Aleutian Islands.

Lynn Canal is a long, straight waterway from the tip of Admiralty Island to the head of the Inside Passage at Skagway, a Tlingit name meaning "home of the north wind." Skagway sits in a rain shadow that receives only 30 inches of precipitation a year—far less than most other southeast sites. What Skagway lacks in rain, however, it makes up for in wind. Here your saltwater journey ends and the road to Alaska's interior begins.

Plan Your Trip

The **Southeast Alaska Discovery Center,** just off the cruise ship dock in Ketchikan, and the **Forest Service Information Center** in Juneau have films, displays, and exhibits. For trip planning, they offer notebooks about backcountry travel, trails, and public-use cabins in **Tongass National Forest** (see below). In Juneau, you can obtain permits for viewing bears at Pack Creek on Admiralty Island. For other permits, contact the Forest Service Information Center.

Big Blue Canoes

With no roads connecting southeast towns and villages, water is the main means of transportation. Everybody—even visiting circus elephants—travels by ferry. Ferries provide a fun way to get out on the water and see fjords and whales while you're en route to towns and fishing hamlets. For a recorded schedule, call 907-465-3940.

Alaska's blue-hulled state ferries, known as big blue canoes, give you a cruise ship experience at a fraction of the cost. For reservations, contact Alaska Marine Highway *(P.O. Box 25535, Juneau, AK 99802. 800-642-0066. www .dot.state.ak//external.amhs).*

Cabin Stays

For an intimate experience of Tongass National Forest and the Inside Passage, rent a rustic cabin—the best deal in Alaska. Tongass offers more than 150 recreational and remote public cabins for $25 to 45 a night. To reach them, you'll have to hike, paddle, or fly. (Some air charters charge $1,000 for a drop-off and pickup.) The cabins sit in alpine meadows, on beaches, near lakes, or at the edges of streams. Some are in prime fishing territory, while others are close to hot springs. For information, contact the National Recreation Reservation Service *(877-444-6777. www.reserveusa.com).* ∎

Breaching humpback whale

Gentle Giants

Whales—huge, mysterious creatures that travel great distances and live in all seven oceans of the world—seem to galvanize humans. Often we see only a flash of them: a flipper, a tail fluke, a vapor plume, an arced segment of back as one swims away. Yet the biggest whale (the blue) is larger than any creature that has ever lived on Earth—and that includes the dinosaurs. At 150 tons, the blue whale weighs as much as 33 African elephants. With seven stomachs, it can eat more than a million calories a day. Its blood vessels are so large that a person could swim right through them.

Like us, whales are mammals: They are warm blooded, breathe air into their lungs, and propagate by live births. Not always have they been revered as gentle giants, however: Whaling ships once plied the world's oceans, hunting down the creatures for their oil-rich blubber, which lit lamps all over the globe. Some of the leviathans earned a not-so-gentle reputation for fighting back. In fact, sailors nicknamed the gray whale "devil fish" for its tendency to turn and attack pursuing ships.

As a result of so much commercial hunting, all of the great whales (except the gray and the minke) are now on the endangered species list. However, scientists have not reliably determined just how many whales there are. "It's a big ocean and water covers most of the planet," explains one marine biologist. "Even in whale country, you can fly for days and because of bad weather or fog you might not see one whale. There is much about whales we don't know."

Fifteen of the world's great whales swim through Alaska waters: the sperm, gray, minke, fin, sei, blue, humpback, bowhead, right, killer, beluga, goosebeak, Bering Sea beaked, giant bottlenose, and narwhal. From the vantage point of a ferry, a cruise ship, or a kayak cruising the coastal waters, you are most likely to spot the black fins of orcas (killer whales) or the acrobatic displays of humpbacks.

Every year, humpback whales make an extraordinary odyssey between their breeding grounds off Hawaii and their rich summer feeding grounds in Alaska. Here they bulk up on schools of herring and small, shrimplike creatures known as krill. Thus do whales, the world's largest creatures, draw their sustenance from some of the planet's very smallest.

Misty Fiords National Monument

- 2.3 million acres ■ 22 miles east of Ketchikan ■ Best months May-Aug.
- Camping, hiking, boating, kayaking, fishing, flight-seeing ■ Access by air or boat only; no visitor facilities ■ Contact Ketchikan-Misty Fiords Ranger District, Tongass National Forest, 3031 Tongass Ave., Ketchikan, AK 99901; phone 907-225-2148. www.fs.fed.us/r10/tongass

MANY CAPTAINS AND SHIP PILOTS remember a time when the "misty fjords" were known only by their individual names—**Rudyerd Bay, Walker Cove, Boca de Quadra.** But in 1978, by presidential decree, these waterways and the surrounding rain forest, lakes, and peaks were christened Misty Fiords National Monument, becoming part of the multiple-use **Tongass National Forest.** At the stroke of a pen, everything within the boundaries of Misty Fiords National Monument was granted fully protected wilderness status.

And what a wilderness it is. There are no visitor facilities here, so you'll have to bring with you everything you could possibly need: tide book, topographic maps, nautical charts, compass, matches, stove, tent, food, and warm clothes. You'll also need rain gear: Misty Fiords receives an average of 160 inches of rainfall a year. Mist and fog will be your frequent companions—even in May and June, when you have the best chance of seeing some sun.

Seen from a boat, the sheer, 3,000-foot-high granite walls of Misty Fiords can resemble the stony pinnacles of Yosemite. Seen from the air, however, the national monument is more like leprechaun country—rolling, rumpled muskeg filled with mountain goats, pocket-size lakes, and waterfalls cascading and tumbling in lacy patterns down long rocky faces to tidewater, or draining one series of alpine lakes into another. In the northernmost corners of Misty Fiords, ancient glacial ice still exists, a reminder of the mighty force that sculpted this beauty.

If you sail up **Behm Canal,** you'll come across an odd pillar of rock rising 230 feet out of the middle of the channel just before you enter Rudyerd Bay. This is **New Eddystone Rock,** a stone fortress that is actually the eroded remains of an extinct volcano. Exploring these waters in 1793, Royal Navy captain George Vancouver named the volcanic plug for its resemblance to the lighthouse on Eddystone Rock in the English Channel.

Nearly half of the Southeast's wild population of chinook (king) salmon are born in Misty Fiords and return every year to spawn. Chinook salmon can be found in the Wilson Arm and its tributaries, the Blossom and Wilson Rivers.

Loon

Opposite: Floatplane on Punchbowl Lake, Misty Fiords NM

Trail to Punchbowl Cove, Misty Fiords NM

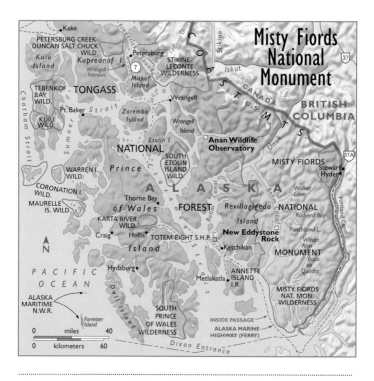

What to See and Do

The grandeur of Misty Fiords National Monument lies in its tranquillity. With thousands of cruise ship tourists docking in Ketchikan every summer, however, it has become a special flight destination. Alas, the drone of small planes is now a familiar sound. Most visitors opt for the one- to two-hour flight-seeing packages, touching down on one of the mountain lakes, or a cruise/fly package from Ketchikan to Rudyerd Bay.

To really slow down your clock, charter a flight to a remote Forest Service cabin in Misty Fiords and stay a few days—or go in with a kayak (*Southeast Exposure, 907-225-8829*). You can also charter a flight that will drop you and your kayak off at your cabin. A good place to start is the **Southeast Alaska Discovery Center** (*907-228-6220*), near the cruise ship dock in Ketchikan. Consult the staff in the trip-planning room for water, weather, and safety information.

Just a few hiking trails thread Misty Fiords National Monument. Among the most popular is the path from **Punchbowl Cove** to **Punchbowl Lake** (1 mile), in the south-central part of the monument. The trail clambers up into alpine lake country, which echoes in early summer with the haunting call of loons. Tiny carnivorous sundew plants grow in the muskeg and acidic bogs here. Their leaves are like glue—handy for snaring their prey of spiders, gnats, and mosquitoes. ■

Anan Wildlife Observatory

■ 35 miles southeast of Wrangell ■ Best months mid-July–mid-Aug. ■ Wildlife viewing ■ Access by aircraft or boat only ■ Contact Wrangell Ranger District, Tongass National Forest, P.O. Box 51, Wrangell, AK 99929; phone 907-874-2323. www.fs.fed.us/r10/tongass/recreation/rec_facilities/ananobservatory.html

RARELY DO THE BROWN BEARS and black bears of southeast Alaska frequent the same feeding areas. (Black bears tend to avoid the larger, more aggressive browns.) However, both species share **Anan Creek,** an ancient Tlingit fishing site that is the largest pink salmon run in the Southeast; it holds as many as 100,000 fish. Brown bears fish upstream in early morning and late evening, while black bears snag salmon on the lower river at midday.

With up to 40 black bears fishing Anan Creek, the site is one of the best places in North America to watch the free-ranging critters up close. A covered viewing pavilion is located just beyond the observatory entrance. You may not see a bear when you first arrive; then, just when you think none are around, a shadow will suddenly emerge from the thickets and grab a salmon out of a dark pool. At other times the bears perch in plain view on mossy boulders or logs.

Food, pets, and camping are prohibited. You may overnight only if you've reserved the Anan Bay public-use cabin. Call the National Recreation Reservation Service at 877-444-6777 to book this highly sought-after cabin up to 180 days in advance; the maximum stay is one week. Air- and boat-charter services in Wrangell and Ketchikan offer day-long and half-day trips for groups of up to eight. For guided trips, contact Alaska Waters Inc. (*P.O. Box 1978 Wrangell, AK 99929. 907-874-2378 or 800-347-4462*) or Stickeen Wilderness Adventures (*P.O. Box 934, Wrangell, AK 99929. 907-874-2085 or 800-874-2085*). ■

Carnivorous sundew plants

Creek Street

■ Half-mile boardwalk to dirt trail ■ Downtown Ketchikan ■ Salmon run in midsummer ■ Walking, bird-watching, wildlife viewing ■ Contact Ketchikan Visitors Bureau, 131 Front St., Ketchikan, AK 99901; phone 907-225-6166. www.visit-ketchikan.com

IN THE HEYDAY OF SALMON, Creek Street was the heartbeat of the rough-and-tumble fishing town of Ketchikan. Built on pilings along the salmon-rich waters of **Ketchikan Creek,** the street was (and remains) nothing more than a wooden boardwalk leading to the brightly painted bawdy houses of such legendary madams as Black Mary and Big Dolly Arthur.

Creek Street, according to a popular saying, was where "both fish and fishermen went up the creek to spawn." A more covert option was the **Married Man's Trail**—a muddy, backdoor path through the woods to the Creek Street establishments. The Married Man's Trail was only partially successful, however: Its habitués were easy to identify by their muddy boots and trouser legs.

Today the legendary runs of salmon are gone, as are the prostitutes and the town fathers who protested their presence. Your route to Creek Street is Stedman Street across from Thomas Basin. For the Married Man's Trail, cross the bridge over Ketchikan Creek on Park Avenue; a sign at the bridge bids you welcome. The boardwalk at Creek Street lies just beyond.

In July and August, take time to linger at the bridge to watch salmon school below the falls. As you watch the fish leap up the falls or navigate the fish ladder alongside, it's hard not to admire the strength and determination with which they power their way upriver. Their payoff is the chance to spawn in the still headwaters of the creek.

Make sure to watch for bald eagles as well: Ketchikan comes from a Tlingit word meaning "wings of the thundering eagle." Scan the tops of dead spruce trees for the birds' white heads. Later in summer, you'll see bald eagles swooping and diving for their favorite meals—the dead and dying fish that are known as spawned-out salmon. ■

Alaska Airways

Waterfowl fly in a V to avoid midair collisions, but this skein also creates an aerodynamic wedge that saves each bird's energy. In the V of Canada geese, for example, each bird rests its wing tip on the vortex of air, or slipstream, rising from the bird's wing in front of it. This enables geese in formation to fly 71 percent farther than a lone goose making the same effort.

Yet geese in flight don't always maintain this aerial pace line, so the echelon may serve a social function as well: It allows young birds to memorize migratory routes, feeding grounds, and predator avoidance strategies.

Totem Poles

Detail, totem pole

LIKE THE CRESTS of medieval knights of Europe, the totems of southeast Alaska declared a family's glory and greatness.

Totems—which traditionally faced out to sea—served other purposes, too. Some were erected for potlatches—great gatherings for feasting, dancing, and the sharing of wealth. Other totems honored the dead. Still others, known as "ridicule" poles, were commissioned by chiefs as a form of public reprimand, perhaps for someone who had not paid a debt or fulfilled an obligation.

Totem poles were never meant to be worshiped, nor were they intended to last forever. Carved from soft, durable cedar trees, they stood in place for the life span of a human (about 60 years or so) before exposure to the stormy weather of the Southeast took its toll. When people had occasion to leave their villages and move elsewhere, they left the poles behind to topple and rot.

As your eye travels up one of these carved cedars, you will see a series of stylized faces—the magical and powerful creatures of forest, sea, and sky. The peoples of southeast Alaska—the Tlingit, Haida, and Tsimshian—have a special relationship to the natural world. Tribe members belong to one of two major groups, the Ravens or the Eagles. Within these groups are clans, each represented by another creature such as the grizzly bear, salmon, orca, wolf, frog, or mosquito.

Since the 1930s an effort has been under way to preserve some of the old totems. There has also been a renaissance in the art of carving new ones. In several places in the Southeast you can see these totems in village settings and watch master carvers at work.

Saxman Totem Park, 3 miles south of downtown Ketchikan on the South Tongass Highway, is a working village. A grand avenue of totem poles—believed to be the largest collection in the world—leads up the hill to the park. For a two-hour guided tour, contact Cape Fox Tours *(907-225-4846).*

The **Totem Heritage Center** *(601 Deermount St. 907-225-5900)* in Ketchikan houses an exceptional collection of old totem poles. Ten miles to the north, on North Tongass Highway, you'll find **Totem Bight State Historical Park.** The park is a recreation of a village site in a beautiful natural setting, right at the edge of the sea. For more information, call the Alaska State Division of Parks and Outdoor Recreation in Juneau *(907-465-4563).*

A ferry or plane ride up the Inside Passage will take you to Sitka, on the

Totem pole in Saxman Totem Park

west coast of Baranof Island—and **Sitka National Historical Park** (*106 Metlakatla St., Sitka, AK 99835. 907-747-6281. www.nps.gov/sitk*). The crowning glory here is the lovely two-mile coastal trail, along which are exhibited numerous totem poles. The trail weaves through forest and along-side river and beach.

In the park, real-life ravens call back and forth overhead. Bald eagles swoop low over the ocean. Then, through the dark but sun-dappled forest, another kind of raven and another kind of eagle appear: Perched high and immobile, their carved cedar faces, as well as those of other animals—frogs, beavers, bears—blend seamlessly into the forests from which they came. ■

Deer Mountain Trail

■ 5 miles long ■ Behind downtown Ketchikan ■ Year-round ■ Hiking, back-packing, bird-watching ■ Contact Southeast Alaska Discovery Center, 50 Main St., Ketchikan, AK 99901; phone 907-228-6220. www.fs.fed.us/r10/tongass

OLD-TIMERS IN KETCHIKAN JEST, "If you can't see the top of Deer Mountain, it's raining. If you *can* see the top of Deer Mountain, it's about to rain." **Deer Mountain** (3,001 feet) is not only Ketchikan's landmark and most popular peak, it is also the town's barometer. One of the soggiest places in all of the Southeast, the town gets about 13 feet of rain a year. Townsfolk say a downpour of nearly 18 feet in 1949 burst the "Liquid Sunshine Gauge" that once stood on the dock.

If you have the rare fortune to visit on a sunny day, make the most of it. The Deer Mountain trailhead is a 30-minute walk from downtown— at the top of Fair Street on Revillagigedo Island. (You can also take a taxi.) But even on a rainy day, the huge canopy of the rain forest—cedar, hemlock, and spruce—protects you from getting too wet. The trail is well maintained with wooden boardwalks, stairs, and bridges, and should take you about four hours to reach the summit. Your very first steps will immerse you in the rain forest experience. Listen for the call of ravens: Their gentle *kloo-klok* sound is distinctive to this black bird that native peoples call the Creator. The raven also makes a kind of hollow, knocking sound that resonates in the forest. Bald eagles are plentiful here, too.

You don't have to go all the way to the top to enjoy the journey, however. The first overlook (a small break in the trees) can be reached in about 45 minutes. Just another mile beyond that takes you above tree line for great views over **Clarence Strait.** ■

Waterfall along Deer Mountain Trail

Bald eagle

Alaska Raptor Center

■ 17 acres ■ Sitka ■ Year-round ■ Bird-watching ■ Adm. fee ■ Contact the center, 1101 Sawmill Rd., Sitka, AK 99835; phone 907-747-8662 or 800-643-9425. www.alaskaraptor.org

VOLTA COLLIDED WITH A POWER LINE. Spike ate a four-inch nail. Gauche sustained a gunshot wound to her left wing. Sunset got electrocuted and was rescued as the sun was going down. Summer and Solstice lost their parents and arrived at the center close to the longest day of the year.

All of these wild "patients" are bald eagles and eaglets. But many other raptors—including golden eagles, peregrine falcons, red-tailed hawks, and great horned and short-eared owls—receive treatment here.

Raptors are defined as birds of prey. Their name comes from the Latin *rapere,* to seize. Indeed, that action best describes the dramatic hunting style of these birds as they plunge from the sky to snatch their prey. Raptors share other characteristics as well. They all have extremely keen eyesight, powerful talons, and hooked beaks that make it easy for them to rip and tear into fur and flesh. Raptors move so swiftly that their victims are usually unaware of their impending doom.

Deadly though they are, raptors themselves lead a precarious existence. Studies show that about 50 percent of them die in their first year out of the nest. Although human activities are partly responsible for this, the young birds' inexperience also plays a role: Misjudging distances can cause fatal accidents. Collisions with trees, poles, boats, or electrical wires can result in a broken wing or leg.

For a raptor, this is a death sentence—unless, by some stroke of good fortune, the bird ends up here at the Alaska Raptor Center. Over the years, the center has successfully returned hundreds of raptors to the wild. As a visitor, you'll be able to tour the facility, see these magnificent creatures up close, and observe the exercise sessions that help prepare and rehabilitate the birds for their eventual release. Tours are offered daily in the summer. ■

Admiralty Island National Monument-Kootznoowoo Wilderness

■ 937,000 acres ■ 15 miles west of Juneau ■ Best months May-Oct. ■ Camping, boating, kayaking, canoeing, fishing, whale-watching, wildlife viewing ■ Access by ferry, small boat, canoe, kayak, or aircraft ■ Contact the monument, 8461 Old Dairy Rd., Juneau, AK 99801, phone 907-586-8790; or Forest Service Information Center, 101 Egan Dr., Juneau, AK 99801, phone 907-586-8751; www.fs.fed.us/r10/chatham/anm

To the Tlingit Indians, this forested and mountainous island has always been Kootznoohoo—"fortress of the bears." It's an apt description for one of North America's premier bear habitats. Early Russian explorers, perhaps all too aware of the proximity of the powerful animals, called it the Island of Fear. In 1794, British explorer Capt. George Vancouver named it Admiralty Island.

Passed by the U.S. Congress in 1980, the Alaska National Interest Lands Conservation Act established 14 wilderness areas in **Tongass National Forest**—and designated Admiralty Island as a national monument. With 678 miles of forested coastline and 67 salmon streams, Admiralty is prime bear habitat. There are no black bears on the island, just brown bears—also known as grizzlies—grown to immense size on the bountiful salmon. Thanks to enlightened conservation, this island gem still supports about one brown bear for every square mile of terrain; that's about 1,700 bears, or almost three times the island's human population.

Most of the 96-mile-long, 25-mile-wide island is a mosaic of open meadow and thickets of old-growth forest—mainly western hemlock and Sitka spruce—that is between 200 and 700 years old. Under the dense canopy, the ground is covered with thick layers of sphagnum moss and brambles. Above tree line (about 1,500 to 2,000 feet) the land gives way to alpine tundra, rocky outcroppings, snow, and ice fields.

Lower down, the ebb and flow of glacial ice over thousands of years has carved out deep, U-shaped valleys. These are now covered by fjords,

GLACIER BAY N.P. & PRES. Gustavus
Mendenhall Glacier
7 Juneau
Mt. Roberts
Gastineau Channel
Oliver Inlet
Mud Bay
ICY Point Adolphus
Cape Spencer
Hoonah
SEYMOUR CANAL
EAGLE M.A.
Admiralty Island National Monument
BRITISH COLUMBIA
T O N G A S S
Pelican
C h i c h a g o f
I s l a n d
ADMIRALTY
Rock Cr.
STAN PRICE S.W.S.
Tenakee Springs
ISLAND
Mole Harbor
TRACY
ARM Fords Terror
A N
Chichagof
N A T I O N A L
CROSS ADMIRALTY CANOE ROUTE
FORDS
P A C I F I C
A L A S K A
Sitkoh Bay
NATIONAL
Mitchell Bay
TERROR
O C E A N
F O R E S T
Angoon
Gambier Bay
WILD.
Kruzof Island
B a r a n o f
MONUMENT
Pybus Bay
T O N G A S S
OLD SITKA S.H.P.
KOOTZNOOWOO WILDERNESS
ALASKA MARINE HIGHWAY (FERRY)
0   miles   30
I s l a n d
N A T I O N A L
0   kilometers   45
Sitka
SITKA N.H.P.
Frederick Sound
INSIDE PASSAGE
ALASKA MARITIME N.W.R.
Kake   Kupreanof I.   F O R E S T
Lynn Canal
Strait
Chatham
Stephens Passage
Endicott Arm
MTS
CANADA
US

forests, and streams—a dynamic landscape that is constantly being re-shaped by sea, wind, rain, and snow.

The island's numerous Sitka black-tailed deer can often be seen along the beach boundaries and open hillsides. Mink, land otters, marten, and beavers are common, too. Blue grouse forage in the understory, Steller's jays flit from branch to branch, and ravens and crows call from the timber. Great blue herons and oystercatchers sometimes stalk the ocean edge; on the wing farther out are common murres, marbled murrelets, surf scoters, pigeon guillemots, and gulls and kittiwakes. You'll see bald eagles everywhere.

Steller sea lions, harbor seals, harbor porpoises, minke whales, orcas, and humpback whales patrol just offshore, occasionally coming within feet of the rocky beaches. The sleek black-and-white Dall's porpoise—one of the fastest cetaceans—can frequently be seen playing in the bow wake of passing vessels.

What to See and Do

Whale-watching is popular in the waters around Admiralty, particularly on the island's south and west sides—and especially in July. Each summer, humpback whales travel here from distant wintering grounds to feed in the rich inshore waters. Their sudden, aerial breaches will amaze you. Experienced charter boat captains know the whale-watching rules and are careful not to harass these endangered animals. Orcas also make an occasional appearance, as do sea lions, harbor seals, seabirds, and Dall's porpoises. Though Dall's porpoises usually travel in groups of 20 to 30, a group of 3,000 was once spotted in Stephens Passage. Sea otters sometimes swim off the north end of the island, but they are not common. The best way to enjoy all of these wonderful marine inhabitants is a multiday cruise that anchors each night in a different bay.

The Forest Service maintains 15 rustic public-use cabins, though all of them are usually reserved months in advance. Some of the cabins are on salt water, others are on lakes, and a few are accessible from the **Cross Admiralty Canoe Route** (see pp. 45-46). To stay in one of the cabins, you'll need all the standard camping gear except a tent. For information, call the Forest Service Information Center *(907-586-8751)*. Thayer Lake Wilderness Lodge *(P.O. Box 8897, Ketchikan, AK 99901. 907-789-5646)* on the west side of the island is the only lodge in the monument, but there is additional lodging in Angoon (see p. 45).

With planning and preparation, anyone can pull off a safe and exhilarating island adventure. An abundance of guides and charter services operate out of Juneau; for a list, contact the Juneau Convention and Visitors Bureau *(888-581-2201)*.

Admiralty Island has three major recreational areas: Seymour Canal, Mitchell Bay, and the Cross Admiralty Canoe Route.

Seymour Canal

Although brown bears can be seen almost everywhere on Admiralty Island, Seymour Canal is the best place to spot them. At the 60,000-acre **Stan Price State Wildlife Sanctuary** on Pack Creek, 30 or so bears regularly fish for salmon or graze in the timber or tidewater marshes. Protected since 1930, these grizzlies pay little attention to people, and no one has ever been injured at the sanctuary. Nearby **Swan Cove** and **Windfall Harbor** *(both accessible only by air or water)* also offer excellent bear-viewing opportunities. Morning and evening are the best times to watch the bears.

Access to the sanctuary is by permit only from June 1 to September 10, with a maximum stay of three days. Permits are especially hard to acquire during the peak viewing season of July 10 to August 20. Contact the national monument for more information *(907-586-8790)*.

You can visit two designated viewing sites: a sand spit at the mouth of the creek and a viewing tower located a mile upstream (the latter is accessed by a groomed trail through beautiful old-growth forest). You can fly, boat, or kayak to the refuge. Once on site, self-sufficiency is the byword. Even day-users need to be prepared for sudden storms that may cancel their flights. No facilities or lodging of any kind exist, and campers are restricted to a nearby island. You'll need a boat or kayak to get to the island's campsite.

The 10,778-acre **Seymour Canal Eagle Management Area** encompasses Tiedeman, Bug, Dorn, and Faust Islands, as well as several smaller islands, in the middle of Seymour Canal. Bald eagles tend to nest in old-growth spruce or hemlock trees within 200 yards of salt water, so you'll see dozens of them here. Admiralty Island averages about one nest for every mile of shoreline—the highest density anywhere in the world.

Paddlers from Juneau can reach the head of the Seymour Canal (which is really a long inlet) courtesy of the tram located at the head of Oliver Inlet, 14 to 18 water

Grizzly Bears, Black Bears, & You

HOME TO AS MANY AS 40,000 black bears and brown bears—also known as grizzlies—Alaska truly is bear country. Physical characteristics distinguish the two species, but color alone is not a reliable indicator. Some brown bears are very dark—almost black. Black bears, meanwhile, can vary from jet black to white; some brown-colored black bears, called cinnamon bears, are often misidentified as grizzlies.

Although black bears usually are smaller than brown bears, size alone is not an ironclad identifier either. By distinguishing the following physical features, you should be able to tell the two apart: Black bears have a long, skinny snout, big ears, no shoulder hump, and short claws; grizzly bears have a dish-shaped face, short ears, a prominent hump, and long, straight claws.

No matter what their claw shape or snout size, all bears are potentially dangerous. Be alert when you're around them, strictly observing the following safety procedures.

Never surprise a bear. Make noise, sing, or talk loudly. Never hike alone. Detour around thick brush.

Never approach a bear. Some bears seem unafraid of people, whereas others feel threatened if approached. Females with cubs should be given an especially wide berth; not for nothing did the she-bear earn her reputation for defensiveness.

Never feed a bear. Bears that associate people with food can be very dangerous. Therefore, keep a clean camp; never cook in or near your tent, and always take pains to store all food and garbage a good distance from your campsite, either high in a tree or in bearproof containers. Anglers should clean their catch well away from camp,

Brown bear and cubs

then dispose of the remains in water.

If you do encounter a bear at close range, remain calm. Talk in a normal voice, raise your arms, and back away slowly. If the bear follows, stop and hold your ground. Whatever you do, don't run; bears can cover the distance between the two of you at 35 miles an hour and, like dogs, will chase a fleeing creature.

What if a bear charges you? Bears often "bluff charge," pulling up within just feet of their adversary. If a grizzly bear grabs you, experts warn, you should not fight back. Instead, fall to the ground, curl up in a ball with your hands behind your neck, and play dead. A mauling from a grizzly usually lasts a matter of seconds.

If you are attacked by a black bear, however, fight back with everything you've got: Sometimes a stout tree limb will see them off. If you fall to the ground and play dead, a black bear might attempt to eat you.

The best defense, of course, is to avoid situations that put you at risk in the first place. State law allows you to shoot a bear in self-defense (and as a last resort). If this happens, you'll be required to file a report. You'll also have to relinquish the animal's hide and skull. In addition, you may face a charge of a different kind if it is suspected that you provoked the confrontation with the bear.

For self-protection, some people carry aerosol "bear sprays" containing the pepper extract capsicum. Although these sprays can deter attacks, they have an effective range of less than 10 yards and are useless in strong winds or heavy rain. Don't spray your gear and your tent with the stuff in hopes of keeping bears away; the odor may actually attract them.

Thankfully, bear attacks are rare. Of the hundreds of encounters that occur each summer, very few result in contact and injury. ■

Admiralty Island

miles from town. Load your kayak or small boat on the tram for the 1-mile overland jaunt. That way, you'll save yourself a long paddle down blustery Stephens Passage to the mouth of the canal. Don't expect a fancy conveyance, however; in fact, don't expect the tram even to have an engine. The Oliver Inlet tram is a do-it-yourself operation: A small cart, big enough to hold a couple of kayaks and gear, is pushed by hand on narrow-gauge rails laid over a boardwalk. Sometimes the hand cart will be at the other end of the route, forcing you to retrieve it first. Still, a 2-mile walk beats 40 miles of paddling through choppy seas.

Mitchell Bay

Many canoers and kayakers head for Mitchell Bay on the "dry" (western) side of the island, which receives a mere 40 to 60 inches of precipitation a year. The Tlingit community of Angoon is the main access point here. Located at the mouth of Kootznahoo Inlet, the bay offers a network of shoals, channels, and small wooded islands for you to explore. (Caution: Strong tides near Angoon can be hazardous to small craft.)

Deer and bears wander the beaches and forests. Harbor seals periscope up above the waves to check out paddlers. The 9-inch-long, black-and-white waterbirds you'll see in the bay are marbled murrelets. Sometimes these little birds flee at the first sign of an approaching boat; at other times they wait until the last second before diving to safety.

There are no developed hiking trails in Mitchell Bay, but its beaches are great for open-ended rambles. You'll find abundant secluded camping spots along the way. Beachcombing at low tide reveals barnacles, limpets, mussels, chitons, anemones, sea stars, sea slugs—and sometimes bears scavenging along the shoreline. Expect to meet local people engaged in fishing and hunting.

With a population of only about 600, Angoon is not set up for tourism. You'll find one or two bed-and-breakfasts, a general store, and a small motel (which is nearly always fully booked in summer). There is no public campground. You can rent canoes and kayaks at the general store. A few charter boats are available for fishing; some also cater to whale-watchers. For information on accommodations and charters, call the Angoon city offices (907-788-3653).

Scheduled seaplane service to Angoon from Juneau is relatively inexpensive, but the Alaska State ferry is the cheapest access if you're toting your own boat and gear. Both the ferry and the seaplanes drop passengers off at a pier about 3 miles from Angoon. You can walk to town, call a taxi,

Stan the "Bear Man"

Stan Price spent 39 years living alongside Pack Creek, becoming a local legend for his ability to live peacefully with the local bears. Sailing a boat he had built in Seattle, Price arrived in southeast Alaska in 1927 and worked as a miner, fisherman, mechanic, and logger before eventually settling at Pack Creek. There, he began to take in and raise orphaned cubs. Armed with only a walking stick (which he used to bop the occasional troublesome bear), Price wandered freely through the area. His ongoing presence habituated the bears to humans.

Although Price died in 1989 at age 90, the descendants of his "pets" still thrill visitors. Near the creek mouth, the crumbling remains of his float house and sheds are a reminder of the "Bear Man," whose philosophy for dealing with his furry neighbors was a simple one: "If you're friends with the bears, they will be friends with you."

or begin your trip right there at the dock.

Cross Admiralty Canoe Route

This 32-mile-long route links Mitchell Bay on the west coast of Admiralty Island with Mole Harbor on the east coast. (Be careful crossing Mitchell Bay; its tides are particularly strong.) Along the way, the route passes through as many as eight lakes, all of them connected by Forest Service portage trails. Relatively easy portages make this a fun and enjoyable trip. A few of the lakes have public-use cabins; others offer only rudimentary campsites.

Along the route, you'll see smatterings of red and Alaska cedar, black cottonwood, subalpine fir, lodgepole pine, and Pacific silver fir, as well as plants such as sedge, prickly devil's club, and skunk cabbage. Watch for deer, bears, beavers, common loons, goldeneyes, and the exquisite harlequin duck.

Don't be surprised to see hummingbirds. Weighing a minuscule one-tenth of an ounce and with a wingspan of less than 4 inches, the rufous hummingbird is Alaska's smallest migrating bird. Named for its reddish brown feathers, the rufous winters in Mexico and travels almost 4,000 miles to get here, arriving in early April—just when the columbines, tiger lilies, and paintbrushes come into bloom. The hummingbirds' tiny size does not mean they stick close to the ground; in fact, they appear to use the same flight lanes—and the same altitudes—as Canada geese.

Fishing for cutthroat trout and Dolly Varden can be excellent here in late spring, during the initial insect hatch. However, you must be extra cautious when fishing or when cleaning or cooking fish. All three activities can attract bears. ■

Tracy Arm-Fords Terror Wilderness

■ 653,179 acres ■ 50 miles south of Juneau ■ Best months May-Sept.
■ Camping, kayaking, wildlife viewing, boat tours ■ Contact Forest Service Information Center, 101 Egan Dr., Juneau, AK 99801; phone 907-586-8751. www.fs.fed.us/r10/tongass

TO SAIL INTO TRACY ARM, you will have to cross a bar left behind by the glacier that once filled this valley. Known as a terminal moraine, the underwater ridge of rocky debris marks the glacier's farthest advance down the fjord. Once across the bar, your tour boat picks its way among icebergs that seem to dance in the turquoise waters. This is one of the loveliest fjords in the Southeast, with steep walls of granite that evoke those of a cathedral.

Tour boats out of Juneau make daily trips to Tracy Arm. Be sure you're out on deck as your captain navigates the 22-mile-long fjord toward two beautiful—and very active—tidewater glaciers, **Sawyer** and **South Sawyer.** All your senses come into play as you listen to the popping noise the ice makes, watch for harbor seals and their pups riding the bergs, and scan the cliffs for mountain goats. If you're lucky, you may see a black bear scavenging for mussels at low tide.

These are fairly good waters for kayaking. Watch the tides, however, and keep a safe distance from potentially rolling icebergs and calving

South Sawyer Glacier, Tracy Arm

glaciers. You'll find more camping spots in neighboring **Endicott Arm** and—because no cruise ships go there yet—a more peaceful wilderness experience. Adventure Bound Alaska *(907-463-2509 or 800-228-3875)* runs a small cruise boat out of Juneau that will drop you off with your kayak at the entrance to Endicott Arm.

At the inland end of Endicott Arm is **Fords Terror.** This narrow, T-shaped fjord was named more than a hundred years ago for an unfortunate sailor named Harry L. Ford, who was a master-of-arms in the United States Navy—and the alarming experience he had here. Rowing a small skiff, he entered the fjord at slack water to carry out a survey of that part of the coast. On his way back out, Ford had to paddle against the outgoing tide, battling the wild currents and whirlpools that swirl about the fjord's entrance. So if you venture here, *Caveat paddlor:* Let the kayaker beware. ■

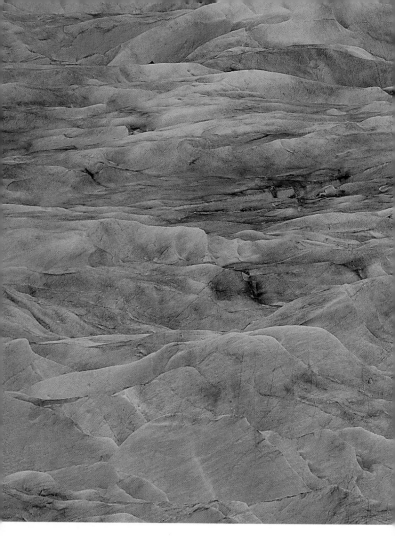

Mendenhall Glacier

■ 12 miles long ■ Northwest of Juneau ■ Best months May-Aug. ■ Hiking, ice climbing, flight-seeing, guided glacier hikes ■ Contact Mendenhall Glacier Visitor Center, Mendenhall Loop Rd., Juneau, AK 99802; phone 907-789-0097. www.fs.fed.us/r10/tongass

FLYING INTO JUNEAU for the first time on a clear day, you may see a startling sight: a monster ribbon of blue-and-white ice creeping down the steep surrounding mountains to the very edge of Alaska's capital city. This is Mendenhall Glacier. Located just a dozen or so miles from downtown Juneau, the glacier plunges steeply from its immense reservoir of ice in the **Juneau Icefield**—in the upper reaches of the Coast Mountains—to near sea level. At its terminus, the face of the glacier is 1.5 miles wide.

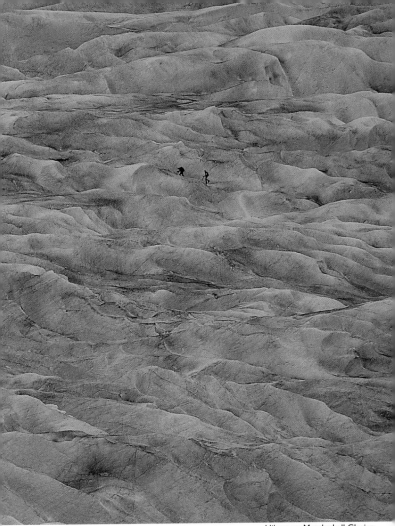
Hikers on Mendenhall Glacier

The best way to experience the glacier and the ice field that gives rise to it is to fly over both. A helicopter can lift you up above Juneau and deposit you on the ice in a matter of minutes.

Atop the glacier, you can take a short walk with a guide. More energetic trekkers can opt for a guided glacier hike and ice-climbing package. Outfitted with an ice ax and a pair of crampons (climbing cleats that attach to your boots), you'll explore a frozen world full of surprises. Jump narrow, deep blue crevasses; drink from tumbling meltwater streams; ascend small ice towers; and marvel at the stark beauty of this wild, icy wonderland.

If your feet prefer to be planted squarely on terra firma, the visitor center at the bottom of the glacier has information about nearby walking and hiking trails. The **Nature Trail** is a gentle half-mile outing, while the 3-mile round-trip **East Glacier Loop** leads to a scenic overlook of the glacier. ■

Mount Roberts

■ 3,819 feet ■ Southwest of downtown Juneau ■ Best months May-Sept.
■ Hiking, parasailing, tram rides ■ Contact Forest Service Information Center,
101 Egan Dr., Juneau, AK 99801; phone 907-586-8751

YOU HAVE A CHOICE TO MAKE ON Mount Roberts: Do you want to rest your
legs, give your heart a workout, or both?

Option no. 1 means the tram. Pick a clear day, go to the cruise ship
dock, hop in one of the cars of the **Mount Roberts Tramway** (they're
painted with traditional Tlingit eagle and raven motifs), and fly halfway
up the mountain, where you'll find a nature center. For information, call
907-463-3412 or 888-461-8726.

Option no. 2 means the 4.5-mile **Mount Roberts Trail,** which starts at
the top of Sixth Street, close to downtown Juneau. After 2.5 miles of forest, the trail emerges above tree line at a spot marked by a large wooden
cross. You're now at about 2,500 feet. From here, you can hike up to Gastineau Peak and then on to the summit of Mount Roberts over steep,
rocky ridges and through flower-filled meadows, enjoying fabulous views
of **Gastineau Channel**—and, perhaps, a splash of airborne color courtesy
of the parasailers who run off Mount Roberts to glide in the thermals.

And, of course, there's always option no. 3—the combo. You can ride
the tram to the halfway mark, then hike the rest of the way (an additional
2 miles or so) to the top of the mountain. ■

Point Adolphus

■ Northern tip of Chichagof Island, across Icy Strait from Glacier Bay
■ Best months late June–mid-Aug. ■ Whale-watching, guided kayaking
trips, sailboat and passenger cruises ■ Contact Glacier Bay National Park
and Preserve, P.O. Box 140, Gustavus, AK 99826; phone 907-697-2230.
www.nps.gov/glba

AT THE HEIGHT OF the Alaska summer, the waters off Point Adolphus in
Icy Strait are the place to watch for humpback whales. The lumbering
leviathans come here for good reason: The ebb and flow of the tides, together with the confluence of waters from Icy Strait, **Glacier Bay** (see pp.
52-57), and **Mud Bay,** churn up rich nutrients that provide a lavish feast
for whales and other marine creatures. Bald eagles and gulls eagerly skim
off whatever is left over.

To spot a whale, scan the surface of the water for a vapor plume about
15 feet high. Watch for tail flukes, too; the humpback almost always
shows its flukes before diving. Turbulence in the water, with gulls screech-
ing overhead, is a good indication of whales feeding. You may even see a
graceful flipper waving and slapping the surface as one of the great beasts
rolls and lunges after schools of fish.

Sea kayaks, Point Adolphus

One of the humpback's most unusual feeding techniques is to catch prey in a bubble net of its own creation. The whale dives down below a school of fish and slowly spirals up around it, releasing air bubbles from its blowhole as it goes. The bubble seine corrals the fish—forcing them into a tight circle. The whale then dives back under to rocket up through the middle of the bubbles, its mouth open wide.

The most thrilling sight of all, however, is that of a humpback whale breaching—a 35-ton ballerina hurtling itself out of the water in a graceful backward arch. Daily boat tours or guided kayaking trips can be arranged from Gustavus or Juneau through Sea Otter Kayak *(907-697-3007).* ■

Hiking at Lamplugh Glacier, Glacier Bay NP and Preserve

Glacier Bay National Park and Preserve

■ 3.3 million acres ■ Park headquarters at Bartlett Cove in Glacier Bay, 65 miles northwest of Juneau ■ Best months May-Sept. ■ Hiking, kayaking, fishing, wildlife viewing, glaciers, cruises ■ Contact the park, P.O. Box 140, Gustavus, AK 99826; phone 907-697-2230. www.nps.gov/glba

> *I sketched and made notes…[then] danced down the mountain to my camp, my mind glowing like the sunbeaten glaciers…. I have been wandering through a thousand rooms in God's crystal temple. Solomon's marble and ivory palaces were nothing like this!*
>
> —John Muir, Glacier Bay, 1879

SUMMER FOG SWEEPS OVER **Icy Strait.** Barely distinguishable in the mist are **Point Carolus** and **Point Gustavus,** marking the entrance to Glacier Bay. On the bridge of the cruise ship, peering through the fog, stand the ship's pilot, the Dutch navigator, the Indonesian helmsman, and the naturalist. The helmsman points to starboard.

A pod of orcas.

Just then, the door to the bridge swings open. In strides the captain—a large Dutchman, usually jovial. Not today. He looks at the weather, scowls, mutters something under his breath. The ship is now in the one place—Glacier Bay—that every tourist on board has come to Alaska to see. Normally, this is where the captain is most in his element: When a glacier calves and sends forth cascades of icebergs, he often bows from the bridge wing to the awed passengers assembled on the decks, as if taking credit for all of nature's wonders.

But not today. Today there is fog.

The naturalist tries to be upbeat. "Think of it this way, Captain," she says brightly, sweeping her arm across a scene that is already changing, as mountain shapes loom and disappear in the drifting banks of fog. "It's just like sailing into a Japanese painting."

The captain thinks. A big smile slowly spreads across his face. For the rest of the day, he can be heard on the decks telling worried passengers in his booming voice, "Think of it this way…."

If Glacier Bay is at its most dramatic when revealing itself in tantalizing sneak previews, today it is positively theatrical. A humpback whale blows in front of the ship, then dives, its heart-shaped flukes sliding beneath the waves. Jagged, snowy peaks rise in a crescendo on the west of the bay. Binoculars trained on the slopes above **Tidal Inlet** reveal a family of mountain goats. A blond grizzly bear prowls the beaches near Gloomy Knob.

The first tidewater glacier on the cruise up the **West Arm** of Glacier Bay is **Reid Glacier.** Then comes the "small," fairy-tale **Lamplugh Glacier,** with its castle towers of ice. The ship noses around **Jaw Point** into the moonscape that is **Johns Hopkins Inlet,** where the ice has only recently retreated and thousands of harbor seals ride the floes. The vessel then turns and sails north to the **Margerie** and **Grand Pacific Glaciers** anchoring the head of the West Arm in Tarr Inlet.

Small thuds sound against the hull. Icebergs. If the Margerie Glacier has been very active, a lot of ice will litter the water, making navigation slow. Finally, the ship comes to rest a quarter of a mile off the face of the Margerie. Here everyone awaits "the white thunder"—what native peoples called the calving of icebergs long ago.

Passengers throng the decks for the spectacle. Groaning, cracking, booming, and echoing, the ice makes an assortment of eerie sounds. "Watch!" says the naturalist. "Watch where little chunks of ice keep falling off the face. A larger piece will probably shear off there." Just then, like a rifle shot splitting the air, a huge tower of ice loses its hold on the glacier's face and crashes, seemingly in slow motion, into the sea. An enormous swell rises toward the ship. Kittiwakes and gulls flock to see what tasty morsels the turbulence has scared to the surface. Out on the bridge wing, the captain turns to his audience and takes a long, slow bow.

Another ship's captain, in another age not so long ago, was rebuffed from entering Glacier Bay by a solid wall of ice. The year was 1778, and

Following pages: Tarr and Johns Hopkins Inlets

Glacier Bay N.P.
& Preserve

BRITISH
COLUMBIA

TATSHENSHINI-ALSEK
WILDERNESS
P.P.

Skagway

Klehini

ALASKA CHILKAT
BALD EAGLE
PRESERVE

HAINES
STATE

TONGASS
N.F.

Alsek

Tsirku Takhin

Haines

FOREST

Grand Pacific Gl.

CARROLL GLACIER

Muir Gl.

Toyatte
Inlet

CHILKAT S.P.

ST. ELIAS MTS

U.S.

Mt. Fairweather
15,320 ft.

GLACIER   BAY

Margerie
Glacier
Johns Hopkins
Inlet

Jaw Point Gloomy
Knob

Muir Inlet

Adams Inlet

Tidal
Inlet

ALASKA

Cenotaph
Island

Fairweather Range

Lamplugh
Glacier

Reid
Glacier

Brady
Icefield

NATIONAL   PARK

TONGASS
ENDICOTT R.
WILD.

Lituya Bay

Gulf   of   Alaska

Lamplugh Glacier

Lamplugh Gl.

Brady Glacier

AND   PRESERVE

Point
Carolus

Bartlett Cove

Gustavus

N.F.

Range

P A C I F I C   O C E A N

Point Gustavus

Icy   Strait

TONGASS N.F.

Cape Spencer

Chichagof Island

Point
Adalphus

0   miles   20

0   kilometers   30

N

Royal Navy captain James Cook sailed right past the bay because it was choked with ice. Before continuing northward on his journey of exploration, however, Cook saw and named 15,320-foot-high **Mount Fairweather,** the crowning peak of the Fairweather Range, whose snow and ice fields feed the rivers of ice that slowly flow down into Glacier Bay. (Cook was the last person, Alaskans contend, ever to see that mountain in fair weather.)

By the time Royal Navy captain George Vancouver sailed into Icy Strait just 16 years later, the landscape had been transfigured: He found a bay almost 5 miles long, filled with "great quantities of broken ice."

In 1879, when John Muir and five companions paddled their canoe into Glacier Bay, they measured the bay at 48 miles long. By 1916, having receded 65 miles up the bay, the Grand Pacific Glacier was in full retreat.

No glacier worldwide has ever done a faster vanishing act. As the ice continues to melt today, the land below it—relieved of its crushing burden—has started to rise (a process known as crustal rebound). Colonizing plants have begun attaching themselves to the previously lifeless rock. A trip up the bay is now like traveling back in time: You can see the changes in vegetation, from lush to sparse, as this land—locked in ice for eons— slowly returns to life.

Ice on the rocks, Glacier Bay NP and Preserve

What to See and Do

Cruising

Contact the park for a list of commercial service providers authorized to operate within Glacier Bay. Most visitors come by cruise ship and spend a day cruising up the west arm of Glacier Bay to the Margerie and Grand Pacific Glaciers. For independent travelers, a day boat tour up the west arm on the *Spirit of Adventure (800-451-5952)* departs from the dock at Bartlett Cove.

Kayaking

Even if your time at Glacier Bay is limited, you should be able to fit in a kayaking trip that ushers you into some of the bay's protected inlets—or way up into the ice. You can arrange drop-offs and pickups for yourself and your boat into the bay's west arm or east arm.

During the summertime, there are six areas designated as non-motorized waters in the bay's two arms that offer kayakers a more authentic wilderness experience. Check with rangers about closure dates and locations. **Adams Inlet,** east off lower Muir Inlet, is a favorite destination. Guided kayaking trips are advisable if you are a novice. Kayaks can be rented at Bartlett Cove from Glacier Bay Sea Kayaks *(907-697-2257)*.

Hiking

If you plan to hike in Glacier Bay, your organized excursions will be confined to three short nature trails through the forest at park headquarters in **Bartlett Cove.** In addition, a shoreline trail leads from the dock to Point Gustavus—a 6-mile one-way trek that affords opportunities to see a variety of intertidal marine life. Be sure to check tide tables before setting out. Beyond these hikes, the decision is up to you.

The trail-less backcountry offers more than a million acres of spectacular terrain. All of the customary Alaska thrills—and many of its trademark dangers—abound: bears, rolling icebergs, glacier crevasses, and fast-changing weather. Never go into the wilderness unprepared. Always consult park rangers about the conditions you're likely to face, the gear you should carry, and the route you intend to follow. ■

The Glacier Bear

Look closely at every bear you see in the rain forests of southeast Alaska, because one of them might just be the state's rarest: the glacier (or blue) bear.

Both names are, in fact, misnomers. The glacier bear does not live on glaciers or ice fields, for it could not find anything to eat there. This seldom seen creature does live *near* glaciers, however; it is most often spotted wandering forest trails, ambling along beaches, or grazing in flower-filled meadows.

Finally, the blue bear is anything but. Its fur is black at the roots but silver at the tips, lending it an overall bluish appearance.

Hubbard Glacier

Why So Blue?

Water has no color. Frozen water often looks white because of the air bubbles trapped inside it during the freezing process. Yet a glacier—a large mass of solid ice—appears blue. Why?

The answer lies in the way the sun's rays travel through the ice. Sunlight is made up of various wavelengths: red and yellow at the long end of the spectrum, blue and violet at the short end. As sunlight penetrates the ice of a glacier, the red and yellow light waves do not react with the molecules of ice; instead, they travel straight through.

By contrast, the short wavelengths—the blue and violet—react energetically with the ice molecules, which scatter them in all directions. One of those directions is toward you. That's why you see blue.

You may also have noticed that glaciers really get the blues on cloudy days, when they take on an an even deeper hue. Here's why: Clouds double the intensity of the ambient light. On cloudy days, blue light waves that are reflected skyward do not travel into outer space. Rather, they are blocked by the clouds and bounced back down to you.

Alaska Chilkat Bald Eagle Preserve

■ 48,000 acres ■ 10 miles northwest of Haines ■ Best months Oct.-Dec. Eagles begin gathering in early Oct. and taper off by Feb. ■ Bird-watching, wildlife viewing ■ Contact Alaska State Parks, Southeast Area Office, 400 Willoughby Ave., Juneau, AK 99801; phone 907-465-4563. www.dnr.state.ak.us/parks/units/eagleprv.htm

FOUNDING FATHER BENJAMIN FRANKLIN was thoroughly disgusted at the animal the young American republic chose as its national symbol. The bald eagle, he declared, was "a bird of bad moral character." Franklin's judgment seems more than a trifle harsh. With its regal white head, enormous wingspan (about 8 feet), and eyes that can detect a target a quarter of a mile away, the bald eagle is a magnificent creature—one that earns its moniker "the king of birds."

After fending off the challenge posed by Franklin's preferred alternative—the turkey—this creature of allegedly suspect morality confronted a much more serious threat: In the early part of the 20th century, the United States declared its own national symbol of freedom a virtual outlaw. Believing that the birds preyed on salmon—and therefore competed with fishermen—the federal government offered a bounty of 50 cents (later increased to two dollars) for every one killed. Between 1917 and 1952, more than 100,000 Alaska bald eagles suffered precisely that fate.

Scientists have since learned, however, that bald eagles posed no threat to the salmon industry; the birds are scavengers, feeding primarily on dying or dead salmon. Thanks in part to that discovery, the bird's rehabilitation in Alaska is now complete. Even though the bald eagle remains on the threatened species list in the rest of North America, it is currently thriving both in Alaska and in Canada.

A visit to the Alaska Chilkat Bald Eagle Preserve will demonstrate just how well the species is doing. Like solemn, hook-nosed judges bewigged in white and robed in black, the birds fly in every fall from hundreds of miles

Bald eagle

away to gather along the banks of the **Chilkat River.** Ask at the ranger station in Haines *(907-766-2292)* for the location of viewing sites that do not disturb the birds.

From October to December, the largest concentration of bald eagles in the world gathers in and around Chilkat. In addition to the 200 to 400 eagles that reside in the preserve year-round, the new arrivals swell the birds' ranks to more than 3,000. You'll see them lining the snowy branches of the cottonwoods, where they sit for hours on end, conserving their energy. Laid out at their feet is a fish banquet: Warm water, welling up from the bottom of the Chilkat River in winter, keeps the river flats ice free, allowing the birds to gorge on spawned-out, dying, and rotting salmon.

The **Valley of the Eagles** is located between Mileposts 10 and 26 on the Haines Highway. The first 26 miles of the highway, which is open year-round, runs from Haines (where the mileposts begin) to Klukwan. Along a 5-mile stretch beside the Chilkat River—between Mileposts 18 and 24—you'll find the **Eagle Council Grounds.** Here, the birds congregate in large numbers along the river flats, making this area the premier spot for viewing them.

Every year, the town of Haines marks the return of the bald eagles with the **Alaska Bald Eagle Festival.** Usually staged during the second weekend of November, the festival features performances by musicians and local artists. Photography workshops and guided eagle-viewing excursions are sometimes offered as well. For information about the festival, contact the Haines Chamber of Commerce *(P.O. Box 518, Haines, AK 99827. 907-766-2203).* ■

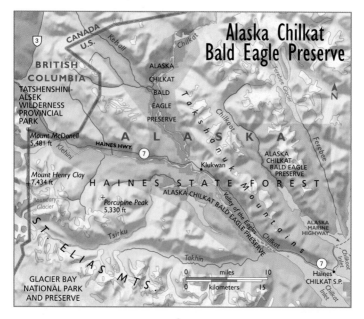

Western Columbines

Chilkat State Park

- Approximately 6,000 acres ▪ South of Haines on the Chilkat Peninsula
- Best months May-Sept. ▪ Camping, hiking, boating ▪ Contact the park,
P.O. Box 430, Haines, AK 99827, phone 907-766-2292; or Haines Visitor Information Center, 2nd Ave., Haines, AK 99827, phone 907-766-2234 (summer).
www.haines.ak.us

A DELIGHTFUL SMORGASBORD for the short-term traveler, seaside Chilkat State Park offers you a chance to scale **Mount Riley**—at 1,760 feet, the highest peak on the Chilkat Peninsula. From the top you'll have lovely views of nearby summits, glaciers, and the Lynn Canal. The climb is not nearly so rigorous as the steep trail up **Mount Ripinski,** the mountain that rises directly behind Haines.

Stop at the Haines Visitor Information Center for maps and directions. Three routes lead to the mountaintop. The easiest to find is the trail off **Mud Bay Road** (2.8 miles to the summit). Allow about 4 to 5 hours round-trip.

For a pleasurable forest and beach walk, head to the park campground (*about 7 miles from town at end of Mud Bay Rd.*). There you'll find the beginning of **Seduction Point Trail** (6.8 miles one way). Across the water, **Davidson** and **Rainbow Glaciers** cascade down the mountains. From the trail you'll have chances to see bears, moose, whales, seals, sea lions, and blue herons. Seduction Point separates the **Chilkat** and **Chilkoot Inlets.** Fit hikers should be able to complete the trail in about nine hours round-trip. The best time to tackle it is in midsummer, when you can take advantage of the longer hours of sunlight. Be sure to check tides before setting out; carry extra water. ▪

Historic Skagway

Klondike Gold Rush National Historical Park

- 13,191 acres ■ Skagway Historic District in downtown Skagway; 33-mile Chilkoot Trail begins in Dyea, 9 miles from downtown Skagway
- Best months late May–mid-Sept. ■ Hiking, backpacking, guided walks, tram rides ■ Contact the park, P.O. Box 517, Skagway, AK 99840; phone 907-983-2921. www.nps.gov/klgo

"GOLD! GOLD! GOLD!" trumpeted the *Seattle Post-Intelligencer* of July 17, 1897. "Sixty-Eight Rich Men on the Steamer *Portland*—Stacks of Yellow Metal!"

Thousands cheered from the Seattle docks as the 68 fortunates carted their gold—wrapped in caribou hides or stuffed in socks, leather satchels, and old jam jars—off the ship. For years, many of these men had been panning the creeks of the Klondike River deep in the Yukon Territory. Like everyone else, they were unprepared for the size of their finds. Throughout the lower 48, news of their auriferous windfall triggered a stampede to the north that had never been seen before—and would never be seen again.

At the height of the madness, **Skagway** was the beginning—and the end—of the Klondike trail of gold. Accessible by sea, the town provided the quickest and easiest routes over the mountains and into the gold-fields. Klondike Gold Rush National Historical Park is unique among national parks. It includes not only historic downtown Skagway—

complete with old wooden sidewalks, cabins, and renovated saloons—but also the trail and mountain pass that thousands of hopeful gold seekers struggled over to reach the Yukon.

"Skagway was little better than a hell on earth," recalled the incorruptible Samuel Steele, superintendent of the North West Mounted Police, after he visited the town. Gunfire rang out through the night, the indomitable Mountie recalled in his memoirs, and bullets crashed through the walls of the boardinghouse where he slept. Cries of "Help!" and "Murder!" punctuated the rollicking music blaring from dance hall doors.

A two-bit con artist named Jefferson Randolph "Soapy" Smith and his gang of hoodlums ruled the town. Soapy had come by the nickname while selling bars of soap earlier in his career, but he just couldn't keep his hands clean: In Skagway, Soapy and his cronies set up bogus businesses practically overnight—barbershops, telegram offices, church fundraising operations—and concocted the most ingenious ways of fleecing hapless newcomers or returning prospectors. By morning, their victims barely had their shirts, let alone the price of a meal.

Soapy's days were numbered, though. On the evening of July 8, 1898, he got wind of a meeting of Skagway's town fathers, who well understood that every dollar he skimmed off the citizenry was a dollar destined never to line their own pockets. The meeting had but one item on the agenda: How to deal with Soapy.

Angered—and armed—Soapy stormed into the meeting. There he was confronted by Frank Reid. Nominally the town's engineer and surveyor, Reid was determined to protect his own shady money-making enterprises—and to eliminate his rival in the bargain. When he accosted Soapy that July night, Soapy responded by pulling a gun. Reid did the same, and both men died as a result of the ensuing gun battle. History has been kind to Reid, however. He and Soapy are buried—one as hero, the other as villain—in the Goldrush Cemetery on the outskirts of town.

Frank Reid's grave, Skagway Goldrush Cemetery

White Pass & Yukon Route railroad

What to See and Do

Explore Skagway

The Park Service visitor center *(daily in summer, reduced hours in winter)* in the old railroad depot on Second Avenue and Broadway offers films, exhibits, ranger talks, and information on conditions along the Chilkoot Trail (see pp. 65–67). Rangers lead excellent walking tours of historic Skagway, which depart several times daily. For a self-guided tour, go to the **Skagway Visitor Center** *(5th Ave. & Broadway. 907-983-2854)* and pick up the "Skagway Walking Tour" brochure. You can also tour by horse and buggy—or even in a vintage car with a costumed driver.

Ride the Train

Once the gold rushers hit Skagway, two routes led into the Klondike. One of them—the **White Pass Trail**—is followed today by the **White Pass & Yukon Route railroad** *(800-343-7373. www.white passrailroad.com)*, which runs from Skagway to White Pass Summit in three hours. In the early days of the gold rush, it went by the name Dead Horse Trail because thousands of the poor creatures fell to their deaths from it while hauling miners' supplies.

The train ride makes for an interesting half-day trip. After the first four miles, the gradient grows unusually steep—some of the grades reach 3.9 percent. The track is the handiwork of a brilliant engineer named Michael J. Heney. In 1898, he constructed a railroad over the Coast Mountains, deemed by most folks as too steep even for a billy goat. Heney's motto: "Give me enough dynamite and snoose [snuff] and I'll build a road to hell."

Hike the Chilkoot

The other route into the Klondike was the 33-mile **Chilkoot Trail,** which you can still walk today (see below). The only footpath in Klondike Gold Rush park, the trail is managed through an agreement between the national park services of the United States and Canada.

If you have only a few hours, try some of the shorter hikes near downtown Skagway. For instance, **Lower Dewey Lake Trail**—which begins on Spring Street between Third and Fourth Streets on the east side of town—is a lovely 0.7-mile walk with an elevation gain of 600 feet. Time permitting, continue to **Upper Dewey Lake** for a total round-trip of 7 miles. ∎

Chilkoot Trail

∎ 33 miles long ∎ Dyea, Alaska, to Bennett Lake, Canada ∎ Best months mid-June–mid-Sept. ∎ Camping, hiking, backpacking ∎ Permit required ∎ Contact Klondike Gold Rush National Historical Park, P.O. Box 517, Skagway, AK 99840, phone 907-983-2921. www.nps.gov/klgo; or Parks Canada, 205-300 Main St., Whitehorse, Yukon, Y1A 2B5, phone 867-667-3910 or 800-661-0486

THE ICONIC IMAGE of the Klondike Gold Rush of 1897-98 is a black-and-white photograph of a line of men and women, each bent double beneath the weight of heavy packs, inching their way up steps carved in the ice—the so-called **Golden Stairs**—to the summit of Chilkoot Pass. The image symbolizes both the hardship and the adventuresome spirit of the times.

Most of the "stampeders," as the gold seekers were known, were city folks, and most of them never found gold. That didn't stop more than 100,000 from slogging their way over the Chilkoot Trail. At the top of the pass (which marks the border between Alaska and British Columbia) awaited members of the North West Mounted Police. To prevent mass starvation in the Klondike, the red-jacketed Mounties made sure that each gold rush-er carried sufficient provisions.

Like one-man bucket brigades, some new arrivals had to climb these steps more than 30 times to ferry their loads into the field. But the effort was worth it: Beyond lay British Columbia, the Klondike, and the city of gold—**Dawson.**

Hiker just off the Chilkoot Trail

For those who love mountains and history, hiking the Chilkoot Trail is a grand adventure even today. Steeping yourself in tales of the gold rush will make the journey that much more fascinating. *Chilkoot Trail: Heritage Route to the Klondike* (by David Neufeld and Frank Norris, Lost Moose Publishing, 1996) provides a fascinating historical account of the gold rush stampeders and the trail.

Long before the gold rush, the Chilkoot Indians used the trail as a trading route from the coast to the interior. The trailhead now starts in Dyea, 9 miles northwest of Skagway. From tidewater and coastal rain forest on the Alaska side, the trail climbs above tree line to high alpine country—and on to the 3,525-foot-high Chilkoot Pass.

The Canadian side is colder and drier than the American side. From the crest you'll descend through open country—high alpine meadows and lakes—before entering the boreal spruce forests surrounding **Lindeman Lake** and **Bennett Lake.** Stampeders spent the winter of 1897-98 building boats on these waters; with the spring thaw, a motley flotilla of more than 7,000 vessels took them through a series of lakes and then down the rapids and currents of the **Yukon River** to Dawson.

You can see remnants of this storied past all along the trail: tumble-down cabins, the ruins of aerial tramways that hauled gear up the mountain, a mysterious stash of canvas boats at the top of the pass, an old boiler, an iron stove, pulley systems. The Park Service has maps and information, as well as the excellent brochure "A Hiker's Guide to the Chilkoot Trail," which is available at the visitor center.

Though the trail length (33 miles from Dyea to Bennett Lake) may

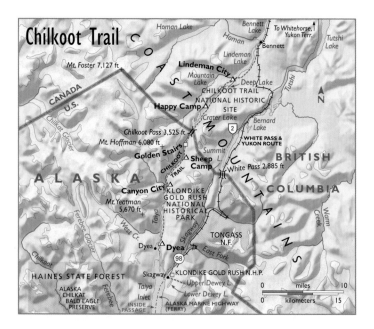

Forest footbridge along the Chilkoot Trail

not seem intimidating, keep your pack light: The route is rugged and steep, and even in midsummer you'll have plenty of snow to cope with. Most hikers take three to five days to complete the trail. Although you are required to register on the U.S. side, the permit is free. There is a fee for the Canadian permit, and Parks Canada limits the number of hikers on the Canadian side to 50 per day, so you'll need to be flexible if you don't have a reservation. The busiest hiking season is July to early August. From June to August, hikers can take a train from Bennett Lake back to Skagway. Service tends to be spotty, so check with the Park Service or the **White Pass & Yukon Route railroad** *(800-343-7373; www.whitepass railroad.com).*

The three-day trip unfolds as follows: Day 1, Dyea to Sheep Camp (13 miles); Day 2, Sheep Camp up the Golden Stairs to the summit and over the pass to Lindeman City (13 miles); Day 3, Lindeman City to Bennett Lake (7 miles).

The five-day trip is a little more leisurely: Day 1, Dyea to Canyon City (7 miles); Day 2, Canyon City to Sheep Camp (6 miles); Day 3, Sheep Camp over the pass to Happy Camp (8 miles) or Deep Lake (10 miles); Day 4, Happy Camp or Deep Lake to Lindeman City (5 or 3 miles); Day 5, Lindeman City to Bennett Lake (7 miles). ■

Russell Fiord Wilderness

■ 348,701 acres ■ At head of Yakutat Bay on northeast edge of Gulf of Alaska
■ Best months June-Aug. ■ Camping, kayaking, glaciers, cruises ■ Contact Sitka
Ranger District, Tongass National Forest, 204 Siginaka Way, Sitka, AK 99835;
phone 907-747-6671

ITALIAN NAVIGATOR ALESSANDRO MALASPINA rejoiced as he sailed from the
Gulf of Alaska into the wide opening of **Yakutat Bay** in the late 1700s.
Though he undoubtedly paused in awe at the sight of the **St. Elias Mountains** (the world's highest coastal mountain range), Malaspina's true ela-
tion had little to do with elevation or aesthetics. Instead, the intrepid
Italian was convinced that he had found the fabled Northwest Passage—
a waterway across North America from the Pacific to the Atlantic.

   With mounting anticipation, Malaspina sailed farther into the bay.
The way ahead began to twist and narrow. Progress slowed. Finally, it
stopped altogether. Blocking his passage was a wall of ice. Malaspina, un-
derstandably, named this part of the waterway **Disenchantment Bay.**

   The great river of ice at the head of Disenchantment Bay is **Hubbard
Glacier.** Ninety-two miles long, Hubbard is the longest valley glacier on
the continent—and the most active tidewater glacier in Alaska.

   The Russell Fiord Wilderness encompasses the Russell and **Nunatak**

Hubbard Glacier, Russell Fiord

Fiords, as well as portions of the majestic stewards that surround them—the St. Elias Mountains. Showing no regard whatsoever for international boundaries, this range crisscrosses from coastal Alaska to interior Canada and back again. It boasts 18,008-foot-high **Mount St. Elias** itself, the second tallest peak in Alaska (only 20,320-foot Mount McKinley—Denali—is higher), and Canada's 19,551-foot-high **Mount Logan,** the second tallest in North America.

A thousand years ago, Hubbard Glacier filled Russell Fiord, Disenchantment Bay, and Yakutat Bay all the way out to the Gulf of Alaska. Since then, the glacier has staged a series of dramatic retreats and advances that few people have been around to witness.

In 1986, by contrast, Mother Nature staged a well-attended drama in this remote corner of the wilderness. During the spring of that year, Hubbard Glacier suddenly surged forward, advancing several hundred feet per day. Ultimately, it sealed off the mouth of Russell Fiord where it meets Disenchantment Bay (in the vicinity of Gilbert Point and Osier Island) with a dam of mud and ice more than 90 feet high. Cut off from the ocean—and topped up with glacier meltwater and rain—the saltwater fjord began to turn into a freshwater lake.

Also isolated from the ocean were a number of seals, porpoises, and other saltwater creatures. The fate of the trapped animals grabbed worldwide attention. Glaciologists, biologists, environmentalists, reporters,

Galloping Glaciers

Most glaciers move just a few inches a day, rarely covering more than several feet a year. Some, however, undergo periods of spectacular advance in which they gallop down a valley at hundreds of feet per day. Scientists call these icy speedsters "surging glaciers."

A surge may continue for two or three years before the glacier lapses into its former quiescence. Some galloping glaciers move forward on a regular basis. Variegated Glacier in Russell Fiord Wilderness, for instance, surges once every 20 years or so. Others advance so infrequently that their surges have never been recorded. Scientists speculate that all glaciers follow some kind of surging cycle.

No one knows precisely what prompts a glacier to sally forth—perhaps an increase in ice thickness or a greater flow of water along its bed. The hotbed of this cold behavior, though, is not in question: More than two-thirds of the glaciers known to gallop on this continent do so in the state of Alaska.

photographers, and broadcast journalists all flocked to the area. For the first time ever, the tiny settlement of **Yakutat** made its way into national weather reports.

Most Alaskans looked on with amusement as the television news showed would-be rescuers in Zodiac boats zipping around newly created Russell Lake, trying to catch the seals and porpoises with nets. Coast Guard helicopters stood ready to ferry the animals over the ice dam to safety. Some of the stranded animals had ideas of their own, however. Marks appeared on the dam that turned out to be those of sliding fins: The seals were rescuing themselves.

The local press had a field day. Participants in the "Great Alaska Seal and Porpoise Chase," as one newspaper headline dubbed it, came up empty-handed; they had succeeded in catching nothing more than a pair of king salmon (out of season), which they promptly barbecued on the beach. This provoked another memorable headline: "Mission without a Porpoise."

Ensuing events justified the commotion. For days, scientists had been predicting the dam would not hold. To capture the projected cataclysm on film, the University of Alaska, the Park Service, and the National Geographic Society set up automatic cameras on **Gilbert Point.** At midnight on October 8, the tremendous water pressure in Russell Lake—now more than 80 feet above sea level—burst the ice dam. A glaciologist camped on Gilbert Point awoke to a fantastic roaring and booming. He later estimated the volume of water rushing out of Russell Lake and into the bay at 35 times the flow of Niagara Falls. It unleashed a massive cavalcade of icebergs that threw up waves 10 to 30 feet high.

In the end, nature had lowered the curtain on this very public spectacle in somewhat private fashion: Because the dam had broken in total darkness, there were no photographs to document the destruction.

Indian paintbrush, Russell Fiord Wilderness

What to See and Do

In summer, cruise ships sailing north through the Gulf of Alaska toward the ports of Seward and Anchorage sometimes visit active Hubbard Glacier. But not always. All that activity kicks out lots of ice, which can make navigation treacherous. You may be lucky, though: If the seas are calm, the winds are in the right direction, and the ship's captain is willing to maneuver through the ice and sail near the face of the glacier, you will have an unforgettable day.

By kayaking and camping in Russell Fiord, you can treat yourself to great views of the icebergs flowing in and out with the tidal currents "like elephants on parade," as photographer Michael Melford once described them. If you choose this option—and especially if it's your first time—go with a guided trip. Don't forget that this is remote wilderness: You can fly in on a chartered floatplane from Yakutat, but once it departs, you and those parading elephants are on your own. ∎

Hubbard Glacier

Mother Hubbard?

Upon seeing the immense face of Hubbard Glacier for the first time, a passenger aboard a cruise ship sailing into Disenchantment Bay approached the ship's naturalist and asked for whom Hubbard Glacier was named. The naturalist, whose sense of humor was as British as his accent, could not resist uttering a one-word response to the passenger's eager inquiry. "Mother."

In actuality, the glacier was named in honor of Gardiner Greene Hubbard (1822-1897), first president of the National Geographic Society. Under Hubbard's direction, in 1890 the fledgling society (founded just two years earlier) had funded an expedition to the St. Elias Mountains led by geologist Israel C. Russell. It was the first scientific expedition financed by the National Geographic Society, and it set the tone for all those that followed.

Hubbard was intensely curious about Alaska. Upon his election as president, he reflected not only the Society's goals but also (as one writer put it) "late 19th-century America's love affair with science" when he spoke of his "desire to promote special researches…and diffuse the knowledge…so that we may all know more of the world upon which we live."

Lituya Bay

■ 16 square miles ■ On the Gulf of Alaska, western shore of Glacier Bay National Park and Preserve ■ Backcountry hiking, kayaking, fishing ■ Best months late May–mid-Sept. ■ Contact Glacier Bay National Park and Preserve, P.O. Box 140, Gustavus, AK 99826; phone 907-697-2230. www.nps.gov/glba

ENCHANTRESS. SIREN. DEATH TRAP. Beautiful Lituya Bay has been called many names, all of them well chosen. For Lituya Bay—the only shelter on a 150-mile-long stretch of the wild northwestern coast of the Gulf of Alaska—is a microcosm of the geologic hazards of the North Pacific.

The little bay is dominated by the backdrop of the majestic, ice-capped **Fairweather Range.** The entrance to the bay (about 350 yards across) is almost sealed shut by a terminal moraine, left behind by the glacier that carved out the bay.

Twice a day, the waters of the Pacific rush in and out of this bottle-neck, setting up a chain of "haystacks"—sailor-speak for standing waves—and pounding turbulence that can overwhelm any ship.

When the French explorer Jean-François de La Pérouse sailed in here in 1786, he sent three longboats from his ship to take depth soundings near the mouth of the bay. With little warning, two of the boats were swept out to sea and crushed. None of the sailors in them survived. On an island in the middle of the bay—Cenotaph Island—La Pérouse buried a bottle containing this poignant message: "Twenty-one brave mariners perished here, Reader. Mingle your tears with ours."

Lituya Bay also lies directly athwart an active seismic fracture zone, the Fairweather Fault. Three fishing boats lay at anchor in the bay on the night of July 9, 1958, when an earthquake rumbled beneath the water. The boats were tossed about like bath toys by a great wave that rolled across the bay and surged onto the land, ripping out trees and advancing 1,720 feet up the mountainside. The wave then roared out of the bay and into the gulf, carrying two of the boats with it. One craft sank, but its crew was rescued. The other boat sank with all hands. (The third managed to stay afloat inside the bay.)

The captain of the third boat described what he had witnessed:

> These great snow-capped giants [the Fairweather Range] shook and twisted and heaved. They seemed to be suffering unbearable internal tortures....At last, as though attempting to rid themselves of their torment, the mountains spewed heavy clouds of snow and rocks into the air and threw huge avalanches down their groaning sides. During all this, I was terrified, rooted to the deck...then I saw a wave come out of this churning turmoil....As we were swept along by the wave over what had recently been dry land and a timber-covered shore, I was sure that the end of the world had come for Sonny and me and our boat.

Miraculously, their boat rode out the monster wave; all hands survived. ■

South Central

DURING THE LAST GREAT PERIOD of the Ice Age, half of
Alaska lay beneath ice. Some 10,000 years later, only 5
percent of Alaska remains so. Today it takes the form
of more than 100,000 glaciers tucked into mountain
passes, tumbling down rocks, winding through valleys,
and crashing into tidewater around the state.

Outside the state's southeastern region and the Alaska
Range, the area with the greatest concentration of glaciers
in Alaska, including one-third of its major ice fields, is

YUKON-CHARLEY
RIVERS NATIONAL
PRESERVE

Charley

N. Fork

Middle Fork

Champion
Cr.

Eagle

⑤

Ogilvie Mountains

DEMPSTER
HIGHWAY

Joseph
Cr.

FORTYMILE
N.W.&S.R.

O'Brien Cr.

Fortymile

Yukon

⑨

⑤

TANANA

Mosquito Fork

S. Fork

Dawson

Klondike

②

VALLEY

ALASKA HWY.

Delta Junction

STATE

W. Fork

Dennison Fork

CANADA

U.S.

Ladue

Stewart

FOREST

②

Tanana

TAYLOR HIGHWAY

⑤

White

Yukon

YUKON

Phelan Cr.
Summit
L.
Paxson

Tok

①

TERRITORY

Sixty Mile

R

A

N

G

E

TOK CUT-OFF

Mentasta Mts.

Slana

②

TETLIN
NATIONAL
WILDLIFE
REFUGE

Wellesley
Lake

RICHARDSON
HIGHWAY

①

Copper

NABESNA ROAD

Nabesna

Chisana

④

K

A

Mt. Sanford
16,237 ft

Nabesna

ALASKA HIGHWAY

Mt. Drum
12,010 ft

WRANGELL-ST. ELIAS

White

KLUANE
GAME
SANCTUARY

①

Glennallen

Mt. Wrangell
14,163 ft

Wrangell Mountains

NATIONAL PARK

Kluane
Lake

KLUANE

EDGERTON
HIGHWAY

④

⑩

Kennicott
N.H.L.

McCarthy

McCARTHY RD.

AND

NATIONAL PARK

Chitina

TRANS-
ALASKA
PIPELINE

Copper

Chitina

PRESERVE

Mt. Logan
19,551 ft

AND RESERVE

Mt. Hubbard
14,950 ft

M

O

U

N

T

A

I

N

S

Bagley Icefield

S

T

.

E

L

I

A

S

M

T

S

.

Cordova

⑩

Bering Glacier

Robinson Mts.

Mt. St. Elias
18,008 ft

FOREST

COPPER RIVER
DELTA STATE
CRITICAL
HABITAT

YAKATAGA
STATE GAME
REFUGE

Malaspina
Glacier

RUSSELL
FIORD
WILD.

Russell Fiord

Kayak
Island

Icy Bay

Yakutat
Bay

Gulf of
Alaska

N

TONGASS
N.F.

0   miles   80

0   kilometers   120

Iceberg, Prince William Sound

the south central, which extends from a breathtaking sea of high mountains in Wrangell-St. Elias National Park and Preserve in the east to the lovely fjord of Kachemak Bay in the west. To the south, on the edge of the stormy Gulf of Alaska, lies Prince William Sound, which contains the greatest concentration of tidewater glaciers in Alaska. To the north, Denali State Park has a front-row seat to the pageantry of the Alaska Range, crowned by the highest mountain on the continent—Mount McKinley.

Over the millennia, huge glaciers carved wide swaths across this land, opening up broad glacial valleys, threaded today by great rivers winding to the sea. Rumbling forward, these massive rivers of ice picked up rocks and debris in their path and scoured the land like giant pieces of sandpaper, pulverizing stone and soil into a fine powder. As the glaciers eventually melted back, they deposited thousands of feet of pulverized rock as sand and gravel in the lowlands. They also left in their wake rolling hills and peaceful lakes.

For more than a million years, strong winds blowing down the Matanuska and Knik Glaciers in the Cook Inlet region picked up silt from the sediment left at the base of these glaciers and carried it across the land in great clouds of dust, depositing it in the lower Matanuska Valley. This silt helped form the rich soil that, along with cool temperatures and the midnight sun, makes the Mat Valley famous for its production of huge cold-weather vegetables: 20-pound zucchini, 70-pound cabbages, and industrial-size carrots, cauliflower, and broccoli.

These conditions have spurred woodland growth, too. The south-central region boasts the second largest national forest in the United States (Chugach National Forest) as well as five mountain ranges—Wrangell, St. Elias, Talkeetna, Kenai, and Chugach—that are home to some of the highest mountains on the continent. It also claims myriad notable glaciers. On the southeastern edge of the region, the Bering Glacier, at 100 miles, is the longest glacier in Alaska. The fan-shaped Malaspina is the largest piedmont glacier (one formed at the base of a mountain), with more than 25 glaciers flowing together to make it bigger than the state of Rhode Island.

These topographical treasures make possible a wide range of outdoor pursuits. You can schuss down daredevil slopes at Thompson Pass or cross-country ski on a peaceful evening in Kincaid Park; beachcomb the remote shores of Kayak Island where the famous naturalist Georg Steller made startling discoveries in the New World; wander for days in wilderness without seeing a soul in Anchorage's backyard, Chugach State Park; or watch the Iditarod Trail Sled Dog Race take off down the Iditarod Trail, that historic mail and gold route.

Fish here are world-class and the populations of migrating birds run into the millions. On the Kenai Peninsula, the Kenai River has one of the world's largest runs of king salmon. Sockeye salmon of the Copper River are highly prized by gourmets for their rich flesh. The Copper River Delta sees not only great runs of salmon in summer but also immense gatherings of birds in spring as they stop here in a feasting frenzy on their way north to nest.

But all of this, just to get you into the glacial lingo, is only the tip of the iceberg. ■

Trumpeter swan, Alagnak Slough, Cordova

Wrangell-St. Elias National Park and Preserve

■ 13.2 million acres ■ 189 miles east of Anchorage, along the Alaska-Canada border ■ Best months June-Aug. ■ Camping, hiking, backpacking, mountain climbing, kayaking, fishing, mountain biking, bird-watching, wildlife viewing, tours, river trips ■ Fishing license required ■ Contact the park, P.O. Box 439, Copper Center, AK 99573; phone 907-822-5234. www.nps.gov/wrst

TOGETHER WITH KLUANE NATIONAL PARK in the Yukon Territory, Tatshenshini-Alsek Provincial Park in British Columbia, and Glacier Bay National Park and Preserve, Wrangell-St. Elias National Park and Preserve protects one of the largest virtually roadless mountain areas in the world. The United Nations has, therefore, designated it a World Heritage site. The biggest park and preserve in North America, Wrangell-St. Elias spans three climatic zones (maritime, continental, and alpine) and encompasses spectacularly diverse landscapes, ranging from rugged, tidescarred coastlines to open tundra to gargantuan ice fields.

Ski-plane winging over Mount St. Elias

Beneath Wrangell-St. Elias, the Pacific plate collides with and dives under the Continental plate, actions that have created faults, earthquakes, massive mountains, and volcanoes. Not surprisingly, some of the world's most powerful earthquakes, including one in 1964 that registered 8.6 on the old Richter scale (see sidebar p. 95), have jolted the region. Nine of the 16 highest peaks in the United States stand sentry along the Alaska-Canadian border, including 18,008-foot Mount St. Elias. And the volcanoes include both dormant (such as Mounts Drum, Blackburn, and Sanford) and active ones. Steam often vents from Mount Wrangell, one of this continent's largest active volcanoes.

The heat within Wrangell-St. Elias's volcanoes contrasts sharply with the ice and snow that perpetually covers about a third of the park. For millennia, ice sheets such as Bagley Icefield (part of the 100-mile-long Bering Glacier) have been edging their way across the landscape where four major mountain chains converge—the Wrangell, St. Elias, Alaska, and Chugach ranges. Included in the hundreds of glaciers that radiate from the park's immense ice sheets are Malaspina Glacier, measuring some 850 square miles, and Hubbard Glacier, North America's longest (92 miles) and most active tidewater glacier.

Ice climbing on Root Glacier, Wrangell-St. Elias National Park and Preserve

Over the eons, some glaciers advanced while others retreated, chiseling serrated peaks and scooping out valleys. The remote Chitistone and Nizina canyons far surpass Yosemite in size and rival it in beauty. Sheer rock walls thousands of feet tall rise above the lower Chitistone canyon; 300-foot-high waterfall spills into the upper Chitistone canyon. Several large rivers, including the Chitina—separating the Wrangell and Chugach ranges—flow into the Copper River, which powers through the Chugach Mountains to the Gulf of Alaska, east of Cordova.

The terrain of Wrangell-St. Elias is challenging in the extreme, which explains why—despite its proximity to Anchorage—it is one of the least visited parks in the state. Vast areas remain devoid of trails, making them inaccessible to visitors on foot. Yet this very difficulty has helped keep this park a secluded, pristine wilderness—one that is well worth the extra effort required to see it.

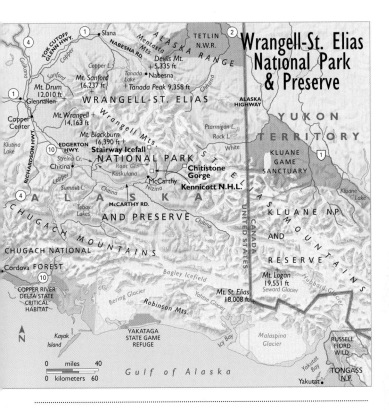

What to See and Do

Wrangell-St. Elias National Park and Preserve is just a day's drive from Anchorage. Follow the Glenn Highway (Alas. 1) northeast to Glennallen.

Although Wrangell-St. Elias has none of the usual national park developments, you can still enjoy a visit through a variety of activities. Lodging and other services for visitors can be found on private land within the park.

Driving

Two gravel roads lead into the park's interior: the **Nabesna** (see p. 87) and the **McCarthy**. Both roads afford views of mountains and tumbling rivers. The McCarthy also leads to historic mining zones, including the ghost town of Kennicott, as well as the town of McCarthy.

To reach the McCarthy Road, take the Richardson Highway 32 miles southeast from Glennallen to the Edgerton cutoff (Alas. 10) and turn left. Follow the paved road 33 miles to the town of Chitina and the park boundary. As you pass through Chitina, stop at the park's visitor contact station, located in a historic log cabin (907-823-2205. *Summer only*).

Inside the park, the paved road becomes 60-mile-long McCarthy Road. This narrow, winding washboard, pitted with ruts, becomes slippery during rainy weather. The road follows the abandoned track bed of the Copper River and Northwest Railroad. Around Mile 17 you'll cross the Kuskulana River via a 525-foot-long, one-lane historic railroad bridge.

Continuing on, you'll drive across the Gilahina River at approximately Mile 28 before reaching the Kennicott River and the end of the road. To visit the old mining town of **McCarthy** or the ghost town of **Kennicott,** you'll have to park your car and walk across the river on the footbridge. On the east bank, follow the road for about a quarter of a mile. The right fork leads to the town of McCarthy (about a mile); the left fork leads to Kennicott (5 miles). On private land in McCarthy you'll find a store, gift shops, lodge, guides, air taxis, and shuttle service to Kennicott.

Either by foot, bike, or shuttle, don't miss the red, weathered, decaying town and millsite of **Kennicott,** which was declared a National Historic Landmark in 1978. Completion of the Copper River and Northwestern Railroad in 1911 spurred full-scale copper and silver production here. Five area mines supplied ore to the now historic 13-story mill, which eventually processed a billion pounds of copper and ten billion ounces of silver.

Miners found three huge copper nuggets in the Wrangells. A two-ton silver nugget from Nugget Creek measured 7 feet 3 inches long, 3 feet 8 inches wide, and 10 inches thick. When the rich ore played out in 1938, the operators abandoned the mine and the railroad. Today the railroad bed provides the base for most of the McCarthy Road.

Hiking

In keeping with Alaska's wild and untamed character, you'll find no manicured trails in the park. A handful of day hikes branch off the McCarthy Road. One is near **Strelna Creek** (Mile 14), leading into the mountains. From McCarthy town you can hike along the south bank of **McCarthy Creek** for about 8 miles; from Kennicott, take 5-mile **Root Glacier Trail** along the glacier toward Stairway Icefall. Neither route is very difficult. On the west side of the Copper River near Chitina try hiking south on part of the old railroad bed that connected Kennicott to Cordova.

Myriad undefiled wonders await intrepid backpackers. Some trekkers fly to bush landing strips, lakes, or alpine areas; others hike in from park roads. No permits are necessary for backcountry travel. Before you head into the wild, however, fill out a "Backcountry Trip Itinerary" form, available at all park contact stations and most air services. Here, you are venturing into true wilderness, where survival skills are paramount.

Due to snow depths at higher elevations, prime backcountry season runs only from June 20 to August 20. Wildflowers such as geraniums, cinquefoil, lupines, and wild roses peak in June and July, the warmest months. Expect rain (and mosquitoes!), and be prepared for snow in any month. In general, the areas above tree line, 3,000 feet, afford the easiest hiking

Kennicott Glacier Lodge, Wrangell-St. Elias National Park and Preserve

and best views. For safety and an added measure of enjoyment, you may want to hire a local naturalist-guide *(Alpine Trekkers 907-822-3634; Kennicott-McCarthy Wilderness Guides 907-554-4444)*.

A wide array of wildlife, including the world's largest concentration of Dall's sheep, inhabits the park. You may also see mountain goats and bison and, on the lakes, trumpeter swans.

Kayaking and Rafting

On the coast, kayakers and campers in **Icy Bay** and **Yakutat Bay** explore waterways teeming with birds such as bald eagles, oyster-catchers, harlequin ducks, Canada geese, and a variety of gulls, as well as marine mammals such as harbor seals, Steller sea lions, and Dall's porpoises.

A panoply of wilderness-rafting companies *(Copper Oar Rafting 907-554-4453; Keystone Raft and Kayak Adventures 907-*

835-2606) offer everything from half-day trips to multiday expeditions down the **Copper River.** Fun trips include a two- to three-hour float on the Kennicott, or a continuation down the Chitina River. Some of the sights and sensations you can expect to encounter along the way include dizzying mountains, steep-walled canyons, dense forests, areas of intense white water, and black bears, bald eagles, and Dall's sheep.

Biking

Though mountain biking opportunities are limited in the park, you can follow rugged, abandoned mining roads and trails. Roads around McCarthy and Kennicott offer some biking. You may find suitable mountain biking on the Nabesna Road and branching creek beds. There are no defined trails. On most routes be prepared for muddy and rocky conditions. Two dry creek beds along the

Alaskan malamute in McCarthy

Nabesna Road—**Lost Creek** and **Trail Creek**—are suitable for mountain biking. Follow them northward and you'll be rewarded with views of the upper Copper River basin.

Mountain Climbing

Mount St. Elias, noted for its spectacular finlike pinnacle, has long captivated explorers and climbers. The National Geographic Society's support of expeditions and scientific research began with the 1890 exploration of the Mount St. Elias region by a party of ten men led by geologist Israel C. Russell.

An ascent of Mount St. Elias should only be undertaken by experienced climbers *(contact the park for outfitter information).* Most of the routes require a charter drop-off. Expeditions typically plan on spending several weeks on the mountain because of the changeable weather patterns.

Fishing

Although you can catch whitefish, lake trout, grayling, and salmon in Wrangell-St. Elias National Park and Preserve, the site is not considered a premier fishing location. That's because it may take 15 years to grow a fish here, so prime areas can very easily become fished out. Still, you're welcome to try your luck in **Rufus Creek** and other road-accessible lakes or streams. Remote but popular fly-in fishing destinations include **Tebay, Summit, Rock, Ptarmigan, Copper,** and **Tanada Lakes.** All anglers age 16 or older must have an Alaska state fishing license; to get one, contact the Alaska Department of Fish and Game *(P.O. Box 47, Glennallen, AK 99588. 907-822-3461).*

Accommodations

Scattered throughout the park, available on a first-come first-served basis, are 14 extremely primitive public-use cabins. Bring everything you need, including sleeping bags and cooking utensils. Leave your cabin cleaner than you found it, replenish any firewood (with downed limbs, not live) that you use—someone's life may depend on it. The only public-use cabin accessible entirely by foot is on **Nugget Creek,** a tributary of the Kuskulana River.

There are private campgrounds and services in local communities outside the park, and two within the park *(McCarthy Lodge 907-333-5402; Kennicott Glacier Lodge 800-582-5128; Copper River Chamber of Commerce 907-822-5555).* ∎

Nabesna Road

■ 45 miles long ■ Northern side of Wrangell-St. Elias National Park and Preserve, access via the Tok Cutoff ■ Best months late May–mid-Sept. ■ Camping, hiking, fishing, bird-watching, wildlife viewing, auto tour ■ Contact Wrangell-St. Elias National Park and Preserve, P.O. Box 439, Copper Center, AK 99573; phone 907-822-5234. www.nps.gov/wrst

FOR TRAVELERS WHO WISH TO VIEW Wrangell-St. Elias National Park and Preserve mainly by car, there is the Nabesna Road. This 45-mile drive begins in Slana *(Milepost 59.8 on Glenn Highway, or Tok Cutoff)*, just outside the park's northern boundary, and winds toward (and eventually into) the Wrangell Mountains to reach the old mining town of Nabesna. Except for its first four miles, the Nabesna is rich in gravel and chuckholes; stop at the Slana Ranger Station *(907-822-5238)* to find out about road conditions. Open from early June to early September, the station also offers information on backcountry travel.

The first few miles of the drive pass through dense, flat, black spruce forest; look for falcon-shaped, northern hawk owls, diurnal hunters of rodents and small birds. Pull off at Mile 7 and walk down to **Rufus Creek,** a popular fishing spot for grayling and Dolly Varden trout. Back on the road again, stop at the lovely pond on the road's northeast side just past Mile 15 for a view of the Mentasta Mountains to the north. On this thinly forested plateau you'll also find seasonal wildflowers, notably lupines, chiming bells, and arnica. Dwarf birch and willow provide cover for willow ptarmigan and arctic ground squirrels. Blueberries and lowbush cranberries reward late summer hikers. In midsummer, moose sometimes feed at ponds such as this.

Wildlife abounds in the park. Early in the spring and late in the fall, some of the 30,000 members of the Nelchina caribou herd often migrate across this road. Occasionally, these animals also can be seen running through dense forest. You may spot a brown bear or two grazing autumn blueberries. In late evening and early morning look for red foxes. On open tundra watch for northern harriers, jaegers, and golden-crowned sparrows. Tundra swans, goldeneyes, buffleheads, and pintail grace many of this region's lakes.

Two of the park's lakes, appropriately named **Twin Lakes,** can be accessed from the pull-off at Mile 28. Just beyond this popular fishing spot, the road begins to deteriorate. A few streams must be forded, so travel beyond this point should be limited to high-clearance and 4WD vehicles. Even drivers of those vehicles should consult park personnel before proceeding. When conditions are right, the drive from here to Nabesna town offers unsurpassed views of the Wrangells, Boyden Hills, and Mentasta Mountains. At Mile 41, a marked trail leads to the **Nabesna River** and to an old airstrip once used by miners to fly out their gold ore. Devils Mountain rises to the left of the trail. With spotting scopes and binoculars, you can see Dall's sheep across the river. ■

Prince William Sound

■ 90-100 miles across ■ Northern edge of the Gulf of Alaska, east of the Kenai Peninsula ■ Best months June-Aug. ■ Camping, kayaking, sailing, fishing, bird-watching, whale-watching, boat tours ■ Fishing license required ■ Contact Chugach National Forest, 3301 C St., Suite 300, Anchorage, AK 99503, phone 907-271-2500; or Glacier Ranger District, Girdwood, phone 907-783-3242; or Cordova Ranger District, phone 907-424-7761; or Seward Ranger District, phone 907-224-3374. www.fs.fed.us/r10/chugach

IN 1899, AMERICA'S CRÈME DE LA CRÈME of scientists and artists boarded a luxury steamship, the *George W. Elder*, in Seattle and headed north for wild Alaska. The allure? Hundreds of miles of uncharted glaciers and coasts, a bevy of new fauna and flora, and the thrilling promise of scientific discoveries. Railroad tycoon Edward Harriman had originally conceived this voyage as a hunting expedition in pursuit of the colossal Kodiak brown bear. But in the sweeping style of 19th-century tycoon-philanthropists, he couldn't resist transforming the undertaking into a grand gesture to the world of science. Loaded on board, along with live turkeys, cows, chickens, and cases of champagne were the tools of the artists' and scientists' trade: tents, canoes, traps, surveying instruments, and painters' canvases.

Like a scientific Noah's Ark, Harriman's expedition included two men from every likely discipline—geologists, botanists, foresters, mining engineers, photographers, artists, and preservationists. Among them was an old Alaska hand, John Muir, whose words "do something for wildness and make the mountains glad" would inspire the creation of national parks.

At the northern reaches of the Gulf of Alaska, the *George W. Elder* sailed past Hinchinbrook and Montague Islands and into Prince William Sound. Sailing to the western side of the sound, the expedition soon found itself, in the words of one member, in a "great ice chest." It held a magnificent treasure of beautiful fjords and breathtaking glaciers for the scientists to examine and record.

As Harriman and his companions approached the Barry Glacier, an uncharted fjord sparkled before them. Known today as Harriman Fiord, this exquisite corner of Prince William Sound is filled with tidewater glaciers laced with waterfalls. A little farther north, amid rafts of sea otters and seals, lay another fjord, whose plunging glaciers Harriman named for the East Coast's Ivy League and Seven Sister colleges, including Harvard, Yale, Bryn Mawr, Vassar, and Smith. Not surprisingly, the inlet itself became College Fiord.

Harriman's expedition was not the first to have explored the sound. More than a hundred years before, in May 1778, English explorer Capt. James Cook sailed into the sound and christened it Sandwich Sound, for the earl of Sandwich. By the time Cook's ship returned to England, however, the earl had fallen from grace, and the name was changed to

Kayaking near Columbia Glacier

The Ice Worm Cometh

At the turn of the 20th century, Robert W. Service, the famous poet who immortalized the Klondike gold rush era, wrote a poem entitled "The Ballad of the Ice-Worm Cocktail." In it, a brash "cheechako" (a newcomer to Alaska) is challenged by old-timers to swallow an ice worm at the bottom of his drink at the Malamute Saloon. Although he chokes it down, the man soon makes a speedy exit. The old-timers roar with laughter at the joke: The worm they slipped into his drink was only a spaghetti noodle inked with two big red eyes.

Like the saloon's mocking patrons, many people believe the ice worm to be a myth. But the joke's on them: There really is an ice worm! True to its name, this tiny black worm lives on coastal glaciers and ice fields in Alaska. Not built to withstand much heat, the ice worm's body hovers around the freezing point of water. How does it survive? On windblown dirt, pollen, and algae. Cocktails at the Malamute Saloon, are not part of its diet.

Prince William Sound to honor the king's third son (later King William IV).

Other events that have transpired in the sound have proved less benign. In March 1964, the largest earthquake ever recorded in North America struck Alaska; its epicenter was here in Prince William Sound. One hundred thirty-one people died and whole towns and villages at the edge of the sea were destroyed by the quake-generated tsunami (see sidebar p. 95).

Twenty-five years later, on the evening of March 23, the loaded oil tanker *Exxon Valdez,* sailing south through the sound from the port of Valdez, requested permission from the U.S. Coast Guard to change sea lanes to avoid icebergs coming off the Columbia Glacier. Shortly after midnight, the ship radioed the Coast Guard again. In what would become one of the great understatements of the day, the captain reported that "We've fetched up hard aground, north of Goose Island off Bligh Reef, and evidently we're leaking some oil."

Approximately 11.3 million barrels of North Slope crude oil spilled into the pristine waters of Prince William Sound. The oil slick swept out into the gulf and from there into lower Cook Inlet, devastating populations of marine wildlife and hundreds of miles of coastal habitats. Thousands of creatures died in the largest oil spill in United States history.

The scientific jury on the long-term consequences to the habitat is still out. But after more than a decade of winter storms and massive environmental cleanup efforts, the effects of the oil spill cannot be seen readily with the naked eye. When the sun shines and the seas are calm, there's no place else on Earth you'd rather be than Prince William Sound. Hundreds of miles of coastline, blue waters, emerald islands, fjords, and rivers of ice tumbling into the sea bewitch visitors.

Prince William Sound

What to See and Do

There are many sights to see in Prince William Sound. If you'd like to spend more than a day here, there are plenty of accommodations. Throughout the sound are dozens of public-use cabins managed by the Forest Service, available for $25 to $45 per night (877-444-6777. www.reserveusa. com). For more information call **Chugach National Forest** and ask for "Public Recreation Cabins: Chugach National Forest Alaska," a 30-page pamphlet that describes each cabin and how to reach it.

You can also overnight at Growler Island Wilderness Camp (907-835-4731 or 800-992-1297), a rustic retreat with cabins and heated tent-cabins. No established campgrounds are to be found, but primitive camping is possible on the islands that dot the sound.

Ferries and Driving Tour

The state ferry system, the Alaska Marine Highway (800-642-0066. www.dot.state.ak//external.amhs), can take you from Whittier to Valdez and Cordova, or from Seward on Resurrection Bay to Valdez and Cordova, and back. The ferry provides much more than transportation—it's communal, festive, and a great way to get out on the water and appreciate the remoteness of the sound. The crossing from Whittier to Valdez takes about seven hours. You can walk or drive onto the ferry. If you take your car, extend your water trip by driving the 350-mile circular route that begins or ends in Anchorage: Done counterclockwise, for example, this entails following the **Seward Highway** to Whittier, driving onto the ferry and crossing to Valdez, then taking the **Richardson** and **Glenn Highways** back to Anchorage—a circuit that can take several days.

Boat Cruises

From the west and the east sides of the sound, one-day boat trips can be arranged to scope out glaciers and whales. Prince William Sound Cruises and Tours *(800-922-1297)* offers boats cruises from Valdez and Whittier.

From Whittier on the western side, you are likely to cruise into **Blackstone Bay, Harriman Fiord,** or **College Fiord.** If you are interested in whales, scan the horizon for the plumes of humpback whales, which can shoot 15 feet high. Or look for the black,

triangular dorsal fins of orcas as they slice through the water.

Traveling out of Valdez, on the sound's eastern side, you can see the spectacular **Columbia Glacier.** One of North America's largest tidewater glaciers, it rumbles down to the sea from high in the Chugach Mountains.

Until 20 years ago, Columbia Glacier lay in almost the same position as when Capt. George Vancouver of the British Royal Navy mapped it in 1794. Around 1980, however, its 300-foot-high face imploded, kicking out massive quantities of ice (which now prevent you from boating close to the glacier). Since then, the glacier has retreated about 7.5 miles. Scientists predict that, within this century, the movement will open up a whole new fjord about 25 miles long.

Facing Columbia Glacier are **Glacier Island** and little **Growler Island.** Air and boat charters allow you to explore the islands' basalt sea caves.

Sea Kayaking, Sailing and Rafting

Alaskans like to explore the sound by kayak, a craft that offers an intimacy with water, beaches, and wildlife impossible to achieve in a larger boat. Outfitters such as Wilderness Alaska *(907-345-3567)* or Alaska Sea Kayakers *(907-472-2534 or 877-472-2534)* can set you up with a kayak or take you on half-day or week-long trips. Novice paddlers should hire a guide.

If you are experienced and go kayaking without a guide, be aware that the weather here is quickly changeable. Though the sound is sheltered from the wild storms of

Skunk cabbage in flower

Sea otter, Kachemak Bay

Soft Gold

With no blubber to keep it warm, the sea otter depends on its luxurious coat for protection against icy waters. Fortunately, it has the densest fur of any mammal. Yet more than 250 years ago, this fur touched off a series of events that nearly wiped out this creature.

In the early 18th century, Russia's Peter the Great commissioned a Danish sea captain, Vitus Bering, to discover if land connected Siberia and North America. On his second voyage Bering reached an island off Alaska's coast (see p. 100). While sailing back to Russia with news of his discoveries, Bering fetched up on the shores of an uninhabited island in what is known today as the Bering Sea. Suffering from scurvy and weakened by cold and hunger, the captain and many of his men died. Sea otters saved the others, who ate the creatures' flesh and kept warm with the fur.

When the bedraggled crew finally made it home, they found people were not as excited by Bering's discoveries as they were by the pelts the sailors had. These unleashed a stampede of hunters, who wreaked havoc on the sea otter population along the Aleutian Chain and into the Gulf of Alaska. The creature's fur became known as "soft gold."

In 1911, with the sea otter nearing extinction, an international treaty gave the creature some protection, the first step to saving it.

the Gulf of Alaska, winds can suddenly whip up and leave you bucking 7-foot seas. Other hazards, typical of Alaska, are in full force here: danger of flipping and cold-water immersion, hypothermia, calving tidewater glaciers, icebergs that roll, strong currents, rough water, and the intrusion of bears, which love peanut butter, salmon, toothpaste, and everything else you've stuffed in your food bags. Stay aware. Alaskan Wilderness Sailing and Kayaking (907-835-5175) offers day trips on small sailboats in the sound.

Just outside Valdez, Keystone Raft and Kayak Adventures (907-835-2606) runs a popular half-day white-water rafting trip on the **Lowe River** through **Keystone Canyon.** ■

Family bonding atop Thompson Pass

Thompson Pass

■ 2,678 feet ■ 30 miles from Valdez at Milepost 26 on Richardson Highway ■ Best months March-April, June-Sept. ■ Hiking, ice climbing, biking, downhill skiing, cross-country skiing, snowshoeing, snowboarding ■ Contact Valdez Visitor Information Center, 200 Fairbanks Dr., Valdez, AK 99686; phone 907-835-2984

HELICOPTER SKIING IN THOMPSON PASS, a past site of the World Extreme Skiing Championships, has boomed as word of the area's favorable skiing conditions has spread. The location of the pass—one of the highest points on the Richardson Highway, where it crosses the Chugach mountain range—has proved ideal. Winter storms roll in from the Gulf of Alaska, piling clouds heavy with precipitation up against the Chugach range to create snowfalls favorable for good powder conditions on the steep-angled slopes cherished by daredevil skiers. In fact, Thompson Pass's snowfalls are legendary: The pass holds the record in Alaska for most snow in a season (81 feet in 1953), most snow in a month (29 feet in February 1964), and most snow in a single day (more than 5 feet in December 1959).

Helicopter guiding services such as Alaska Backcountry Adventures (*907-835-5608 or 888-283-9354. March-April*) set skiers atop mountains for a day of schussing down breathtakingly precipitous slopes. Although local guides are knowledgeable about avalanche risks, you, too, should be trained to assess dangers, know precautions, and bring appropriate gear.

If you're into ice climbing, the **Valdez** area has one of the largest concentrations of ice routes in the world. Several, among them the enticingly named Wowie-Zowie, Hung Jury, and Bridal Veil Falls, can be found in **Keystone Canyon** right off the highway. The **Valdez Ice Climbing Festival** *(907-835-2984)* draws top national and international climbers every February to compete on the frozen waterfalls of Keystone Canyon en route to Thompson Pass.

If you prefer summer activities, you'll find the meadows and mountains here great for summer walks. The pass, which lies above tree line, is covered with lovely alpine wildflowers such as fireweed, lupine, and mountain harebell. In the **Worthington Glacier State Recreation Area** *(907-262-5581)* at Milepost 28.7 of the Richardson Highway you'll find the one-mile-long **Worthington Glacier View Trail,** which will take you right to the edge of this picture-postcard glacier. From here you can pick a ridge, a meadow, or a hill and set out on your own walk. There are also guided hikes along the ridges of Thompson Pass; contact Thompson Pass Treks, the guiding service of the Thompson Pass Chalet *(907-835-4817. www.alaskagold.com/tpass/scenic.htm)*. Guides can offer historical information on the area and identify plants and wildlife along the way.

Bikers can tour the pass along the **Richardson Highway.** There are no formal off-road trails, but the vistas from the road are spectacular. ■

The Great Alaska Earthquake of 1964

On the evening of March 27, 1964, the strongest earthquake ever recorded in the history of North America struck Alaska. From its epicenter in Prince William Sound, the earthquake sent shock waves over an area 500 miles wide, releasing twice as much energy as the San Francisco Earthquake of 1906 and moving more earth horizontally and vertically than previous quakes. In the month that followed, residents suffered through some 9,000 aftershocks, registering more than 6.0 on the Richter scale.

The earthquake, which measured 8.6 on the Richter Scale (9.2 on the revised moment-magnitude scale used today), led to the deaths of 131 people. But it wasn't the quake itself that claimed 90 percent of those lives; it was the tsunamis—or ocean waves—generated by it. So powerful were these tsunamis that their effects were felt as far away as Antarctica.

The word "tsunami" is Japanese for "harbor wave," though the more scientific definition is "seismic wave." In the 1970s, the United Nations officially adopted the Japanese term to describe the phenomenon of ocean waves created by an earthquake, a large landslide, a volcanic eruption, or a man-made nuclear explosion.

In the wide open ocean, a tsunami can travel up to 600 miles per hour. The tsunamis created by the 1964 earthquake rushed into Prince William Sound in enormous waves—some reached 90 feet high at the point where they crashed onto the shore. The tsunami savaged the Alaska coast from Cordova all the way to Kodiak, destroying entire towns.

Chugach National Forest

■ 5.6 million acres ■ Coast and islands of Prince William Sound and parts of Kenai Peninsula ■ Best months March-Sept. ■ Camping, hiking, backpacking, boating, white-water rafting and kayaking, skiing, fishing, horseback riding, snow-mobiling, skiing, bird-watching, whale-watching, wildlife viewing, glaciers ■ Fishing license required ■ Contact the national forest, 3301 C St., Suite 300, Anchorage, AK 99503, phone 907-271-2500; or Glacier Ranger District, phone 907-783-3242; or Cordova Ranger District, phone 907-424-7761; or Seward Ranger District, phone 907-224-3374. www.fs.fed.us/r10/chugach

PRESIDENT THEODORE ROOSEVELT created Chugach National Forest in 1907, when the national forest system was still in its infancy. Encompassing fjords, lakes, islands, glaciers, mountains, and vast stretches of trees, the national forest sweeps across the coasts and islands of Prince William Sound, covering 3,500 miles of coastline from the Bering Glacier on the northeastern edge of the Gulf of Alaska to the salmon-choked waters of the Russian River on the western half of the Kenai Peninsula.

Like Tongass National Forest near Juneau, the Chugach is a temperate rain forest. Translation: Cherish sunny days! Always, there is an abundance of rain and snow. MacLeod Harbor on Montague Island, located at the entrance to the sound, holds the Alaska record for the most rainfall in a year: nearly 28 feet in 1976. It also holds the record for a single month: November 1976 swam in 6 feet of rain. The alpine tundra—as low as 2,000 feet elevation in Chugach National Forest—is free of snow only a few months a year. As you can see, it won't do to trip lightly into this country. Come prepared for wet and cold, even in summer. Clouds and fog are dramatic, storms even more so.

Chugach's heights are raw and rugged with sculpted rock, glaciers, and imposing peaks. Below the peaks, Chugach comprises deep coastal forests of spongy moss and dark green trees—spruce and western hemlock—interspersed with aspen and birch that turn beautiful shades of yellow in the fall. Buttercups, columbine, and Indian paintbrush all flourish in the short growing season here.

The forests, coasts, and slopes abound in bears and moose. With the exception of Montague and Hinchinbrook Islands in Prince William Sound, black bears are found everywhere in Chugach National Forest. You can see them foraging for berries and carrion on the open slopes or digging grasses and catching fish in the intertidal zones. Brown bears, which can outweigh black bears by 800 pounds, prowl the eastern shore of Prince William Sound on the Copper River Delta and the Kenai Peninsula, where moose and small herds of caribou roam as well. In winter, shy and lovely Sitka black-tailed deer wander onto island shores in the sound to feed on beach grasses. As the snows disappear, the deer follow the green growth up the mountainsides, feeding on skunk cabbage and blueberry bushes. On rocky outcroppings much higher up, you may spot

Flattop Mountain viewed from Chugach National Forest

clusters of white dots, identifiable through binoculars as Dall's sheep. Look for them particularly around Kenai Lake on the rocks of Langille Mountain. Mountain goats live on steep cliffs, closer to salt water. Try spotting them high up on the mountainsides of Prince William Sound and the Copper River Delta. A host of smaller mammals wanders the forest: coyotes, lynx, red fox, wolverines, porcupines, red squirrels, and beavers.

A star-studded cast of marine mammals swims through Prince William Sound and the Gulf of Alaska, such as fin, gray, humpback, and killer whales, Dall's porpoises, and sea otters.

And birds? Come at the right time in spring, and you'll hit the jackpot: Within the space of only a few hours, thousands fly overhead. The Copper River Delta is a resting and staging area for millions of birds migrating north in late April and May. More than 200 species of resident and migratory birds find their way to these rich intertidal banquet tables.

What to See and Do

Since there's so much to see in Chugach National Forest, you might want to stay overnight and spend several days exploring. Dotted throughout Prince William Sound and Chugach National Forest are dozens of public-use recreational cabins available for rent. For more information call the Forest Service and ask for the 30-page pamphlet describing each cabin and how to reach it: "Public Recreation Cabins: Chugach National Forest Alaska." Call the National Recreation Reservation Service for reservations (877-444-6777) or visit www.reserveusa.com.

Hiking

From the Sterling and Seward Highways, you can access more than 200 miles of trails on the **Kenai Peninsula** (see pp. 122-23), many of which may also be used by horseback riders. For other walks in the national forest, seek out *55 Ways to the Wilderness*, by Helen Nienhauser, which can be purchased from the Alaska Natural History Association (907-274-8440).

Boating

For sailors, kayakers, anglers, canoeists, and white-water rafters, Chugach National Forest offers a wealth of white-water rivers, quiet alpine lakes, beautiful fjords, and hidden coves.

Kayakers can take day-long or multiday trips out of Valdez, exploring the waterfalls of **Shoup Bay** or paddling around **Sawmill Bay** with its mountainous backdrop. Guided trips, hosted by Alaskan Wilderness Sailing and Kayaking (907-835-5175) or Pangea Adventures (907-835-8442) depart from Valdez and Whittier. Rentals are available from both if you'd like to explore on your own.

Keep in mind when planning trips that this water is surpassingly cold. Water sucks the heat out of your body 20 times faster than air. After ten minutes in these ocean waters, a person begins to lose mobility. If you are a beginner, go with a guide. If you are experienced, don't get too cocky. Alaska has the highest drownings per capita of any state.

Horseback riding by Kenai Lake

Fishing

From salt to fresh water, there's plenty of secret and not-so-secret places to fish in the Chugach. But with 3,500 miles of coastline, you can wet a line on an empty beach with only seals and sea otters as company. Popular destinations include **Billy's Hole** in Long Bay, where you may spot brown bears in mid-July; **Eickelberg Bay,** known for its stunning granite peaks; and **Finski Bay,** where you can explore sea caves and hike to alpine lakes or Glacier Island.

You can charter a motorboat out of Whittier or Valdez *(contact Valdez Convention and Visitors Bureau 907-835-4636 or 800-770-5954)* and head into deeper water, where reeling in a 200-pound halibut is not unheard-of. In June and July, you can stand shoulder to shoulder with other anglers on the **Russian River** when the red salmon swim in en masse.

If you're a freshwater angler, you can escape by floatplane *(Ketchum Air Service 907-243-5525 or 800-433-9114; www.ketchmair .com)* to a remote lakeshore cabin, paddle out in a canoe, and toss out a line. Or you can hike to great fishing on lakes and streams all the way from the Kenai to the Copper River. Many of the Kenai rivers and streams are migration routes for Dolly Varden trout, rainbow trout, and silver, king, and red salmon. Other freshwater fish found in these waters are arctic grayling, burbot, lake trout, and cutthroat trout.

Glacier Viewing

Lying just 55 miles south of Anchorage, **Portage Glacier** is the national forest's most popular

Sockeye salmon from the Russian River

attraction. The **Begich, Boggs Visitor Center** on Portage Glacier Road offers interpretive displays on area glaciers and natural history *(907-783-2326. Daily in summer, weekends in winter).*

Columbia Glacier, out of Valdez on the eastern side of Prince William Sound, is one of the largest tidewater glaciers in North America; several years ago it began a dramatic retreat, opening up the fjord in front of it (see p. 92). You can sail or paddle to the glacier, nosing among small icebergs. Just remember to stay a respectful distance (at least a quarter of a mile) from the face of any glacier or large iceberg. Because an iceberg is constantly melting, it is unstable and can roll at any time.

Bird-watching

The **Copper River Delta** outside the town of Cordova in eastern Prince William Sound is an extraordinarily lush and diverse ecosystem fed by several glacial rivers. In late April and early May, hundreds of bird-watchers descend with their rubber boots and binoculars for the annual **Copper River Delta Shorebird Festival** to watch millions of migrating birds. Nearly the entire world population of western sandpipers cruises through here in the company of thousands of other shorebirds, swans, sandhill cranes, raptors, and geese. The local Audubon Society chapter *(907-424-7260)* often sponsors a cruise with naturalists from Valdez to Cordova during the festival. ■

Kayak Island

■ 25,600 acres ■ 62 miles southeast of Cordova on eastern boundary of Chugach National Forest ■ Camping, hiking ■ Contact Cordova Ranger District, Chugach National Forest, P.O. Box 280, Cordova, AK 99574; phone 907-424-7761. www.fs.fed.us/r10/chugach

AS YOU CRUISE UP the Gulf of Alaska from the head of the Inside Passage, Kayak Island rises sharply out of the sea, a harbinger of more sheltered waters ahead in Prince William Sound. The island acquired its present name in the 1800s, when Russian explorers decided that it resembled the skin boat of the Eskimo. Before that time it had been known as St. Elias, a name bestowed upon it by Danish sea captain Vitus Bering, who landed briefly on the island in 1741 (see sidebar p. 93).

Aboard Bering's ship was a serious, young German scientist named

Georg Wilhelm Steller, who had prepared for this moment—the first landfall in an unknown land—for ten years. To Steller's shock and rage, the captain allowed him only ten hours on shore. Despite his disappointment, however, he made the most of the brief time granted him—and thereby secured himself a place in history. He collected as-yet-undiscovered plants, recorded the finds of a native cache, and identified the western cousin of the American blue jay, now named Steller's jay. Later, he described in exhaustive detail and accuracy relatively unknown mammals such as the Steller sea lion, the northern fur seal, and a giant manatee (now extinct) known as the Steller's sea cow.

Kayak Island is remote and far flung, and that's the beauty of it. A wealth of flotsam washes onto its shores, making it ideal for beachcombing. Indeed, currents propel floating treasures to Alaska from all over the Pacific Ocean. Cargo ships crossing the gulf have been known to lose containers overboard whose whimsical contents—rubber duckies, plastic tugboats, and frogs—are still surfing their way onto beaches across the state. When a container of Nike shoes went swimming, Alaskans went booty hunting—combing beaches, matching feet, and swapping sizes. Beachcombers wandering the tide line on Kayak Island have been known to find "pearls of the sea" (fishermen's glass floats), handcrafted wooden casks, and even messages in containers from distant lands. Tracking such flotsam not only delights the treasure hunter but provides a gold mine of information for oceanographers on currents, winds, and seas.

Although you can travel to Kayak Island by boat, the easiest way to get there is by helicopter or small plane, chartered in Cordova. Contact the Cordova Chamber of Commerce *(907-543-2911)* for a list of outfitters and charter services. ∎

Steller sea lion

Hiking the Turnagain Arm Trail, Chugach State Park

Chugach State Park

■ 495,000 acres ■ 12 miles south of Anchorage via Seward Highway ■ Year-round ■ Camping, hiking, backpacking, mountain climbing, river kayaking, paragliding, fishing, mountain biking, cross-country skiing, backcountry skiing, snowmobiling, snowshoeing ■ Parking fee at some access points ■ Fishing license required ■ Contact the park, HC 52, Box 8999, Indian, AK 99540; phone 907-345-5014. www.dnr.state.ak.us/parks/units/chugach

WHAT MAKES THIS PARK so extraordinary? It's wild. And, surprisingly, this extreme wildness—almost half a million acres of it—lies in the backyard of the metropolis of Anchorage, home to a quarter million people. In Chugach State Park's 30-year history, all the rangers combined have not come close to walking, let alone exploring, every corner and valley of it. Many summits are unnamed, and a few of them are still unclimbed. Most valleys and headwaters in the park's interior receive only a few hardy visitors all year long. Yet half the population of Alaska lives on the boundary of Chugach State Park, mere minutes from its rivers, creeks, and trailheads.

There's a price for that proximity. Residents here frequently discover moose chomping away in summer vegetable gardens. And these uninvited dinner guests don't disappear with summer's end; the critters can be seen trimming trees all winter long. Of greater concern to residents than the moose, however, are the bears. Every year, both black and brown bears from the park mosey around the homes on the hillside, wreaking havoc and creating some heart-stopping moments for people in the vicinity. Despite these occurrences, most Alaskans would live nowhere else. The joy of seeing an animal in the wild—even if it's peering in your windows—is a gift.

Chugach State Park is bounded to the north by the Knik Arm and to the west by the city of Anchorage (on the edge of Cook Inlet). Scenic Turnagain Arm forms the park's southern boundary; here pods of white beluga whales can be spotted throughout the summer. Knik Glacier and Chugach National Forest (see pp. 96-100), the second largest national forest in the United States, combine to constitute the park's eastern limit.

Mountains, their peaks rising dramatically from sea level to more than 8,000 feet, compose the vast majority of the park. If you're hiking, you will get above tree line very quickly. In these high alpine meadows, myriad miniature flowers blossom at your feet—moss campion, dwarf fireweed, mountain harebells, shooting stars, buttercups, and dwarf dogwood. Come late summer, you'll find a wealth of blueberries, raspberries, crowberries, and cranberries.

Humans aren't the only ones interested in such fruit, however. If you are picking berries, look up periodically to make certain you haven't been joined by a bear. Take heed on a summer's evening if you hear a piercing whistle; it may be a fat, gray-brown hoary marmot, frozen motionless on a rocky perch, trying to warn his colleagues of an approaching brown or black bear. Other mammals in the park include wolves, lynx, foxes, ermines, coyotes, mountain goats, river otters, flying squirrels, mink, muskrat, and beavers. In addition, some 2,000 Dall's sheep scramble around the rocky summits of the park.

In the lowlands, you wander through birch, spruce, aspens, poplars, and willows. Up higher, near tree line, you begin to see wondrously stunted, gnarled, bonsai-like forests of mountain hemlocks—a reminder that this is not always hospitable terrain. Winds blow as hard as 130 miles per hour during winter storms. Raw peaks loom in primeval grandeur. On a long, mild summer evening, with the sun setting near midnight, the views from any one of the park's ridges and peaks can be stunning. On a clear day, you can see Mount McKinley 130 miles to the north, the volcanoes of the Alaska Range 100 miles to the west, and the Kenai Peninsula, across Turnagain Arm, to the south.

Although the mountains on the front range of the park are small by comparison with those in the park's interior—about 3,500 to 5,000 feet—they look majestic from the time they acquire their first dusting of snow in the fall to the time they take on their deep mantle of whiteness in the winter. With the approach of summer, green life returns, inching its way up the slopes. June is statistically the driest month of summer, but "termination dust"—an Alaskan euphemism for "the first snow"—can fall as early as mid-July.

To get deep into this park you have to work a little bit, and you must be sufficiently versed in backcountry camping skills to fend for yourself. People die every year in this park. Opportunities to get lost or get into trouble are legion—from crevasses, avalanches, river crossings, bear encounters, hypothermia, frostbite. Check with park rangers for the latest weather advisories. No matter how mild or sunny the weather is at the time you start out, always carry a day pack with water, some high-energy food, an extra fleece, wind/rain jacket and pants, hat, gloves, map, matches or lighter, basic first aid supplies, knife, mosquito repellent, sunglasses, and a flashlight.

What to See and Do

Chugach State Park has dozens of access points. The old federal building in downtown Anchorage houses the Alaska Public Lands Information Center *(605 West Fourth Avenue. 907-271-2737)*. Here you can obtain maps and books about the park, as well as information on trails and cabins. The center also offers exhibits on other parks, refuges, and forests throughout the state.

Hiking

To make the two-hour climb to the most popular peak on the Anchorage horizon—3,550-foot-tall **Flattop Mountain**—head for the Glen Alps parking lot: From the Seward Highway, go east on O'Malley Road, then continue east via Hillside, Upper Huffman, and Toilsome Roads. Though polka bands, dancers, wedding celebrants, winter campers, and summer solstice revelers have all gained Flattop's summit, getting there is no stroll. On the mountain's flanks, climbers train every winter and spring to get in shape for Mount McKinley. Watch out for some

steep pitches below the summit.

Be careful as you scramble up these slopes. Climbers jokingly call the region's volcanic rock "metamorpha-grunge-it" or "Chugach crud." Hikers and climbers discover the aptness of those monikers the moment they reach for a solid handhold and get a fistful of rotten rock instead.

If you prefer flatter walking, try the 12-mile-long **Powerline Pass Trail,** which also begins at the Glen Alps parking lot. The trail dips below **False Peak** and follows the **South Fork Campbell Creek.** If you are so inclined, head across the valley and up **Little O'Malley Peak** (3,257 feet). Should the next valley (the **Middle Fork Campbell Creek**) beckon as well, cross the wide stretch of open land known as the "football field" and descend to **Williwaw Lakes,** a pretty place for overnight camping or a picnic.

On the southern boundary of the park where the Seward Highway winds beside Turnagain Arm, the beautiful **Turnagain Arm Trail** runs 9 miles along the side of the mountains, paralleling the high-

What colossal incisors you have!

Eagle River Nature Center

Located in Chugach State Park near the rushing waters of Eagle River, this former log-cabin lodge has been renovated and is now a nature center. The Eagle River Nature Center *(907-694-2108. Parking fee)* has an active year-round naturalist program from wildflower and mushroom walks in summer to animal tracking and watching for northern lights in winter. There are exhibits on animals, and displays on the natural history of Chugach State Park as well as self-guided nature walks, trail maps for independent hikers, and telescopes for spotting Dall's sheep on the mountain crags.

For good views of Hurdy Gurdy, Cumulus, and Polar Bear Peaks, amble down the 3-mile **Albert Loop Trail** that takes you alongside the river and offers beautiful views of the valley. The **Rodak Nature Trail** is less than a mile long and has interpretive signs about the natural history of the valley. On the trail, you'll find a viewing platform that overlooks a beaver pond. In late August, you can watch spawning red and silver salmon.

A hundred years ago, gold miners and trappers seeking the interior would cross from Girdwood on Turnagain Arm over **Crow Pass Trail** past Raven Glacier and down into Eagle River Valley. This was a dangerous route in winter, with "avalanches up the yinyang" as one former park ranger described it. It's still perilous in winter today.

If you're going for the full experience (the 26-mile Iditarod/Crow Pass Trail from the Girdwood side of the mountains into Eagle River Valley) do it in summer. From Girdwood, take Crow Creek Road to its end to reach the trailhead. Lots of bears live here, both black and brown, and midway through the trail there's an exciting fording of Eagle River.

For visitors wishing to spend a few days in the area, the center rents a cabin and yurt, which are located 1 to 2 miles along the Iditarod Trail near Eklutna Lake. You will have to carry in any supplies that you need because the cabins are accessible only on foot.

To reach the nature center from downtown Anchorage, take the Glenn Highway to Eagle River Road at Milepost 19. The center is 12 miles down the road—about a 45-minute drive.

Chugach Mountains off Glenn Highway

way and providing mostly flat walking. The railroad route in the days before any roads connected Anchorage and Seward, this trail brims with raspberries, highbush cranberries, and watermelon berries. It also offers spectacular glimpses of Turnagain Arm and the Kenai Mountains. You can access the trail at numerous trailheads along the highway between Mileposts 115 and 106. The 3.3-mile section from Potter Creek to McHugh Creek is the easiest walking. The 6.1 miles from McHugh Creek to Rainbow Valley and beyond to Windy Corner are more difficult, but they offer excellent views. A map of this interpretive trail is available at the Potter Creek trailhead at Mile 115.

For a steep, vigorous hike embroidered by spectacular wildflowers such as lupine and chocolate lilies, trek up **Bird Ridge** along Turnagain Arm to the lookout point—about 1.5 miles; the trailhead is at Milepost 100.5 of the Seward Highway. If your knees are in less than mint condition, take along a pair of ski poles to steady yourself on the descent.

If you walk part of the historic **Iditarod Trail** (see pp. 139-143) over Crow Pass to Eagle River, you'll cross over **Yakedeyak Creek.** It got its name in the mid-1970s when a troop of Girl Scouts was restoring the old trail, which entailed building a bridge over an unnamed creek. The girls spent so much time talking about a name for it that Doug Fesler, the young park's very first ranger, said, "You've been yakking so much about it, why don't you name it Yakedeyak." And so they did.

In the north, the 13-mile-long **Lakeside Trail** at Eklutna Lake (*accessed via Glenn Highway*) meanders along the gently rolling eastern shore from one end of the lake to the other. It is good not only for hiking but for mountain biking and cross-country skiing.

Climbing

Humor, Respect, Honor, Terror: A spectrum of human experience in these mountains is recorded in their names. Trappers and miners traveling the Iditarod Trail from Girdwood to Eagle River named a string of peaks in the Chugach range for birds, such as Magpie, Camp Robber, Gray Jay, Raven, Crow, Finch, Bunting, Roost, and Golden Crown. (One ridge, valley, and creek in the park are named for a bird that doesn't even live in the Northern Hemisphere— Penguin.)

Aspiring mountaineers dubbed some of the highest peaks in the park's interior with a basketful of B's: Baleful, Bold, Bashful, Benevolent, Boisterous, Bellicose, Baneful, Bounty, and Benign. At 8,005 feet, Bashful is the tallest mountain in Chugach State Park. "Bold, Bashful, and Baleful Peaks," says former park ranger Fesler, "are rights of passage for young climbers. There's lots of rotten rock, definite exposure, and you need ropes. They're very rugged and not easy to get into."

The technical route up **Eklutna Glacier** ascends over Inferno Pass by Mount Soggy, Devil's Mistress, and Mount Beelzebub. A second technical climb ascends Bird Ridge to **The Beak** at 4,730 feet, then climbs 240 feet higher to its true summit at **Bird's Eye Peak** before descending a mere 10 feet to Tail Feather Peak. Contact the park for specific route information, keeping in mind that the duration of any climb varies with its difficulty and the climber's experience level.

Boating

Carved out by glaciers, 7-mile-long **Eklutna Lake** is by far the largest lake in the park. Ensconced between jagged 7,000-foot mountains, it offers a wealth of recreational opportunities. You can kayak or row its length. *(Beware of the wind; get off the lake as soon as it comes up.)* You can rent a kayak in Anchorage or from Lifetime Adventures *(907-746-4644. www.lifetimeadventures.com)*, the park's concessionaire. With no boat ramp, however, you'll have to carry your craft at least 100 yards to the water's edge.

Eagle River is the only river in the park suitable for canoeists, kayakers, and rafters. The put-in is at Milepost 7.5 on the Eagle River Road. From here downstream to the first bridge is Class I and II water, which calls for basic navigating skills. The trip will take about three hours.

Pull out at the left bank before the bridge. Unless you are a veteran paddler and have scouted the rapids, do not venture below the first bridge. Experienced boaters have died in the Class II and III white water that runs between the first and second bridges. ■

Alaska Native Heritage Center

■ 26 acres ■ Northeast Anchorage, north of intersection of Muldoon Road and Glenn Highway ■ Year-round ■ Walking, folk performances, arts and crafts demonstrations, films, cultural exhibits ■ Adm. fee ■ Contact the center, 8800 Heritage Center Dr., Anchorage, AK 99506; phone 907-330-8000 or 800-315-6608. www.alaskanative.net

WHEN THE FIRST white men came to these shores more than 250 years ago, the native peoples of Alaska called themselves different names. Eventually, however, the world came to know them as Eskimos, Aleuts, and Indians. Today the Alaska Native Heritage Center proudly celebrates the diversity in their heritages. This living museum, which opened to the public in 1999, gives visitors an opportunity to marvel at the ancient ways, preserved by master artists, carvers, boatbuilders, storytellers, dancers, and weavers.

"Qayaqs and Canoes: Paddling into the Millennium" was the theme for the heritage center's second year. Throughout the summer, as visitors watched, master boatbuilders—some of them the last keepers of this ancient knowledge from diverse native cultures throughout Alaska—built eight beautiful crafts. People also told stories of their cultures through these traditional watercraft used for hunting, trading, and traveling.

Techniques for building boats varied from one region to another. In the north and southwest, the land has few trees. To the Inupiaq and

Tlingit dancer, Alaska Native Heritage Center

Yup'ik Eskimo people there, a boat—a *qayaq* (kayak) or a *umiaq* (open boat)—was a hunter's most prized possession. People built these ocean-going crafts from driftwood found along the beaches and covered the vessels with seal hide and walrus skin. The Athapaskans, Indians of the interior, made lightweight canoes out of bark stripped from birch trees. In the southeast, where cedar trees grow to dizzying heights, Tlingit and Haida people fashioned an entire dugout war canoe from the wood of a single cedar.

In September 2000 the center celebrated the ceremonial launching of the boats. "Today we sing, dance, and our hearts soar like the geese overhead," rejoiced Margaret Nelson, president of the Alaska Native Heritage Center. When the boats were launched in Kachemak Bay for a blessing, the assembled guests saw a salmon finning ahead of the crafts. For these first peoples of Alaska who have rejoiced at the return of the salmon every year, it was a good omen.

Each year, the center sponsors activities designed to tell the outside world about native cultures, which are still thriving in villages all over Alaska. Themes include the art of dance, the art of hunting and gathering traditional foods, and the art of healing through medicinal plants. Another theme—"Furs, Feather, and Fiber"—features the art of making traditional clothing such as seal-gut parkas, mukluks, and Chilkat dancing blankets.

If you watch the dances, you may be invited to join in. Don't be shy. As one Yup'ik elder said, "Long ago, dance was precious; it was something great. If one dances hard it is like taking away bad things—cleansing oneself, trying to be happy."

Or as a song from Tooksook Bay in southwestern Alaska warns: "You have to dance or you'll get moldy." ■

Tony Knowles Coastal Trail

■ 11 miles long ■ Anchorage, along the shores of Cook Inlet ■ Best months May-March ■ Hiking, walking, orienteering, biking, mountain biking, inline skating, cross-country skiing, snowshoeing, skate skiing, skijoring, bird-watching, wildlife viewing, wildflower viewing, races ■ Contact Municipality of Anchorage, Parks and Recreation, P.O. Box 196650, Anchorage, AK 99519; phone 907-343-6397

THOUGH NOT STRICTLY a wilderness trail, this paved coastal route (named for Alaska's governor) is still one of the most beautiful pathways in the state. The trail takes you on an urban-to-wilderness journey, as it follows the **Cook Inlet** shoreline for 11 miles, from the railroad station downtown, past skyscrapers, old neighborhoods, pocket parks, and private flower gardens to the forest and ridge ski trails of **Kincaid Park** (see p. 112). You'll also pass native wildflowers, bushes, and trees.

The trail begins near the railroad station at Ship Creek *(2nd Ave. and*

Biking along the Tony Knowles Coastal Trail

G St.), though you can also access it at various points along the way. Signs at the trailhead tell the story of Anchorage's beginnings as a tent town of about 2,000 workers who had come to build the railroad in 1915.

The view from the trail is spectacular. The low peak known as the Sleeping Lady (Mount Susitna) lies on the northwestern horizon; to its right rises the highest mountain on the continent—Mount McKinley. If you're a dawn or dusk walker, you'll enjoy the long pink sunrises and fiery sunsets over the Alaska Range.

And, of course, the waters of Cook Inlet run the length of the trail. The upper Cook Inlet near Anchorage has the second greatest tidal fluctuation (38.9 feet during spring tides) in North America next to the Bay of Fundy in Nova Scotia, which varies 50 feet during spring tides (see p. 118). There are no white sandy beaches; when the tide is out, it exposes large expanses of mudflats. These have their own unique beauty, but are highly dangerous, with a quicksand consistency. Don't walk out here.

From the trail, you may see pods of beluga whales surfacing in the waters of the inlet. You may even spot a gray whale in summer. Other animals you may meet along the trail include moose, lynx, bears, porcupines, muskrat, and foxes. The likelihood of happening across such creatures depends on the time of day and the amount of foot traffic on the trail. It's easier to spot moose in the early morning or evening because they may bed down during the day. Nocturnal animals such as lynx begin to appear at twilight.

Activities are well represented, too. Informal and formal ski races are held throughout the winter, while summer brings many runs and youth races incorporating all or part of the trail.

On a sunny, summer evening in June, the Tony Knowles Coastal Trail is a festive and friendly place—something like a big outdoor town party. On other days, however—when the wind is howling or the cold off the water sends daggers through your parka—you'll have it all to yourself. ■

Kincaid Park

■ 1,517 acres ■ West end of Raspberry Road in Anchorage, between the airport and Turnagain Arm ■ Best months May-March ■ Hiking, walking, jogging, mountain biking, cross-country skiing, snowshoeing, whale-watching, sledding, biathlon range ■ Fishing license required ■ Contact Municipality of Anchorage, Parks and Recreation, P.O. Box 196650, Anchorage, AK 99519; phone 907-343-6397

TO THE DELIGHT OF ITS INHABITANTS—particularly when the stories are funny and have a happy ending—wildness still lurks in the heart of Anchorage, Alaska's most populous city. One night in 1989, for example, local resident Bruce Talbot was skiing on a lighted trail in Kincaid Park when a great horned owl swooped down and stripped him of his hat, gloves, coat, vest, and shirt. Fortunately, Talbot managed to get away with only a few minor scalp wounds and a pair of talon marks on his back—and with his pants.

In meetings that are customarily far less eventful, skiers and other visitors to the park do encounter wildlife every day, among them moose, lynx, coyotes, foxes, ermines, nesting pairs of eagles, squirrels, and even the occasional black or brown bear. Offshore, in the **Cook Inlet,** beluga and gray whales swim, and may be spotted particularly in summer. Plenty of other sea creatures live in the inlet, including chinook and coho salmon that draw fishing boats to the area.

Mountain bikers and walkers enjoy the 11-mile **Tony Knowles Coastal Trail** (see pp. 110-11), which ends behind the outdoor center, locally known as The Chalet. From this vantage point along Point Campbell, recreationists take pleasure in the sight of Mount Foraker and Mount McKinley (Denali) to the north and Mount Sustina across Cook Inlet to the northwest. Just off the coast lies Fire Island.

In the winter, skiers flock to the park's 60-mile network of world-class ski trails (30 are lighted against the long winter night). Over the years, high school students racing these trails have unofficially named them. Sometimes a cardboard sign would get tacked up on a birch tree, replaced later by a fancy wood-burned version from a student's shop project.

As with so many things in life, the unofficial names have stuck. **Compression** earned its name because, said one expert skier, "you can really feel the G-forces on the descent." Feel the chill and the temperature plummet when you ski into the depression known as **Icebox,** the lowest elevation of the park. Skiers love riding the **Roller Coaster,** a series of undulating hills and corners, while **Stairway to Heaven** is a seemingly unending, but beautiful, climb.

Across town, an additional network of cross-country trails laces **Hillside Park** and **Far North Bicentennial Park** *(accesses off Tudor Rd. and Abbott Rd.).* City dwellers don't need to go far for alpine action either. The adjacent **Hilltop Ski Area** *(907-346-2167)* offers easy downhill runs for skiers and snowboarders alike. ■

Potter Marsh

■ 564 acres of wetlands ■ 11 miles south of Anchorage, just off Seward Highway ■ Walking, bird-watching, salmon viewing ■ Best months April-Oct.
■ Contact Alaska Department of Fish and Game, 333 Raspberry Rd., Anchorage, AK 99518; phone 907-267-2100. www.state.ak.us/local/akpages/FISH.GAME/wildlife/region2/refuge2/acwr.htm

TUCKED BETWEEN THE MOUNTAINS and the salt water of Turnagain Arm, Potter Marsh is an oasis for birders and photographers. Part of the **Anchorage Coastal Wildlife Refuge's** 32,476 acres of tidal flats, the marsh mingles fresh and salt water, providing a nutrient-rich banquet for winged and finned creatures alike.

Some 90 species of birds frequent the marsh. Canada geese are among the first dinner guests in spring, arriving in their V-formation flight patterns. Also in the spring, the arctic tern—which makes an extraordinary 20,000-mile-round-trip each year from Alaska to Antarctica—appears. It hovers over the marsh spotting for fish, its graceful forked tail helping it balance in the breezes. There's plenty of competition at mealtime. You can see belted kingfishers plunge downward and snatch the fish with their beaks. Fish here include salmon and char.

If you time your visit for late May or early June, you may see a fascinating display—the courtship ritual of the red-necked phalarope. The more brightly colored female (a reversal in the bird world) sashays around the male. But after she seduces him and lays the eggs, reality sets in. Then it's "Bye, Honey. Good luck!" and she's off down the beach to court another, leaving the duller-colored male to sit on the eggs.

To reach the marsh head south from Anchorage on the new Seward Highway. After the Rabbit Creek Road turnoff, signs will direct you to parking. You access the marsh via a half-mile boardwalk. ■

Potter Marsh

Seward Highway

■ 127 miles long ■ Anchorage to Seward ■ Year-round ■ Hiking, biking, snow-mobiling, downhill skiing, cross-country skiing, wildlife viewing, glaciers ■ Contact Chugach National Forest, 3301 C St., Suite 300, Anchorage, AK 99503; phone 907-271-2500. www.fs.fed.us/r10/chugach

ONLY ONE ROAD—the Seward Highway—leads south from Anchorage, but it's a doozy: It snakes along exquisite Turnagain Arm, past the rich bird life of Potter Marsh, through Chugach State Park and into Chugach National Forest, past the ski slopes of Alyeska and the Portage Glacier, into the Kenai Mountains, over Turnagain Pass, along the edge of Kenai Lake, and past Exit Glacier. After all that—a drive of about three hours if no stops are made—the Seward Highway winds up at Resurrection Bay, the jumping-off point for Kenai Fjords National Park (see pp. 119-124).

As you drive along the edge of **Turnagain Arm,** you can marvel at its backdrop of mountains and valleys. The body of water came by its name in 1778, when British explorer Capt. James Cook sailed up it in search of the elusive Northwest Passage believed to lead directly from Europe to the riches of the Orient. On his third and final voyage of discovery, he had to turn his ship around yet one more time in these waters—a disappointment he captured in the name Turnagain River (later renamed Turnagain Arm).

On the north side of Turnagain Arm, the Seward Highway forms a boundary to Chugach State Park (see pp. 102-108). Check out the scene at **Beluga Point** at Milepost 110. If you're there about a couple of hours

Turnagain Arm near Portage Glacier

after Anchorage's low tide, you may witness waves of salt water called tidal bores rushing down the arm (see sidebar p. 118). In summer, you may spot the colorful sails of windsurfers on the water or glimpse surfacing pods of white beluga whales.

You'll likely see Dall's sheep picking their way along the cliffs near **Windy Corner,** known for its exposure to its namesake breezes. From here and many other turnouts (look for the Alaska hiker signs), numerous trailheads give access to some lovely hiking along the **Turnagain Arm Trail** (see pp. 104-107) and its bird's-eye views of Turnagain Arm. A new interpretive overlook at **Bird Point,** at Mile 96, juts out into the ocean. From here you can hike or bike the recently completed 6-mile paved **interpretive trail** to Girdwood, part of the old Seward Highway (it was bypassed with the building of a new highway in 1998). It also makes an easy bike ride with pretty views of the arm. Bike rentals are available at either end of the trail. For information call Chugach State Park *(907-345-5014).*

Like many towns in Alaska, **Girdwood** (Mile 90) got its start from gold. Skiers turn off here for Alyeska Ski Resort *(907-754-7669),* with its challenging downhill runs. It's the only ski resort in the country where you can schuss down powdery slopes with views of an ocean (albeit a frozen one) directly below. At Mile 79 is the turnoff to **Portage Glacier** (see pp. 99-100) and iceberg-filled Portage Lake. Thanks to its easy access, this glacier draws more tourists than any other attraction in the state. Your best view, depending on weather and ice conditions, may be on board one of the daily Portage Glacier Cruises *(907-783-2983).*

At one time, Portage Glacier extended as far as where the Chugach

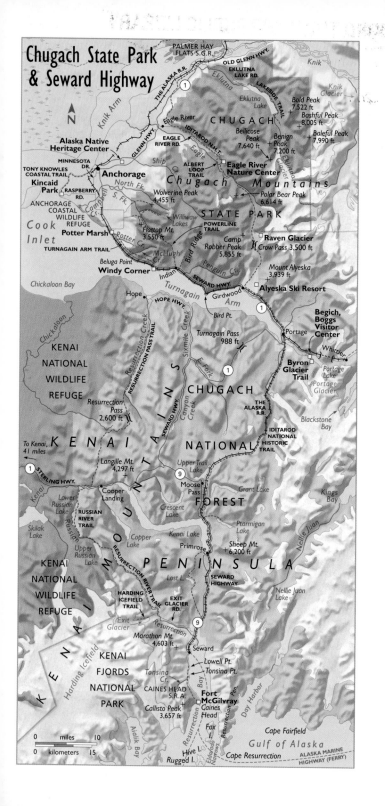

Dall's Sheep

Named for pioneering naturalist William H. Dall, these sheep are one of Alaska's most common species of large mammals. Numbering perhaps 70,000 statewide, they prosper in dry inland mountain ranges, seldom living in the wetter, snowier coastal ranges. Their habitat is characterized by grazing meadows and slopes adjacent to cliffs.

Although the sheep's white coloration provides winter camouflage, biologists theorize that the color also mitigates the heat from the unrelenting summer sun in the animal's treeless alpine habitat.

The sheep's normal life span is 10 to 12 years. Adults weigh between 150 and 250 pounds. Both sexes grow horns—rams' are large and curling; ewes' are short, slender, and slightly curved. During breeding season, which runs from November into December, the males sometimes break their horns as they battle each other head-on for the right to mate.

Look for Dall's sheep along the Seward Highway, 20 miles south of Anchorage; on Sheep Mountain; Mileposts 110 to 120 of Glenn Highway; and near Cooper Landing, Milepost 45 of Sterling Highway.

National Forest's **Begich, Boggs Visitors Center** now stands *(907-783-2326. End of Portage Glacier Rd. Daily in summer, weekends in winter)*, and the entire lake was filled with ice. The glacier has since retreated more than 4.5 miles. The visitor center offers films and exhibits on the forest and glacier, as well as information about local hiking. The short (less than 1 mile) **Byron Glacier Trail** near the visitor center is a level and easy walk for all ages. Here you get a close view of the hanging valley glacier, the snowfields left by winter avalanches, and the silty glacial creek formed from the glacier's meltwater. Black and brown bears, moose, marmots, and bald eagles all inhabit Portage Valley.

Back on the highway from Portage, the road winds into the mountains and crosses 988-foot-high **Turnagain Pass,** a popular cross-country

Tidal Bore

With one of the largest tides in the world, Cook Inlet fluctuates more than 35 feet between low and high tide. The ebbing tide runs so strongly against the rising tide that it temporarily dams up the water until the incoming tide literally bursts into the narrow inlet. The tide then advances as a wave or wall of water known as a tidal bore.

Such waves form in shallow, tapering inlets where the water levels fluctuate greatly between low and high tides. In North America, tidal bores occur in only two places: the Bay of Fundy in Nova Scotia, and the upper Cook Inlet near Anchorage in the narrow Knik and Turnagain Arms. In Turnagain, the most dramatic of the two arms, the bore can travel 10 to 15 miles per hour and reach a height of 6 feet.

The bore begins forming at the mouth of Turnagain Arm about one hour after each low tide for Anchorage. Its journey to the end of the arm takes a little more than five hours. One of the best places to view these bore tides is along the Seward Highway about 30 miles south of Anchorage. You'll find pull-offs here. The best time to be at this viewpoint is about two hours after Anchorage's predicted low tide.

skiing and snowmobiling area in winter. For a list of licensed snowmachine outfitters, contact the Glacier Ranger District (907-783-3242).

Past Turnagain Pass, an interesting side trip is the 34-mile round-trip cutoff road at Mile 57 to **Hope,** a quaint old gold-mining town on the southern edge of Turnagain Arm. Cyclists also prize it for its highly scenic nature and low auto traffic.

Before the turnoff to Kenai and Homer on the Sterling Highway, you'll pass a sprinkling of alpine lakes. Continue to **Moose Pass,** so named for an oft-told episode in which a cantankerous moose refused to budge, forcing a musher to detour his dog team.

Shortly before you reach Seward, turn off at Mile 3.7 for **Exit Glacier.** Nine miles of driving and half a mile of walking will take you to the foot of this river of ice, flowing down from the Harding Icefield. It is the only glacier you can drive to in **Kenai Fjords National Park** (see pp. 119-24).

At the end of your journey, Seward sits on Resurrection Bay, an important ice-free port and sea link from the coast into the interior of Alaska. It is Mile 0 on the historic gold rush and mail route, once known by the early mail carriers as the "Seward-to-Nome Trail," known today as the **Iditarod National Historic Trail** (see pp. 139-43).

You should take precautions while driving the Seward Highway. Keep your headlights on at all times. Take special care on the twisty section of road between Potter Marsh and Portage, which is often struck by high winds and subject to avalanches and mud slides. Be prepared to slow for animals: Moose often bolt across the highway and Dall's sheep sometimes come down near Windy Corner and Beluga Point. ■

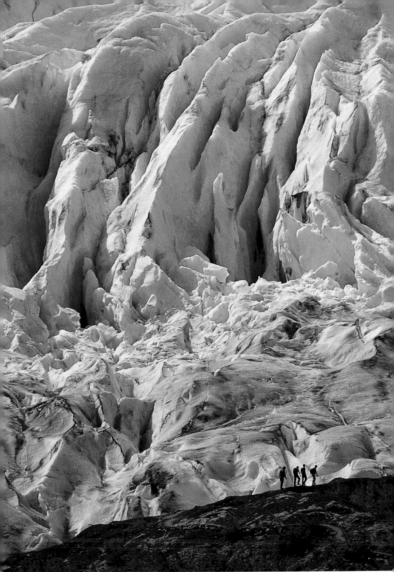

Hikers at Exit Glacier

Kenai Fjords National Park

■ 669,500 acres ■ 130 miles southwest of Seward on the southwest Kenai Peninsula ■ Best months May-Aug. ■ Camping, hiking, boating, kayaking, fishing, cross-country skiing, bird-watching, whale-watching, wildlife viewing, wildflower viewing, glaciers, boat tours, nature walks ■ Adm. fee to Exit Glacier ■ Fishing license required ■ Contact the park, P.O. Box 1727, Seward, AK 99664; phone 907-224-3175. www.nps.gov/kefj

ONLY A GEOLOGIC HEARTBEAT removed from the last great period of the Ice Age, the immense Harding Icefield dominates the moonscape face of this park. Pierced only by peaks of granite called nunataks (Eskimo for

Fierce Fireweed

Though Alaska's official flower is the tiny blue forget-me-not, many people think it should be the fireweed. Brilliantly framed against coastal green forests and ice blue glaciers, the crimson flower brightens Alaska meadows, woods, and roadsides. Yet its first blooming brings a kind of wistfulness: The opening of its last flowers in August signals the end of summer. The cold autumn days that follow turn the leaves of the fireweed a flaming orange-red.

Fireweed is a tenacious, quick-growing herb. When fire ravages the countryside, fireweed is one of the first plants to recolonize the devastated area. As a result of its deep roots, which usually escape damage, it is quick to grow, bringing life back to the land.

"lonely peaks"), the Harding Icefield covers 700 square miles and is nearly a mile high and hundreds, perhaps thousands, of feet deep. Robing the Kenai Mountains in snow and ice, it is the reservoir for the spectacular glaciers here that rumble toward the sea. In this park, nearly three dozen named glaciers and a host of unnamed glaciers dangle in high mountain valleys, spill down rock faces, and plunge into the headwaters of fjords.

Kenai Fjords National Park encompasses nearly 65 percent of the Harding Icefield, as well as islands, peninsulas, and fjords. These narrow inlets of water formed as the globe warmed after the last ice age, causing the world's glaciers to begin melting back. Salt water rushed in to fill the U-shaped valleys left by the retreating ice.

A narrow fringe of spruce and hemlock forest, with fireweed, lupine, and dwarf dogwood, grows along the coast on land reclaimed from the ice. Among the thriving growth, however, are "ghost forests," a legacy of the great earthquake of 1964 (see sidebar p. 95). The land dropped 7 feet, swamping the beaches and coastline of Resurrection Bay and killing huge stands of spruce trees with salt water. Bleached by the sun, scoured by weather, and preserved in salt, these ghostly trees stand like eerie sentinels in tribute to the power of that event.

Life, fortunately, abounds elsewhere. The waters of Resurrection Bay and the fjords are rich with marine life. Groups of jellyfish like the gossamer-white moon jellies and huge, orange-yellow, lion mane jellyfish float just beneath the surface of the water. Freshwater and saltwater fishes found here include all five species of Pacific salmon, Dolly Varden trout, halibut, lingcod, and rockfish.

The most gigantic creatures on the planet—whales, such as the fin, minke, gray, humpback, and orca—submarine through waters surrounding the park all summer long. Humpbacks are the most readily spotted. If you are fortunate enough to see one breach, it's like watching a graceful 35-ton ballerina doing a pirouette. Humpbacks come back to Alaska every year from their warmer water breeding grounds in Hawaii and Mexico to bulk up on schools of the tiniest fish on the planet, such as krill and herring. The smaller, eight-ton orcas, with their distinctive black-and-white markings and triangular dorsal fins slicing through the water, are also highly visible here.

Harbor seals, sea otters, and sea lions may be spotted, too. But the western population of Steller sea lions in the North Pacific declined by 80 percent in the late 1990s—a fall so fast that this population (found from Prince William Sound to the Aleutian Islands) is considered endangered. The eastern population, ranging from Prince William Sound south through southeastern Alaska, has been classified as threatened. The population crash may stem from the overfishing of their food sources, pollution, or warmer ocean temperatures. You can still see these chubby, noisy creatures on their haul-outs in the Chiswell Islands, which neighbor the park and belong to the **Alaska Maritime National Wildlife Refuge.**

What to See and Do

The waterfront in Seward is the headquarters for the park as well the embarkation point for all-day boat tours. It is also the southern terminus of the railroad to Fairbanks and Milepost 0 on the historic gold rush and mail route "Seward-to-Nome Trail," more familiarly known today as the Iditarod National Historic Trail (see pp. 139-143).

Camping
In summer, there are three public-use cabins along the park's coast that are available. In winter, there is one for rent at Exit Glacier.

Hiking
Exit Glacier is the only glacier in the park to which you can drive. A gravel road leading to the glacier intersects the highway about 4 miles north of Seward (turn at Mile 3.7); from there it's another 9 miles to the Exit Glacier parking lot (open early May, weather permitting; winter access to glacier by cross-country skis or snowmobile).

At the parking lot, you'll find a ranger station with information about the area. A paved pathway leading to several trails can be found at the parking lot as well.

Proceed down the paved pathway about a quarter mile to a kiosk with information about the glacier. At the kiosk, turn onto the dirt trail that leads to the glacier's outwash plain. Another quarter-mile walk brings you to the foot of the impressive ice giant. Don't get too close to the glacier, however. A tourist was killed here in 1987 when she posed for a photo beneath overhanging ice. Remember glaciers are always moving.

From the outwash plain, a half-mile nature trail leads you back to the ranger station. The trail's interpretive signs provide information on glaciers, moraines,

Hiking with the Gods

IN ANCIENT GREEK and Roman mythology, immortals entered Mount Olympus, the home of gods and goddesses, through the Great Gate of Clouds. Hiking in Alaska, traveling upward through the clouds of its many mountain peaks, you may feel as if you, too, are entering the heavens as you come upon an enchanting mountain lake or stand on a summit and look out over the land below.

Despite the vastness of Alaska, there are few official trails. **Chugach State Park** (see pp. 102-108) and the **Kenai Peninsula** probably have the best network of developed trails in Alaska because they are near the greatest population of the state.

In Chugach State Park, **Wolverine Peak** is a popular day hike (10.5 miles round-trip). Named by climbers for wolverine tracks seen in the snow at its summit, this mountain affords great views of Mount McKinley and the Alaska Range, Cook Inlet, and the rugged peaks of the Chugach. Dall's sheep often wander over its summit into the next valley. You can pick up the trail for the peak from the Prospect Heights trailhead above Anchorage.

South of Anchorage, 26.5 miles along the Seward Highway and Turnagain Arm, is the start of the trail up **Bird Ridge**. With southern exposure, this trail is one of the first to be free of snow in spring (about April). You'll emerge from the trees quickly for fabulous views over Turnagain Arm. You can climb farther to the top of the ridge or walk about 20 minutes to an alpine meadow, have a picnic, luxuriate in the views, and lounge around as your spirit dictates.

At the end of Turnagain Arm is the turnoff for Girdwood and Alyeska Ski Resort. **Mount Alyeska** is fun to hike in summer: The route goes up a toll road, along a tumbling river, and past some bushes with tasty blueberries to reach alpine meadows.

The 38-mile (one-way) **Resurrection Pass Trail,** an old gold miners' route on the Kenai Peninsula, crosses the mountains from the little town of Hope to just south of Kenai Lake. The trailhead is just southeast of Hope on the airport road. The route takes about three to five days of hiking. Reservations are required to overnight in public-use cabins along the trail (877-444-6777; www.reserveusa.com).

Near the end of this trail on the Kenai River side is the trail to **Lower** and **Upper Russian Lakes,** extremely popular fishing territory for

Scaling Flattop Mountain

sockeye salmon in June and July. You'll find trails for both hikers and anglers. The former use the **Lower Russian Lake Trail** (6 miles round-trip), which connects to the **Upper Russian Lake Trail** (24 miles round-trip). Anglers access the river via a separate trail. Both lakes have public-use cabins.

En route to Seward are two exquisitely beautiful destinations: Ptarmigan and Lost Lakes. You pick up the trail (6 miles round-trip) to **Ptarmigan Lake,** a turquoise jewel twinkling in a mountain setting, at Milepost 23 on the Seward Highway. To access the **Lost Lake Trail**—set in high alpine meadows of forget-me-nots and wild geraniums and a sprinkling of other small lakes and mountain tarns—drive to Primrose at the eastern end of Kenai Lake or to the other Lost Lake

trailhead near Seward. Or start at one end and make the traverse to the other. The round-trip to Lost Lake is about 14 miles; the traverse is 16 miles. Even as late as early July there can be still a fair amount of snow.

For more information on trails and trailheads, the Alaska Public Lands Information Center *(605 W. 4th Ave. 907-271-2737)* in downtown Anchorage, has an array of maps and books.

Remember, this is wilderness. It's best to go prepared and rely on yourself. If your knees aren't what they once were, take collapsible ski poles for climbing and descents. No matter what the weather, even if you are going only for the day, take a backpack with water, extra food, warm clothing, rain gear, map, lighter, and basic first aid supplies. ■

and plant and animal succession.

You also might take the half-mile loop trail, which begins at the kiosk and wanders up alongside the glacier before coming back down to either the outwash plain or the paved trail.

Hardier hikers will enjoy the well-marked, 7-mile round-trip **Harding Icefield Trail,** reached by taking the **Main Trail** from the Exit Glacier parking lot. The Harding Icefield Trail climbs about 2,500 feet through alpine terrain. This is a six-to-seven-hour trip, so wear warm clothing and good hiking boots, and carry plenty of food and water.

Fishing

The popular Seward Silver Salmon Derby (*Seward Chamber of Commerce 907-224-8051*) is held each August in Resurrection Bay. Everywhere you can see flashes of silver leaping and slapping the water on their journey toward the rivers to spawn.

Boat Tours

Take one of the popular day trips out of Seward into **Resurrection Bay.** They cruise into **Aialik Bay** or **Northwestern Fjords** and around the **Chiswell Islands.** The best time to go—especially if your goal is to spot a humpback whale—is June to mid-August. Other creatures you're likely to spy are sea otters, harbor seals, and sea lions.

Bird-watching

Many different species of seabirds return every year to nest on the Chiswell Islands, including common murres, horned and tufted puffins, and pelagic and red-faced cormorants. The murres, which look like little black-and-white penguins (but are not related) and the puffins (those clown-faced birds with the bright orange beaks) are part of the Alcidae family. You can easily recognize puffins by their chubby bodies and massive colorful bills. They are good divers and good fliers—once they get airborne. The characteristics that make these birds adroit at diving, such as heavier bones (water pressure on deep dives would crush hollow bones), make them amusing to watch when they are trying to get their heavy tanks off the surface of the water.

Cormorants, those gothic-like black birds, are renowned fishers. They are the only waterbirds that have no preen gland. (This secretes a waterproof fluid.) Therefore, they cannot "oil" their feathers like alcids. While this allows them to dive deeper and catch more fish because they are less buoyant, the down side is that their feathers get waterlogged. They can get chilled and hypothermic if they do not stay close to land and dry out occasionally. So, you will often see them sunning on the rocks with wings outstretched. ∎

Marmot, Exit Glacier Trail

Mount Marathon

■ 4,603 feet ■ Seward ■ Best months June-Sept. ■ Hiking, mountain race
■ Contact Seward Chamber of Commerce, P.O. Box 749, Seward, AK 99664;
phone 907-224-8051. www.sewardak.org

BLOOD, GUTS, AND GLORY are what Marathon Mountain means to many
people. A bar bet in 1915 sent the first runners racing up its slopes to "the
rock"—the mountain's lower summit at 3,022 feet. Nowadays (specifi-
cally, every Fourth of July), Seward hosts the **Mount Marathon Race.**
Some 30,000 revelers—ten times the town's winter population—arrive to
watch the scramble for the lower summit and back, a plummet over rock,
shale, and snow that one contestant described as "a controlled free-fall."
The record from the center of town to "the rock" and back is 43 minutes
and 23 seconds, set in 1981 by former Olympic skier Bill Spencer.

But you don't have to be a racer to venture up the mountain. By
following the trail that begins near the center of town, you can enjoy a
four-hour round-trip hike to the rock. Pick up a map at the visitor information center at the north end of town *(Milepost 2 on Seward Hwy.)*
before you set out.

Although the terrain is steep, and at times you may be reduced to all
fours and pulling yourself up by tree roots, the hike is a rewarding one.
On a clear day in summer, you will see grand sweeping views over other
mountain peaks, glaciers, and the breathtaking fjord of Resurrection Bay.

Be advised that the mountain always has some snow on its higher
reaches, and that snow arrives lower down in October and stays until
May. This makes the steep slope slippery, so take ski poles to stabilize
yourself. In addition, check in town for avalanche warnings, or call the
Alaska Mountain Safety Center *(907-345-7736).* ■

Alaska SeaLife Center

■ Downtown Seward on Resurrection Bay ■ Year-round ■ Bird-watching,
wildlife viewing, exhibits, films ■ Adm. fee ■ Contact the center, Mile 0, Seward
Hwy., P.O. Box 1329, Seward, AK 99664; phone 907-224-6300 or 800-224-
2525. www.alaskasealife.org

THE DEVASTATING OIL SPILL from the *Exxon Valdez* in 1989 (see p. 90) provided further urgency to a movement already under way to fund a world-
class facility in this northern climate for marine research, rehabilitation,
and public education. In 1998, the Alaska SeaLife Center was born here
on the edge of Resurrection Bay, a bridge from land to ocean. As you enter on the first floor, you will see a mural depicting the species of marine
creatures that were injured by the oil spill.

More a research facility than a traditional tourist site, the center nev-
ertheless offers a natural setting for viewing seabirds and marine mam-

Steller sea lion, Alaska SeaLife Center

mals both above and below the water's surface. At the huge underwater windows, toddlers and adults stand mesmerized by gliding, diving, dancing Steller sea lions. The creatures' large eyes and long whiskers help the sea lions hunt food in the dark depths of the ocean.

At the habitat pools, it's fun to watch as biologists feed the comical diving seabirds collectively known as alcids. Black-and-white, the murres look like penguins, but they are not related at all. Unlike those Southern Hemisphere birds, these can fly—even underwater. You can easily pick out the orange-beaked puffins with the small tank-like bodies, flapping their wings like underwater bats while using their feet as rudders. Pigeon guillemots look like tiny, silver-gilded stealth bombers beneath the water. But when they resurface, fish in mouth, and shake the water off their feathers, they transform back to their softer, duller black, with white wing bars. Now they seem flashy only when you glimpse their bright red feet.

The newest additions to the seabird habitat, red-legged kittiwakes, are not divers but excellent fliers; they are rarely seen outside some remote Aleutian Islands or the Pribilofs in the Bering Sea. With brilliant white feathers, dark gray wings, and scarlet legs and feet, they are a treat to watch as they fill the air above the habitat pool. ■

Caines Head State Recreation Area

■ 6,000 acres   ■ 4.5 miles from Seward on west side of Resurrection Bay
■ Best months June-Sept.   ■ Camping, hiking, backpacking, boating, kayaking,
fishing, bird-watching, wildlife viewing, wildflower viewing   ■ Fee for cabins
■ Fishing license required   ■ Contact Alaska Department of Natural Resources,
Division of Parks and Outdoor Recreation, Kenai/Prince William Sound Area
Office, P.O. Box 1247, Soldotna, AK 99669; phone 907-262-5581.
www.dnr.state.ak.us/parks/units/caineshd.htm

THE OLD ADAGE THAT TIME AND THE TIDE wait for no one is borne out by
the 4.5-mile coastal trail from Seward to Caines Head in the Caines Head
State Recreation Area. Three miles of the trail along the beach can be accessed only at low tide. If you're caught there during high tide, you may
find yourself doing a bit of cold-water swimming—a dangerous prospect.
Before you venture out on the trail, therefore, pick up a tide table from a
local sporting goods store or newsstand. Rangers advise you to start your
journey at least two hours before low tide to be on the safe side.

The trailhead begins at Lowell Point, just south of Seward. The first
1.5 miles take you along clifftops and through forests of spruce, alder, and
western hemlock on a footpath edged in summer by lupine, dwarf fireweed, beach peas, dogwood, and cow parsnip. The trail drops steeply
through berry bushes and devil's club to the bridge over Tonsina Creek.
Keep your eyes open; this is prime black bear country. Among the many
other creatures you may spot are sea otters, harbor seals, salmon, whales
(humpbacks and orcas), puffins, oystercatchers, and, at a distance, mountain goats (bring binoculars).

A quick jaunt through open woods takes you across another bridge
and to the beach. As with many beaches in Alaska, this is not the fine,
white sand variety but shale, gravel, and rocks. On a sunny day, the view
across the bay is a stunning panorama of glaciers and the mountain
peaks of the Resurrection Peninsula.

Hike the next 3 miles of beach from Tonsina Point to North Beach
only at extreme low tide, and plan to return at the next low tide. Alternatively, you might choose to spend the night before journeying back
to Lowell Point. There are campsites and cabins (at Derby Cove, Porcupine Glacier, or Spruce Glacier) available; reservations are required for
the latter.

One interesting place to explore is abandoned **Fort McGilvray,** on the
650-foot-high promontory of **Caines Head** at the entrance to Resurrection Bay. Fort McGilvray was built to defend the Port of Seward against
enemy attack—no abstract threat, considering that by 1942 Japanese
ground forces had captured two tiny Aleutian islands.

Although Resurrection Bay never saw combat, there were a few un-
confirmed reports of enemy submarines in the Gulf of Alaska. You can
access the fort on your own, but take a flashlight with you—and use
caution in navigating the tunnels and underground passages. ■

Fox Island

■ Approximately 3 square miles ■ 14 miles southeast of Seward, in Resurrection Bay ■ Best months May–mid-Sept. ■ Hiking, kayaking, bird-watching, whale-watching, wildflower viewing, berry picking, boat tours ■ Contact Kenai Fjord Tours, CIRI Alaska Tourism, 2525 C St., Suite 405, Anchorage, AK 99503; phone 907-276-6249 or 800-478-8068. www.kenaifjords.com

ON THE OLD TOPO MAPS OF 1951, Fox Island goes by its French reincarnation—Renard Island. French or English, there are no foxes left on Fox Island. No bears either. Without that furry, four-legged competition, picking the island's incredibly fat blueberries in late August is that much sweeter.

During the height of the tourist season in summer, boat tours from Seward stop at Fox Island every day, usually for about an hour—long enough for you to enjoy a salmon bake lunch. Unfortunately, that precludes a hike to the top of **Fox Island Peak** (its unofficial name), which takes about an hour one way, with a bit of a mountain goat scramble at the end. The spectacular bird's-eye views over **Resurrection Bay** from atop the peak make the climb worthwhile. If you'd like to make an extended journey to the island, reserve one of the eight guest cabins on the island through the Kenai Fjords Wilderness Lodge *(Alaska Tour & Travel 800-208-0200)*.

You can get an intimate water perspective by taking a guided kayaking trip to the north or the south of the island *(Sunny Cove Sea Kayaking 907-224-8810)*. For the more adventurous, the coast of the entire island (12 miles) can be circumnavigated in about four hours on a calm day. You'll paddle past natural rock arches, sea caves, and ghost forests left by the 1964 earthquake (see sidebar p. 95). Watch for puffins, orcas, sea otters, bald eagles, jellyfish, cormorants, and humpback whales.

Fox Island is sedimentary rock, a marked contrast to nearby **Hive** and **Rugged Islands,** which are granite, and **Cape Resurrection** to the east, which is pillow basalt. On rare occasions, orcas (killer whales) can be found around Fox Island's flat sculpted stone, sometimes swimming in to massage themselves on the rocks in the shallow beach waters. Human beachcombers enjoy skipping pieces of the flat rocks over the water.

In 1918, the famous American artist Rockwell Kent spent a winter on the island with his young son and an old Swedish trapper and fox farmer, an experience he immortalized through words and drawings in *Wilderness: A Journal of Quiet Adventure in Alaska*. Kent's fascination with this island world is an apt evocation of the many reasons why Alaska's wilderness continues to exert its inexorable pull on visitors today: "I crave snow-topped mountains, dreary wastes, and the cruel Northern sea with its hard horizons at the edge of the world where infinite space begins. Here skies are clearer and deeper, and for the greater wonders they reveal, a thousand times more eloquent of the eternal mystery than those of softer lands." ■

Fishing on the Kenai

Kenai River

■ 82 miles long ■ On Kenai Peninsula, from Kenai Lake to Cook Inlet ■ Year-round. Best in summer for fishing and boating ■ Camping, hiking, white-water rafting, canoeing, fishing, bird-watching, wildlife viewing ■ Fishing license required ■ Contact Kenai River Center, 514 Funny River Rd., Soldotna, AK 99669, phone 907-260-4882; or Alaska State Parks, P.O. Box 1247, Soldotna, AK 99669, phone 907-262-5581. www.dnr.state.ak.us/parks/parks.htm

FROM THE LOVELY, ICY GREEN WATERS of Kenai Lake, nestled in the Kenai Mountains, this extraordinary river tumbles over rocks and through rapids from one lake to another, winding its way down from the mountains and into the salt water of Cook Inlet.

Though visitors can go white-water rafting and canoeing, the big lure of the Kenai River is salmon fishing. One of the largest races of king salmon on the planet swims through these waters. Four of five Pacific salmon species—chinooks (kings), sockeyes (reds), cohos (silvers), and humpies (pinks)—return every year to spawn.

The challenge of the Kenai is that no river running through any city in the world has ever sustained such a world-class run of fish. You have only to think of the great rivers of the world to understand the uniqueness of the Kenai. These fish pass by the doorstep of hamlets, cities, highways, bridges, and sewage treatment plants. And though they arrive in the tens of thousands, their river world is exceedingly fragile: The territory most critical to the life of juvenile salmon extends just 15 feet from the riverbanks. Here the young fish live in the grasses, snags, and overhangs, feeding, foraging, and hiding out. They depend on these riverbanks to be wild and undeveloped, yet anglers throng some banks in such numbers that their pursuit has been dubbed "combat fishing."

A decade ago, the Kenai River was on a downward curve. Erosion of riverbanks and increased development were both taking their toll. Then,

A Dickens of a Catch

When he wrote *Barnaby Rudge* in 1841, Charles Dickens had no idea that one of his characters—the flirtatious Miss Dolly Varden—would gain immortality in the hearts of Alaskan fishermen. Named for the pink-spotted dress the character wore, Dolly Varden trout are popular sport fish—olive green with brilliant pink, orange, and red spots.

Like salmon, Dolly Varden are born in fresh water, live most of their lives in salt water, and return to fresh water to spawn. Found in North America and eastern Asia, the trout follow salmon to feed on their eggs. This habit imperiled the trout's existence in the first half of the 20th century. Believing Dolly Varden a menace to their industry, the powerful congressional salmon lobby persuaded the government to offer bounties for the fish, which were destroyed by the thousands. Reason and science finally combined to end the misguided practice.

in 1977, a special management team for the Kenai River took shape to address these issues and ensure the river's health. Since that time, planning efforts have brought together many diverse user groups to discuss not only the river and its wildlife resources but also the entire watershed, tributaries, and associated wetlands. Today the river is a healthy place for salmon and a great vacation destination for anglers. (Word to the wise: King salmon fishing may be catch-and-release in the near future.)

Where you fish on the river depends on the type of experience you're after. The **Lower Kenai River,** below the town of Soldotna, is prime king salmon territory, so it's no surprise that the banks bristle with fishermen and the waters are filled with boatloads of anglers, motoring upriver or drifting down. The first run of kings begins in late May; the second run usually arrives in late June or early July. Kenai kings often weigh 50 to 85 pounds. Indeed, the Kenai produced the largest king salmon ever caught—a 97-pounder.

The **Upper Kenai River** is more serene and more scenic. Circled by mountains, the upper river offers a radically different experience from fishing in the lowlands. It's strictly a drift fishery, with guides rowing down the river in drift boats. Their quarry: Salmon and rainbow and Dolly Varden trout. Several companies offer guided fishing, rafting, and natural history trips down the rapids of the Upper Kenai to **Skilak Lake,** a scenic place to camp, boat, and watch for wolves, bears, and moose.

Nearly 400 fishing guides ply the Kenai. Some guides are more conservation minded and ethical than others. One of the most highly respected guiding services is Alaska Wildland Adventures *(800-478-4100).* The permit coordinator *(907-260-4896)* for the state division of parks at the Kenai River Center can offer advice on other top fishing guides on the Kenai River, as well as information about additional recreation opportunities.

Choose wisely, and come to the Kenai with respect. Only by working together can we preserve here what has been lost elsewhere in the world. ▪

View of Redoubt Volcano from Ninilchik

Kenai National Wildlife Refuge

- 1.96 million acres, including 1.35 million acres designated as wilderness
- Kenai Peninsula ■ Best months May-Sept. ■ Camping, hiking, backpacking, boating, canoeing, cross-country skiing, fishing, bird-watching, wildlife viewing
- Fishing license required ■ Contact the refuge, P.O. Box 2139, Soldotna, AK 99669; phone 907-262-7021. www.r7.fws.gov (Kenai NWR link)

CREATED IN 1941 TO PROTECT the area's moose and the wild lands over which they ranged, this refuge was originally known as Kenai National Moose Range. It became the Kenai National Wildlife Refuge in 1980, with expanded lands and a new mission: to protect habitat for all wild creatures in its boundaries. The refuge now covers half of the Kenai Peninsula. Most of that acreage holds a special wilderness area designation, meaning that refuge managers use "least intrusive methods" to administer the area.

Moose, the biggest members of the deer family, still have star status here—no surprise, considering their size: Alaska moose are the largest in the world. The biggest bulls weigh up to 1,500 pounds. Their racks, or antlers, may extend 6 feet across and weigh 70 pounds when dry (125 pounds when wet). These they use to impress females during the fall mating season and fend off challengers purely by displaying the size of their weaponry. Such an exhibit, biologists say, is intended to "win the war without fighting a battle." Come December, the males shed their antlers. Other mammals found on the refuge include caribou, bears, otters, wolverines, porcupines, wolves, snowshoe hare, beavers, and lynx.

Sixty-seven bird species make their homes here. Among them are trumpeter swans, whose white feathers were once so prized that the birds became endangered by the early 1900s. Their populations rebounded in the 20th century, and they are now off the endangered list. More than 80 percent of the world's population of trumpeter swans live in Alaska today.

The Kenai National Wildlife Refuge encompasses **Skilak Lake** and **Tustumena Lake.** The latter, a watery blanket of 117 square miles, is one of Alaska's largest. The refuge holds some 4,000 lakes all told; many of them harbor rainbow trout, grayling, and arctic char.

What to See and Do

To reach the refuge's visitor center and headquarters in Soldotna, turn left off the Sterling Highway onto Funny River Road, then turn right on Ski Hill Road and follow it to the end. You'll find a trove of material, including maps, dioramas, books, videos, and information on canoeing, hiking, and camping.

Hiking

More than 50 miles of established trails and routes thread the refuge. The **Keen Eye Trail,** a mile-long nature walk that begins at the visitor center, wanders through a boreal forest of spruce and birch to reach a small lake. Interpretive signs along the way help you see the woods through different eyes. Most hiking trails in the refuge are found in the **Skilak Wildlife Recreation Area** around Skilak Lake and are road accessible. Many lead to good fishing lakes; follow the trail to **Lower Fuller Lake** to fish for grayling from the banks.

Other trails can be found in *Kenai Pathways,* published by the Alaska Natural History Association and available in the visitor center.

Canoeing and Kayaking

Nationally recognized wilderness routes singled out for their extraordinary wildlife and recreation, the **Kenai Canoe Trails** comprise two systems in the northern wetlands area of the refuge. The **Swan Lake Canoe Route** links 30 lakes into a journey of 60 miles; it gets the most day use of the two. The **Swanson River Canoe Route** weaves 40 lakes and 50 miles of river for an adventure of 80 miles.

The canoe trails take off from Milepost 84 of the Sterling Highway. Pick up a description from refuge headquarters or buy *The Kenai Canoe Trails* by Daniel Quick there. Guided tours are available only around Skilak Lake *(Alaska Wildland Adventures. 800-334-8730; www.alaskawild land.com).*

The country here provides scenic views of spruce and birch forests mirrored in clear, cold waters. On large lakes you'll be able to see the snow-crested Kenai Mountains rising in the distance. Blueberries and lowbush cranberries brighten the landscape in summer. As you paddle by lakeshore and riverbank, look for the refuge's famous moose, as well as coyote, wolves, bears, and birds such as loons, green-winged teal, mallard, mergansers, and eagles. The sounds of nature, undimmed by the outside world, are one of the great joys you'll experience on this journey.

Afternoon breezes can whip up a frenzy of whitecaps—Skilak and Tustumena can become especially nasty—so get off the lakes if the wind starts to blow.

Rafting

A great day outing is to float the Kenai River from Cooper Landing to Skilak Lake with a guided rafting trip *(for outfitter information, contact the refuge).* First, you float down the peaceful upper river discussing natural history with your guides, who will point out sockeye salmon, moose, Dall's sheep, and bald eagles. Next comes the thrill of negotiating the rapids through

Country store, Alaska style, in Seldovia

the canyon. Floating into Skilak Lake is a grand ending. If you are lucky, you may see moose, coyote, wolves, or even bears en route.

Bird-watching

With the refuge providing habitat for more than 67 species of resident birds—including three-toed woodpeckers, sharp-shinned hawks, and great horned owls—birders will feel right at home.

You may also see sandhill cranes, some of the world's tallest and leggiest birds, with long necks and droopy tail feathers. Males are known for their stately courtship rituals: They flourish their wings, dance about, toss sticks in the air, and bob their heads.

In wetlands and marshes and on ponds and lakes, listen for the trumpeter swan's call, which sounds like a loud French horn. ∎

Homer Harbor

Kachemak Bay State Park and State Wilderness Park

■ 380,000 acres ■ Southern tip of Kenai Peninsula ■ Best months May-Sept.
■ Camping, hiking, backpacking, mountain climbing, boating, kayaking, fishing, bird-watching, wildlife viewing, wildflower viewing, berry picking, clam digging, glaciers, tours ■ Fee for public-use cabins ■ Fishing license required ■ Access by small plane or boat only ■ Contact Alaska State Parks, Kachemak District, Mile 168.5 Sterling Hwy., Homer, AK, phone 907-235-7024; or Division of Parks, Kenai Area Office, P.O. Box 1247, Soldotna, AK 99669, phone 907-262-5581. www.dnr.state.ak.us/parks/parks.htm

SWEEPING IN FROM THE Gulf of Alaska, the sea ebbs and flows into the magnificent fjord known as Kachemak Bay, on the southern end of the Kenai Peninsula. It rushes into smaller bays, coves, and lagoons; laps onto rocky beaches and into tide pools; and caresses the edges of a coastal rain forest. From ocean to beach to forest to cottonwood meadows filled with wildflowers to clear, alpine lakes, the Kachemak Bay State Park and the Kachemak Bay State Wilderness Park rise in a crescendo to the tips of mountains capped with ancient ice fields and draped in robes of glaciers.

Kachemak Bay State Park, which has more biodiversity found within its boundaries than almost any park in the world, became a state park in 1970 to protect the area from logging. Today, it is the flagship for a remarkable fleet of state parks, rivaling the best parks on the planet.

On the southeast side of Kachemak Bay, the parks' boundaries stretch from Tutka Bay, China Poot Bay, Sadie Cove, Halibut Cove Lagoon, all the way to the edge of Aurora Lagoon. This thin strip of coastline sees most of the parks' visitors. Here you will find a few trails, campsites, and public-use cabins. Beyond is trailless wilderness, where you may never see another soul for weeks.

Although both parks are really treated as one, the wilderness park was added later in 1972. It encompasses mountain peaks, glaciers, and large bodies of water such as Port Dick, Tonsina Bay, One-Haul Bay, and Bootlegger Cove. All of these face the Gulf of Alaska and are exposed to stormy weather. The park takes its wilderness designation seriously: There are no trails within its boundaries.

Commercial fishermen, homesteaders, cabin dwellers, and artists call this bay home. The sea influences much of the artwork here, often in surprising ways: Artist Diana Tillion paints in octopus ink. "The ocean is so powerful and unyielding," says Tillion, whose studio sits on Ismailof Island in Halibut Cove. "I use octopus ink to paint things of great intensity. To me, it's a living color."

What to See and Do

Water taxis, ferries, and floatplanes are available in Homer. Contact the parks for a list of authorized operators, or visit the park's website.

Boat Tours
Known locally as the Kachemak Bay ferry, the *Danny J (Central Charter 800-478-7847)* is a colorful former fishing boat that makes two trips a day to **Halibut Cove,** on the south side of Kachemak Bay just outside the state park boundary. The first departure usually

Homer charter-boat crew and their record-setting halibut   *Following pages:* Gull Island

passes near **Gull Island,** which is not technically in the park. It is home to a large colony of kittiwakes, as well as a host of tufted puffins, cormorants, and murres. A larger tour boat, the *Rainbow Connection (907-235-7272),* carries tourists down Kachemak Bay to the fishing village of **Seldovia** via Gull Island every day. For fishing, marine-wildlife tours, or ferry service to Kachemak Bay State Park, call Inlet Charters *(907-235-6126).*

A Shrimpy Sex Life

Those cocktail-size pink shrimp that show up in salads or hors d'oeuvres everywhere come from Alaska's waters, where they lead sex lives much more complex than you may have imagined (if you'd bothered to think about it at all, of course). At one stage in its life, a pink shrimp is male; at another, it is female; and at still another it is something in between.

All pink shrimp are born as males. In the third year of their lives, the male shrimp gradually become female through a series of changes called molts that take place over a six-month period. Once the sex change is complete, shrimp remain females for the rest of their lives. Thus the pink shrimp population is maintained by young males and older females, leading certain envious humans to claim that the lucky critters have the best of both worlds.

Hiking

Kachemak Bay State Park has several developed trails. For an easy, flat walk through a mature spruce and cottonwood forest, take the 3.5-mile **Grewingk Glacier Trail** from your water-taxi drop-off at Rusty Lagoon outside Halibut Cove to Grewingk Lake at the foot of the glacier.

Hikers seeking a stiffer challenge might set off for **Poot Peak** (also called "Chocolate Drop" for its distinctive, kisslike shape), which can be seen from Homer. With a water-taxi drop-off at the head of Halibut Cove Lagoon, you can make the challenging climb to the lower summit and then descend in four hours' total time. *(upper summit climb recommended only for those with rock-climbing training).*

If you prefer a more leisurely pace, this is also a fun place for overnight camping. For a good campsite, walk to **China Poot Lake,** located 2.6 miles from the trailhead at Halibut Cove Lagoon. Leave your backpack in camp the next day and climb the Chocolate Drop unfettered.

Natural History Tours

At Peterson Bay, the **Center for Alaskan Coastal Studies** *(907-235-6667. www.akcoastalstudies .org)* is a nonprofit organization dedicated to the study of marine and coastal ecosystems of Kachemak Bay through educational outreach. Naturalists lead beach walks and conduct programs on tide pools, rain forest flora and fauna, geology, and marine land. On the way to the center, you will pass by Gull Island. ■

Dog mushing along the Iditarod National Historic Trail

Iditarod National Historic Trail

■ 2,400 miles (trail); 1,151-1,161 miles (race) ■ Seward to Nome (trail); Anchorage to Nome (race) ■ Best months Feb. (Iditasport competition), March (Iditarod Race) ■ Mountain biking, snowmobiling, cross-country skiing, snowshoeing, dog-mushing, dog-mushing rides, Iditasport competition, Iditarod Race ■ Contact Iditarod Trail Sled Dog Race Headquarters and Visitor Center, Mile 2.2 on the Knik-Goose Bay Rd., P.O. Box 870800, Wasilla, AK 99687; phone 907-376-5155. www.iditarod.com or www.anchorage.ak.blm.gov/inhthome.html

THE FAINTHEARTED WILL NOT FEEL AT HOME on the Iditarod Trail. Running along the original gold rush trail and mail route from Seward to Nome, the Iditarod crosses two major mountain ranges—the Alaska and the Kuskokwim—then runs up the mighty Yukon River, west to the Bering Sea, and over the frozen ocean to the gold rush town of Nome on the Seward Peninsula. Wind-chill temperatures can drop to minus 130°F. Yet every March, men, women, and dogs test their endurance against the elements in one of the last great races in the world: the Iditarod Trail Sled Dog Race, which runs from Anchorage to Nome.

Along the way, dogs and mushers battle ferocious winds, blizzards, overflow, and the constant danger of frostbite as they careen and twist down steep mountain passes. Sometimes competitors slide into open water along winding creeks, getting a soaking in ice-cold water. Mushers fall off sleds and get dragged behind until they can stop the dog team. People get battered and sleds break, necessitating repairs before continuing. Sleep deprived, mushers experience wild hallucinations of freight trains roaring toward them down this wilderness trail or competitors flashing by in silver lamé bodysuits. Still, they return, year after year, to compete.

With their natural insulation and tough feet, the dogs fare much better than people. When the weather gets extreme, they can curl up in a ball and tuck their noses under their tails to keep warm. Wiser by far than their mushers, they know when enough is enough and say so—by sitting down. Many's the lead dog that has saved its master from catastrophe—such as mistakenly mushing a whole team into deep overflow or into open leads in the Bering Sea during whiteouts and blizzards. Mushers

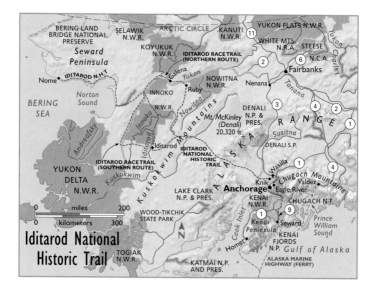

BERING LAND
BRIDGE NATIONAL
PRESERVE
Seward
Peninsula
Nome• IDITAROD N.H.T.

SELAWIK
N.W.R.
ARCTIC CIRCLE
KANUTI
N.W.R.
YUKON FLATS N.W.R.
KOYUKUK
N.W.R.
IDITAROD RACE TRAIL
(NORTHERN ROUTE)
WHITE MTS.
N.R.A.
STEESE
N.C.A.
Fairbanks

BERING
SEA
*Norton
Sound*
INNOKO
Galena
Ruby
Yukon
NOWITNA
N.W.R.
Nenana
Tanana

YUKON
DELTA
N.W.R.
Andreafsky
Innoko
N.W.R.
Nowitna
Kuskokwim Mountains
•Iditarod
IDITAROD RACE TRAIL
(SOUTHERN ROUTE)
Kuskokwim
Mt/McKinley
(Denali)
20,320 ft
DENALI
N.P. &
PRES.
A   L   A   S   K   A
Susitna
DENALI S.P.
RANGE

IDITAROD
NATIONAL
HISTORIC
TRAIL
Wasilla
Knik
Chugach Mountains
Valdez•
LAKE CLARK
N.P. & PRES.
Anchorage•
Eagle River
KENAI
N.W.R.
CHUGACH N.F.

0   miles   200
0   kilometers   300
**Iditarod National
Historic Trail**
WOOD-TIKCHIK
STATE PARK
N
TOGIAK
N.W.R.
Kenai
Peninsula
•Seward
Homer•
KENAI
FJORDS
N.P.
*Prince
William
Sound*
Gulf of Alaska
ALASKA MARINE
HIGHWAY (FERRY)
KATMAI N.P.
AND PRES.
Cook Inlet

agree that the dogs are the true athletes here. They are bred for speed and
distance. While they might settle into loping along the trail at 9 to 10
miles per hour, they can reach a starting speed of 25 miles per hour just
a few yards out of the chute.

No one today questions the huskies' ability to run a 1,000-mile Alaska
trail. That wasn't the case in 1973, when Joe Redington, Sr., founded the
race. Newspapers called him a dreamer, and even other mushers doubted
that the animals could make it. But Redington—who would mush a dogsled team to the top of Mount McKinley six years later—knew they pos-
sessed the necessary strength and endurance. It wasn't only the dogs that
people worried about. At the first race, recalls 1978 Iditarod champion
Dick Mackey, "Wives and sweethearts were weeping at the starting line,
wondering if they would ever see their loved ones again." (They did; no
musher has died on the trail, but many have come close.) Today the Iditarod Race has a multimillion-dollar budget and thousands of volunteers
from trailbreakers to veterinarians and a flotilla of pilots and planes
called the Iditarod Air Force.

The route along which competitors race came into being after gold
was discovered in Nome in 1898. With the boom came a need to transport passengers, gold, and mail to and from the ice-free port of Seward.
Dog mushers and mail carriers aptly named this route the Seward to
Nome Mail Trail, a designation that became official in 1908 when the
Alaska Road Commission conducted a survey of the trail. At that time,
the Iditarod Trail was the name for only a spur route running a few miles
from the main trail to the gold town of Iditarod, which had sprung up
halfway between Anchorage and Nome. Eventually, the entire trail became known as the Iditarod. Today's historic trail comprises side trails

Iditarod Trail Sled Dog Race: The banner's race mileage is symbolic; 49 signifies the 49th state.

and connecting trails—about 2,400 miles in all—and crosses both private and governmental lands. The Bureau of Land Management is responsible for coordinating its management.

The word *iditarod*, meaning "distant place," is now synonymous with great adventure and long-distance dog racing. But the Iditarod Race itself is more than a challenging adventure. It is also a tribute to the spirit of the early mail carriers and gold rushers and a commemoration of the 1925 "race for life." When a diphtheria epidemic broke out in Nome that year, dogs and mushers ferried the lifesaving serum—wrapped in fur against the cold—along part of today's race route from Nenana to Nome. Mushers and dogs raced through nights and 60°F-below-zero weather with the precious serum and made it to Nome in a record time of five days, seven and a half hours of relay mushing.

What to See and Do

Visit **Iditarod Trail Sled Dog Race Headquarters and Visitor Center** to steep yourself in stories of races and racers past.

Run, Ski, Bike, or Snowshoe

Beginning the last week of February, the **Iditasport** *(907-345-4505. www.iditasport.com)* is many races in one: the Iditasport (130 miles), the Iditasport Extreme (350 miles), and the Iditasport Impossible (1,100 miles). Choose human-powered transportation—bike, skis, snowshoes, or your own two feet—and race against others in your category. Training is critical, and you must be prepared for the extreme cold.

Be an Idita-Rider

Bid for a seat in the sled of one of the starting mushers for the Iditarod Race in March and experience the excitement of the first 11 miles of this 1,000-mile (plus) trail. (After Mile 11, the rider jumps off and the musher goes on.) Bidding opens in November by phone, mail, or in person at Iditarod Headquarters, and closes on the last Friday of January.

Watch the Iditarod

On the first Saturday in March, howling dogs, eager to run, can be heard all morning as mushers get ready at the starting line of "The Last Great Race" in the heart of Anchorage on Fourth Avenue. It's the best show in town. Get there early to watch, then position yourself along the race route to see the famous Alaska huskies doing what they do best: running! After racing from Fourth Avenue to Eagle River, mushers and handlers truck their teams to Wasilla, approximately 40 miles northeast of Anchorage, for the official start of the race the next day. (The Anchorage start is ceremonial, and the first day's leg from there to the VFW post in Eagle River is not factored into the overall time to Nome.) This is as festive as the first day of the race, and there's plenty of room to get really good views. This is the final farewell. After all the hoopla, mushers and dogs are happy to finally get out of town and on the trail to Nome.

If you've seen the beginning of the race, you should try to see the end. About nine days after the start, the front-runners come in under the famous burl arch.

Iditarod is Nome's Mardi Gras. At the finish line, Nome draws mushers, media, and groupies from all over the world. Iditarod time is something to behold with everything from frozen turkey bowling to pick-up dog-mushing races and golfing on the frozen Bering Sea. For information, contact the Nome Convention and Visitors Bureau (P.O. Box 240, Nome, AK 99762. 907-443-6624). Or you can visit the center, located a few yards from the finish line.

Go Dog-mushing

Should you come anytime during winter, not just Iditarod time, folks here can recommend dog-mushers who offer sled rides to fit your itinerary. Go for an hour, a day, or even a week for the unforgettable experience of following a powerful

Sled dogs

On Togo, on Balto!

"What athlete in Alaska runs 1,000 miles, eats raw meat, and sleeps naked in the snow?" This was a question posed by *Alaska Airlines Magazine* to all its readers flying north several years ago in March for the Iditarod Sled Dog Race. If you guessed the Alaska husky, you'd be right. These animals are considered the true Olympians of the race. Names of famous or endearing dogs from this trail will long be remembered: Togo, who ran the longest stretch of the 674-mile "Serum Run" from Nenana to Nome in 1925, and Balto, who ran the final leg of the Serum Run.

In 1978, in a startlingly dramatic finish, this race of more than 1,000 miles was won by a single second. Dick Mackey and Rick Swenson, having mushed the Iditarod Trail across Alaska, were racing neck and neck down Front Street in Nome. Swenson crossed the finish line first, but Leo Rasmussen, the official finish-line checker (who also happened to be mayor), proclaimed Mackey the winner. The reason? Mackey's lead dog's nose had been the first to cross the finish line. Queried later about his decision, Mayor Rasmussen retorted, "Well, you don't take a picture of the horse's arse, do you?"

team of dogs while listening to the soft, syncopated padding of their feet, their gentle breathing, and the quiet of the forest trails and open meadows.

Hike the Trail

If you're here in summer, you can hike small portions of the trail; most of the rest is covered with tundra vegetation and plagued with mosquitoes. From Seward, you can hike or bike the first 2 miles of the trail through town, which are paved. The 30-mile section from Girdwood to Eagle River (known today as the **Crow Creek Trail**) is hikable and runs near the Bering Sea, giving you a chance to glimpse walruses or seals. ■

Kayaker's-eye view of Nancy Lake State Recreation Area

Nancy Lake State Recreation Area

- 22,685 acres ■ 67 miles north of Anchorage on George Parks Highway
- Year-round. First snowfall usually late October; midwinter temperatures can reach minus 40°F; lakes ice-free by end of May ■ Camping, canoeing, fishing, snowmobiling, cross-country skiing, snowshoeing, dog-mushing, bird-watching
- Adm. fee for vehicles ■ Fishing license required ■ Contact the recreation area, Mile 1.3 Nancy Lake Parkway, P.O. Box 10, Willow, AK 99688, phone 907-495-6273; or Mat-Su Area Office, HC 32 Box 6706, Wasilla, AK 99654, phone 907-745-3975. www.dnr.state.ak.us/parks/units/nancylk/nancylk.htm

GLACIERS ONCE COVERED this broad river valley. Upon retreating, they left myriad lakes, swamps, and drumlins—that is, oval hills of glacial drift. The names of the lakes tell various stories: of creatures (Owl, Lynx, and Butterfly); of fortunes lost (Little Noluck and Big Noluck); of native peoples and pioneers who fished, hunted, and settled here in the 19th century. Shem Pete Lake, for instance, commemorates a Tanaina Indian who came to the area seeking the mythical "Nicholai Lode" of gold. Ardaw Lake honors "Russian Mike" Ardaw, a one-time officer in the tsar's cavalry who had hung up his saber to become a fur trapper at Nancy Lake.

Nancy Lake State Recreation Area, with its lake-dotted woods, summer mists, and peaceful waters, is just a 90-minute drive from Anchorage, via the Glenn and George Parks Highways (*entrance at Milepost 67.3 on Parks Hwy.*). Most outside visitors to Alaska pass by with nary a backward glance as they race north for Mount McKinley, the tallest mountain on the North American continent. For Alaskans, however, the area is a winter weekend paradise or a summer evening getaway. It doesn't have the grand drama or big views for which Alaska is so famous, but you will find it has a serenity and symphony all its own.

One of the nicest times to go to the recreation area is in spring (late May, in Alaska). Bright green foliage is just starting to tinge the willows. The beavers—slapping their tails and working the banks for sticks and branches—are busy repairing their dams from the catastrophes of winter. And with a host of songbirds—warblers, sparrows, flycatchers—contributing the background chorus, the loons have returned to nest, casting their eerie calls back and forth to their mates.

It is with this "long cry in the still of the night," as Alaska chronicler John McPhee once described it, that "the loon authenticates the northern lake. The cry...is a sound that seems to have come up a tube from an unimaginably deep source—hardly from a floating bird. It has caused panic, because it has been mistaken for the cry of a wolf, but it is far too ghostly for that. It is detached from the earth."

For those who like to hike, the 3-mile (one way) **Red Shirt Lake Trail** gives occasional glimpses of **Nancy Lake** as it traverses the tops of glacial drumlins and moraines. For those who wish to overnight, there are back-country campsites at Red Shirt Lake. You can pick up the trailhead at the entry to South Rolly Lake campground at the end of the Nancy Lake Parkway. In winter, be careful of overflow on lakes and streams, and watch for hypothermia and frostbite.

Canoeists may want to paddle down **Lynx Lake Loop,** a popular 8-mile chain of lakes that can be navigated in a day or in a leisurely weekend. The lakes support populations, wild and stocked, of rainbow and Dolly Varden trout, northern pike, and whitefish. The loop begins at Tanaina Lake Canoe trailhead *(Milepost 4.5 on park road)*.

If you would like to overnight at the recreation area, you can rent a rustic cabin on a nightly basis *(for reservations, call 907-745-3975)*. You can also car camp at **Nancy Lake campground** *(Mile 66.5 on Parks Hwy.)* or **South Rolly Lake campground** *(end of Nancy Lake Pkwy.)*. Be careful not to strip bark from trees or cut living trees for fires; you'll find plenty of downed wood on the ground for campfires. ■

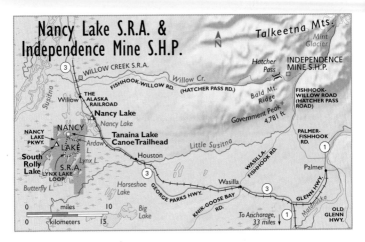

Independence Mine State Historical Park

■ 761 acres ■ 67 miles northeast of Anchorage ■ Year-round; road over Hatcher Pass from Independence Mine to Willow side usually closed by snow Oct.–July ■ Hiking, cross-country skiing, sledding, snowboarding, paragliding, berry picking, tours ■ Fee for use of groomed cross-country ski trails ■ Avalanches can close Hatcher Pass Rd. in winter. Chains or 4WD are advisable ■ Contact the visitor center (open seasonally), phone 907-745-2827 or Alaska Division of Parks, HC 32, Box 6706, Wasilla, AK 99654, phone 907-745-3975. www.dnr.state.ak.us/parks/parks.htm

NESTLED IN A BEAUTIFUL BOWL of meadows and wildflowers such as bluebells, wild geraniums, and arctic sandworts, and surrounded by jagged peaks and wonderful hiking ridges, Independence Mine offers a fascinating historical journey through one of Alaska's hard-rock gold-mining operations. Independence Mine in the Willow Creek Mining District was one of Alaska's greatest gold producers in the 1930s, and the old mine buildings and equipment are preserved today in this historical park located in the Hatcher Pass area. You can see tumbled-down shafts high above on the mountainsides and ruins of gold mines drilled or blasted deep into the mountains.

A narrow, dirt road, twists alongside Willow Creek and leads you up to Hatcher Pass. The river flows down from Mint Glacier and still carries traces of that elusive, glittering pay dirt that lured so many hardy souls into this country. In winter, Hatcher Pass gets generous amounts of snow, making it a great destination for early and late cross-country skiing (and suspectible to avalanches of serious proportions).

What to See and Do

To reach the park, drive past Palmer on the Glenn Highway. At Milepost 49.1 take Fishhook-Willow Road, which turns into the Hatcher Pass Road as it winds along Little Susitna River up the canyon into the mountains. At Mile 17, continue straight on to the access road to Independence Mine, another 1.2 miles.

The **visitor center,** located in the old mine manager's house, is open daily in summer (*usually June–mid-Sept.*). You can view the center's interpretive displays, then set out on an amble around the park on the self-guided **Hard Rock Trail.** Guided tours (*fee*) take you inside the mine buildings.

Hiking

Located above tree line, this is a wonderful area for alpine hiking in all directions. In summer, if you want to give yourself a head start on the elevations, drive to the highest point—**Hatcher Pass** at 3,886 feet—and climb to the top of a ridge for beautiful views and a pleasant aerobic workout. There

Independence Mine, Hatcher Pass

are no set trails here so just pick a ridge and head for it *(road to the pass is steep, narrow, and often muddy, making it unsafe for campers or trailers).* There are more established trails elsewhere; check out the popular day outing to **Reed Lake,** about 6 to 8 miles. There you can boulder hop, watch cascading waterfalls, and look for ptarmigan, marmots, and eagles.

Backcountry Skiing
In winter, skiers flock to Hatcher Pass because it usually has skiable snow long before (and long after) most other places near Anchorage. Come here to cross-country ski on groomed trails or carve your own route up the mountains with cross-country, mountaineering, or telemark skis.

Always use caution. As the experts say, "Pay attention to the clues Mother Nature is giving you." Avalanches are frequent and have buried several backcountry travelers here in past years. ■

Denali State Park

■ 325,240 acres ■ North of Anchorage, Milepost 131.7 to 169.2 on George
Parks Highway ■ Year-round ■ Camping, hiking, backpacking, orienteering
white-water kayaking, canoeing, fishing, mountain biking, cross-country skiing,
snowshoeing, wildlife viewing ■ Contact the park, HC 32, Box 6706, Wasilla,
AK 99654; phone 907-745-3975. www.dnr.state.ak.us/parks/units/denali1.htm

WEDGED BETWEEN THE TALKEETNA MOUNTAINS to the east and the spectacular Alaska Range and Mount McKinley to the west is Denali State Park,
Alaska's third largest. Down the park's middle runs George Parks Highway, the major link between Anchorage and Fairbanks. A little exploration
reveals a landscape varying from wetlands and small lakes to forest to
alpine tundra. The 35-mile-long north-south Curry and Kesugi Ridges
form the backbone of the eastern half of the park, where alpine plants
dominate. The swift Chulitna River flows through the western half. Expanded to its present size in 1976, Denali State Park shares a boundary
with its larger neighbor, Denali National Park and Preserve (see pp. 166-
180), assuring protection for this intact ecosystem.

   Although the mixed habitat supports a variety of wildlife, including
common loons, moose, black and brown bears, beavers, and marten, few
are seen because of thick vegetation. Denali comprises forests of cottonwood, white spruce, and paper birch with an understory of alder, cow
parsnip, tall grasses, currants, and spiny devil's club. Dense thickets of
birch and alder clog open areas. In the summer, the park sprouts wild
geraniums, lupine, fireweed, dogwood, and prickly rose.

   Characterized by a cool and rainy weather fanned by southerly winds,
Denali State Park's short summer has temperatures that average in the
mid-60s, with lows into the 40s. Moderated by the relatively warm coastal
climate, normal temperatures range between 30° F to zero, but winter
lows can dip below minus 25° F. The 30 inches of yearly precipitation results in 180 inches of annual snowfall. First snows dust the park in early
October, and above 2,500 feet snow often remains into July. Cross-country skiers delight in the deep, persistent snowpack.

What to See and Do

If you're just passing through on
a clear day, you can stop at a number of great roadside vantage
points along the Parks Highway
that offer breathtaking vistas of the
heart of the Alaska Range. **Denali
Viewpoint South,** at Milepost
135.2, may be the finest view anywhere of the Alaska Range and

Mount McKinley. On clear days
even the most jaded highway travelers stop here. This pristine panorama includes distant Ruth Glacier
valley and the Chulitna River. An
interpretive bulletin board at this
site names the mountains and other terrain features.

   Drive on to Mile 147.1 to enter

Kayaking on Byers Lake, Denali State Park

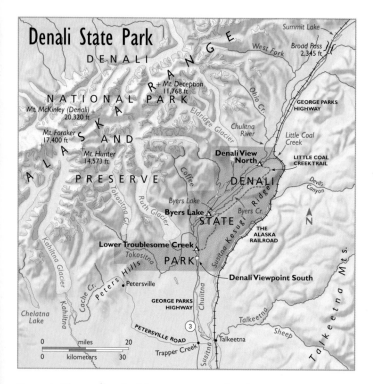

the park. The small park **visitor center** offers natural history displays and information, and sells maps, books, and bug spray.

Camping

You have four campgrounds from which to choose: Lower Troublesome Creek, Byers Lake, Byers Lake Lakeshore, and Denali Viewpoint North.

Lower Troublesome Creek with twenty campsites is just off the Parks Highway at Mile 137.2.

The park's busiest campground and main attraction, **Byers Lake** has 68 woodsy drive-in and walk-in campsites near the lake. Byers also has a boat launch, picnic areas, day-use parking, well water, and park trailheads. Caution: Black bears wander the camp-

ground, so bear-country camping rules are strictly enforced. Check with a ranger for rules.

Two public-use cabins on Byers Lake are available by advance reservation (in writing or in person only). One is a rustic log structure with a sod roof and is drive-up. The second cabin can be accessed on the southwest bay by canoe or by a short half-mile walk. You can get a great view of the mountains from the front window.

A short canoe paddle or a 1.8-mile hike gets you to **Byers Lake Lakeshore Campground.** Here six sites capture the essence of the forest and lake, with wondrous views of Mount McKinley and surrounding spires. Try swimming from the clean granite sandbars at the inlet stream.

Spend a clear night at the **Denali Viewpoint North Campground,** at Mile 162.7. This wayside offers superlative mountain vistas, 23 campsites, picnic tables, outdoor exhibits, a paved, fully accessible botany loop trail, and a small memorial to a World War II aircrew that crashed on Mount Deception in 1944. In midsummer the campground may be noisy and busy during mild weather, but the walk-in tent sites offer some seclusion and a chance to awaken to impressive views of mountains painted with alpenglow.

Autumn cranberries, Denali State Park

Hiking

Even if just driving by **Lower Troublesome Creek trailhead,** stop and take the 10-minute walk (0.6 mile) to the **Chulitna River** with its superb riverside views of the Alaska Range. Deer fern, locally called "fiddleheads," carpets the forest. Watch for beaver cuttings. Look for salmon at the creek mouth. You'll also find numerous red berries but one is the poisonous baneberry, so don't eat any.

Just north of the highway bridge (Mile 137.6), you'll find the beginning of the **Upper Troublesome Creek Trail.** If you hike the entire 15 miles to Byers Lake, you'll follow the creek for the first 8.3 miles before climbing Kesugi Ridge and eventually descending to the lake. For a more difficult hike, continue on the trail from Byers to Little Coal Creek, another 21 miles. Plan on spending at least a night or two in the backcountry. All overnight hikers are urged to use bear resistant food containers.

Caution: Upper Troublesome Creek Trail is closed from mid-July to September because of concentrations of bears feeding on salmon. Heed the warnings: People have been seriously injured here.

If these long treks don't appeal, you can take a 4.2-mile hike that begins at **Byers Lake Campground trailhead** and leads to the alpine zone via the **Tarn Point Trail.** The hike becomes rigorous as you ascend Kesugi Ridge near the end. On top of the ridge enjoy sweeping 360-degree views from Broad Pass to the Talkeetna Mountains.

Backpackers and day-hikers access Kesugi and Curry Ridges from several trailheads. The most northerly, **Little Coal Creek Trail,** Mile 163.9, gains only 715 feet and offers the easiest access to the alpine. Spectacular, unencumbered vistas of the Denali massif await hikers here. You'll see glacial erratics (boulder size to house size deposited by long-vanished glaciers) and kettle ponds. In season you'll find blueberries, lichens, and myriad wildflowers such as lupine and fireweed. Watch for bears and other wildlife (mountain goats are rarely seen, report any sightings to rangers). The nearly 5,000-foot-high **Curry Ridge** you traverse is one of several longitudinal faults that parallel the Alaska Range.

Backcountry Hiking

For rugged adventurers and orienteerers, a cross-country hike into the trail-less **Peters Hills** in the western end of the park is a journey away from the summer crowds. For the hardy, the summits of the lightly visited Peters Hills offer views across the Tokositna River to Mounts McKinley, Foraker, and Hunter.

You can access the Peters Hills area from the end of the 40-mile-long, gravel Petersville Road, which intersects the Parks Highway at Trapper Creek, Mile 114.9 (*Caution: seasonal flooding and chuckholes. Beyond Forks Roadhouse, Mile 19 Petersville Road, 4WDs recommended*). This scenic route, with good views of the mountains at various locations, leads through homesteads and areas of pristine forest to the historic Cache Creek/Petersville mining district. Backpackers use some of the abandoned vehicle trails at the very end of the road as routes into the hills. Watch for bears, and always let a ranger know when you're venturing into the interior of the park—and when you plan to return.

Boating

Outboard motors are prohibited on Byers Lake, but you can launch your canoe or rent one. Common loons and trumpeter swans frequent the lake—but take care not to disturb nesting birds. Several outfitters offer float trips on the Chulitna, as well as other area rivers (*Susitna Expeditions, Ltd. 800-891-6916; Denali View Raft Adventures 907-733-2778; Alaska Wilderness Recreation and Tourism Association 907-258-3171*).

Fishing

Byers Lake supports red salmon, arctic grayling, lake trout, and burbot, but fishing is poor. Most successful fishermen troll deep for lakers. Rules prohibit fishing for salmon on Byers Creek upstream from the Parks Highway bridge. At high water the creek can be floated, but it's tricky and must be finessed. ■

Foxtail grass

Male sockeye salmon in spawning colors, Summit Lake

They Shall Return

The salmon is a remarkable creature. Born and reared in fresh water, the fish migrates to salt water, where it spends most of its life. Then, somewhere thousands of miles out in the ocean, an internal biological alarm summons it home again. Swimming nearly nonstop (sometimes from 2,000 miles out in its ocean pastures), the salmon navigates back to the very river of its origin.

Upon entering fresh water, the salmon fights the current and limited time to find its way back to its native stream, to the very gravel bar where it was born. There it spawns—and, ten days later, dies.

Salmon runs are precisely timed; they typically occur within one or two days of last year's run. Why? We don't know. Nor do we understand how salmon find their way back home or manage to time the journey so exactly. Some scientists believe salmon make their way through the ocean by using celestial navigation or magnetic orientation, or by recognizing underwater landmarks. Once this extraordinary fish reaches its river of origin, its strong sense of smell guides it upstream to its home (each river has a unique chemical composition and therefore a unique odor).

A salmon's journey is filled with hazards and predators, none more efficient than man. Of the 4,000 eggs a sockeye salmon lays, for example, only four will survive to maturity. Of these, only two will make it back upriver to spawn. The modern salmon fishery in Alaska is so efficient that almost all salmon entering a major river system could be caught if no limits were imposed. That means an entire generation of salmon could be wiped out in a single season.

Forecasting when and where to close the fishery and how many salmon should be allowed "to escape" the nets of fishermen is an inexact and often controversial science. Sometimes it borders on an art form—with intuition and luck thrown in. But the goal remains simple: to allow enough salmon up the rivers to spawn, so that the salmon will always return.

Denali Highway Scenic Drive

■ 135 miles long ■ Connects Richardson Highway with Parks Highway
■ Open mid-May–Oct.; weather permitting ■ Camping, hiking, white-water rafting, canoeing, fishing, biking, wildlife viewing, berry picking, auto tour
■ Contact Glennallen Field Office, Bureau of Land Management, P.O. Box 147, Glennallen, AK 99588; phone 907-822-3217. www.glennallen.ak.blm.gov/Denali Hwy/denali.html

WHEN IT OPENED IN 1957, the Denali Highway provided a new avenue of overland access to Mount McKinley (now Denali) National Park. Before then, the Alaska Railroad provided the only park access. The new highway, however, was made of gravel, and few people wanted to rattle and roll over it. Today, most of Denali Highway remains a gravel road; only the first 21 and the last 3 miles are paved. For that reason, many

Rumbling past Mount Sanford

motorists still avoid it, missing out on mountain scenery, tundra vistas, and a variety of wildlife and recreational opportunities. You can also travel the Denali Highway on two wheels *(Alaska Bicycle Adventures 907-243-2329).*

Denali Highway has many pullouts where you can stop to admire the view, hike down a trail, plop your canoe in a river, or camp. Although you can drive east to west or west to east, the mileages given are approximate measurements from Paxson Lodge, Milepost 185.5 on the Richardson Highway and Milepost 0 on the Denali Highway.

From a turnout at Mile 3.5, you can spot **Summit Lake** to the north. Drive another 3 miles and pull over for a view of 13,832-foot **Mount Hayes** piercing the northern sky. The Wrangell Mountains, about 78 air miles to the southeast, come into view around mile 13: 16,237-foot **Mount Sanford** is the prominent peak on the left, 12,010-foot **Mount Drum** on the right, and 14,163-foot **Mount Wrangell** in the center.

Steam sometimes vents from Mount Wrangell, the northernmost active volcano on the Pacific's Rim of Fire.

Mile 16 marks the eastern boundary of **Tangle Lakes Archaeological District.** For the next 22 miles the highway passes through an area containing more than 500 archaeological sites, some dating back at least 10,000 years. Artifact collecting is strictly prohibited.

If you're interested in stopping to camp, try **Tangle Lakes Campground,** just beyond pavement's end at Mile 21. Its 25 campsites are assigned on a first-come first-served basis. Here you can put-in to float a segment of the Delta Wild and Scenic River (see pp. 158-59). Back on the road a short distance west, you'll find a wayside that offers access to the upper Tangle Lakes system. For accommodations, contact Tangle Lakes Lodge *(907-688-9173);* for guided floats, contact Paxson Lake Alpine Cabins *(907-822-5972).*

The second highest highway summit in Alaska (the first is Antigun Pass on the Dalton Highway in the Brooks Range), 4,086-foot **Maclaren Summit,** is at Mile 35. Two miles to the west pull over and enjoy the mountain and river panorama. If you diligently scour the slopes with binoculars, you might spot caribou or even a grizzly bear.

Before you reach the Maclaren River bridge, Mile 42, you'll see several small lakes and ponds. These kettle ponds formed when chunks of ice below ground melted, leaving depressions that filled with water. **Maclaren Glacier** is about 16 miles north of the bridge. Four miles on, the **Crazy Notch** cuts through a lateral moraine deposited long ago as the Maclaren Glacier receded. This natural snow catchment closes the Denali Highway in winter with huge snowdrifts.

Harvesting salmon roe at Paxson hatchery

Wetlands on both sides of the road for the next 15 miles support a variety of waterfowl, including trumpeter swans, northern pintail, common loons, and Barrow's goldeneyes. The rise that you drive along at Mile 59 is an esker, a sinuous ridge of sand, gravel, and rock deposited by a glacier. Watch for moose and red fox.

A 1,036-foot-long bridge spans the **Willow Creek** at Mile 79.5, a major drainage flowing south from the Alaska Range, through the Talkeetna Mountains to spill into Cook Inlet.

About 6 miles after the bridge, pull over at the small hill on the north side of the highway and make the short climb toward the top. Stunning views of 12,339-foot

Mosquito netting: Not a bad idea up here

Makeup of a Mosquito

Her wings beat so fast they create that shrill whine that every camper dreads. If you've been in Alaska for even one summer, you've probably had a taste of her—or, more accurately, she's had a taste of you.

"She" is the female mosquito, and she's the Dracula of the insect world. Born in watery environments such as lakes or soggy tundra, female mosquitoes grow from larva to adult in about two weeks. As adults, they are really quite peaceful—until it is time to mate, when the female literally goes out for blood, the substance that helps produce her eggs.

Contrary to popular belief, the mosquito does not really bite. Instead, using an intricate network of cutting and pumping parts that would dazzle a hydraulic engineer, she unsheathes her needle mouth and slices through your skin with a sort of surgical saw. The itchy bumps that result are caused by the anticoagulant she injects into your blood, which allows her to smoothly suck it out. Yes, she's ruthless, but take heart: The female mosquito's life span is only six weeks long. Though you may feel like the only victim, she's not picky: Human, caribou, or wolf—any blood will do.

Mount Deborah, 11,940-foot **Hess Mountain,** and the **Susitna River Valley** will reward you. From a pullout at Mile 95 you'll find a great place to photograph the Monahan Flat and the snowcapped summits beyond. In autumn this area has great blueberry picking.

If you're ready to stop for the night, try **Brushkana Creek Campground** at Mile 104, which has 22 campsites available on a first-come first-served basis. If you are willing to walk a mile or two along the creek, you'll find some secluded spots for good grayling fishing.

For the final 20 miles or so, the road parallels the silt-laden **Nenana River** that turns north and flows through the Alaska Range. River runners enjoy canoeing this upper stretch. Look for a put-in point near Mile 117 *(18 miles from Cantwell)*. You can take out at a number of points along the Parks Highway north of Cantwell. After the first road bridge you come to, the river becomes swift and challenging. Novices should take out at the bridge *(Mile 215.7 on Parks Hwy.)*.

Pavement begins again 3 miles from the junction with the Parks Highway. Some 2 miles to the west lies the town of Cantwell and the entrance to Denali National Park 25 miles to the north. ∎

Delta Wild and Scenic River

- 62 miles long including 20 miles wild, 24 miles scenic, 18 miles recreational
- Alaska Range ■ Best months mid-June–mid-Sept. ■ Camping, hiking, white-water rafting and kayaking, canoeing, fishing, bird-watching, wildlife viewing
- Contact Glennallen Field Office, Bureau of Land Management, P.O. Box 147, Glennallen, AK 99588; phone 907-822-3217

FLOWING THROUGH THE SCENIC Amphitheater Mountains and the foothills of the Alaska Range, the Delta River offers views of tundra, boreal forest, distant glaciers, and 13,832-foot Mount Hayes. River runners often see waterfowl such as pintail, mallard, and goldeneyes. They may also glimpse red foxes, beavers, moose, caribou, bears, and ptarmigan. Bald eagles nest along the river, and northern harriers fly over the tundra and wetlands.

Because of road access at both ends, experienced boaters enjoy this two- to three-day trip. Experience is a must: The Delta River is not for novice boaters. On the upper stretches you'll have to run Class II to IV rapids and portage around hazards that include boulders, jagged rocks, waterfalls, and downed trees. Even the experienced should take precautions such as scouting the rapids below portages and at the river's confluence with **Eureka Creek.** Begin at Tangle Lakes Campground at Milepost 21, Denali Highway, west of Paxson. Here you'll find a boat launch and lodging.

The first 9 miles of the trip pass north through three of the placid **Tangle Lakes,** connected by shallow channels of slow-moving, clear wa- ter. At low water you might need to line your boat through the channels for short distances. The Delta River flows north out of Lower Tangle Lake and continues 20 miles from the outlet to the take-out point. The first shallow 1.25 miles are rocky and rated Class II to III. Following this first segment, and before you reach Wildhorse Creek, the river enters a wide canyon where you'll have to portage around unnavigable waterfalls. Watch the right-hand bank for the sign marking the portage. Here, a half-mile maintained trail takes you over steep, rocky terrain.

Below the falls, the river narrows and speed increases. Boaters must have white-water experience to float the next mile of rocky, Class II to III rapids. If you're lacking experience, line this section. Below the rapids you'll find 12 miles of slow, meandering Class I water. At its confluence with Eureka Creek, the Delta becomes cold, silty glacial water. At high water or after storms, strong crosscurrents can tip a canoe. The last 7 miles to the take-out point are often shallow and braided with numerous channels and gravel bars. The water is swift and generally Class II. Most floaters take out near **Phelan Creek** (*Milepost 212.5 on Richardson Hwy.*), a river distance of 29 miles from the put-in. Watch for the take-out sign on the right bank. By road it is 49 miles back to Tangle Lakes. While it's possible to travel from Tangle Lakes to the town of Delta Junction, the river becomes very swift with high standing waves and powerful hydrau- lics. Only experts should attempt **Black Rapids,** rated Class III to IV. ■

Delta River and the Alaska Range foothills

The Interior

North wall of Mount Hunter from base camp, Mount McKinley

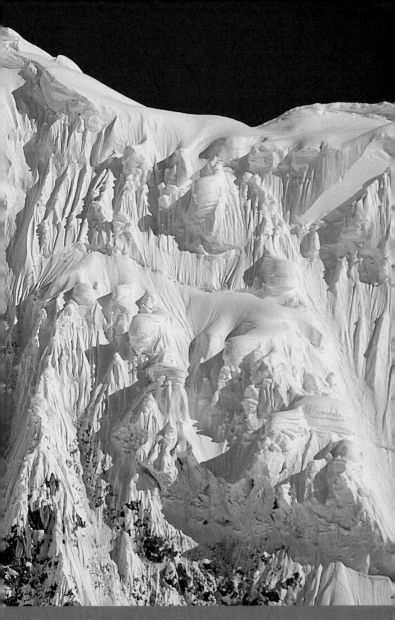

Bounded by two great mountain ranges—the glacier-skirted Alaska Range to the south and the austere Brooks Range to the north—Interior Alaska sprawls westward from the Canadian border. The Interior covers an area of approximately 170,000 square miles, larger than the state of California.

Between the blue spires of these distant ranges rise hundreds of lower summits, laced with wandering valleys, wetlands, boreal forest, tundra, and wide basins stretching

Base camp, Mount McKinley

a hundred miles or more. Almost two dozen great rivers, dominated by the Tanana, Porcupine, and Yukon—the state's longest—muscle through what is truly a republic of rivers. Rarely is a traveler a mile or more from one of the many streams that extend over the entire land in a delicate network of channels . Rivulets merge into streams and streams merge to form rivers often clouded by the silt of dissolving mountains.

Wolves, moose, caribou, grizzly bears, Dall's sheep, lynx, wolverines, marten, and foxes roam the countryside. In spring and fall, salmon struggle upriver to their spawning grounds, attracting predators of all kinds. In summer the Interior's wetlands and forests harbor millions of migrant birds, but by late autumn only a few hardy species, such as ravens and grosbeaks, remain to cope with winter. Despite its wide variety of wildlife, the Interior supports very few animals when compared on a per-acre basis with habitats in more temperate zones.

Forewarned by survival stories such as those chronicled by Jack London, early travelers and prospectors prepared carefully for any expedition into the Interior—then took their chances. Here winter comes early, daylight wanes, and temperatures regularly dip to life-threatening lows. (Minus 80°F, the official record low, was the coldest day in a month that averaged minus 52°F.) The first frost typically occurs in September and the spring thaw does not begin until mid-April. Summer brings its own challenges: ravenous mosquitoes, uncrossable floods, immense wildfires, muskeg swamps, and surprising heat. On June 27, 1915, at Fort Yukon, just north of the Arctic Circle, the thermometer officially topped 100°F.

Latitude and topography together create these weather extremes. At the summer solstice, Fairbanks enjoys almost 21 hours of daylight; the shortest day of the year lasts only four hours. A consequence of these long, severe winters is that much of the Interior buckles with permafrost, or perpetually frozen ground. Despite annual precipitation of less than 20 inches, the underlying ice holds water at the surface, creating ponds and marshes but limiting tree growth. Black spruce on wet muskeg may be only 12 feet tall but 150 years old. Only six tree species grow in the Interior: white spruce, black spruce, tamarack or western larch, paper birch, balsam poplar, and quaking aspen. Common forest plants include prickly rose, highbush cranberry, bluebell, monkshood, and fireweed as well as sphagnum mosses with their permafrost-insulating properties.

The Alaska Range effectively seals the Interior from moderating maritime influences. Extending in a great arc from Cook Inlet north through the Mount McKinley massif, the Alaska Range turns east and runs to the Canadian border, an overall distance of 650 miles. Snow perpetually covers the peaks above 8,000 feet and great glaciers grind downward from the summits. The range in its present form emerged from beneath sea level about ten million years ago, a mere tick of the geologic clock. This immense cordillera is the aftermath of a collision between the North American and Pacific plates. Whenever one plate slides along another, strike slip faults develop (the Denali Fault is one). When two continental plates collide, inexorable forces build massive mountain ranges. Abundant granitic intrusive rocks and lava flows along the crest of the Alaska Range indicate that remelting of collided materials was common. Remelting helped elevate the light granitic rocks of the range's highest peaks; it also partly explains why Mount McKinley's south peak is hard granite whereas its north peak is 56-million-year-old marine sedimentary rocks.

Over millennia, tectonic forces buckled the land. Basins and lakes filled and then emptied. Powerful rivers were rerouted; ancient ice sheets oscillated. Much of this change proceeded gradually, but it was punctuated by the occasional catastrophic event.

One hundred million years ago, the rocks atop 20,320-foot-high Mount McKinley rested on the ocean floor. Since then, the mountain has emerged from the depths to become the highest peak in North America. Geologists are not sure why Denali, as the Athapaskans called the "high one," is so massive. Looming 18,000 feet above its 2,000-foot base, McKinley claims the highest vertical relief of any mountain in the world. Its great height may be related to its location at a bend in the Denali Fault system—a place where the crust probably thickened as one crustal block shoved against another. Yet another theory suggests that a buoyant block of continental crust, dragged under the continent by subduction, is pushing up from below.

Colossal forces may have built these mountains, but glaciation gave them the aspect we see today. Layers of snow accumulated year after year and compacted into ice. As glaciers grow heavier, they move downslope, scraping and gouging the rock over which they pass. This glacial erosion contributes to the rugged, jagged appearance of the Alaska Range. As glaciers recede, they leave behind scarred rock walls, U-shaped river valleys, and giant debris piles called moraines. Most of the great glaciers—some of them 20 to 30 miles long—flow down the south and west side of the Alaskan Range. Storms generally approach from the Pacific and dump their moisture as they pass over, or are blocked by, the mountains.

Leave the road's beaten path and you'll experience the Interior more completely—exquisite in every season. A winter visit holds particular magic, inviting you to marvel at the cosmic cold as you gaze heavenward at the dancing aurora borealis. ▪

Denali National Park and Preserve

■ 6.03 million acres ■ Entrance: Milepost 237 on George Parks Highway
■ Park road open late April–early Oct., depending on weather ■ Camping,
hiking, backpacking, mountain climbing, white-water kayaking, cross-country skiing, wildlife viewing, dogsledding ■ Road-access limitations ■ Adm. and user
fee; permit required for backcountry camping ■ Contact the park, P.O. Box 9,
Denali Park, AK 99755; phone 907-683-2294. www.nps.gov/dena

JUDGE JAMES A. WICKERSHAM had a plan: He would achieve fame by being
the first to climb Mount McKinley. So, in 1903, he started out with a
party of four handpicked to deliver him to the summit. Their dreams
ended abruptly on the Peters Glacier. Above them rose an unstable—and
therefore unscalable—wall of ice thousands of feet high, now known as
the Wickersham Wall. Admitting defeat, they turned around. Not far
from the base of the mountain, however, they found a spectacular conso-
lation prize: gold.

Throughout Interior Alaska and the Yukon Territory, a gold strike (or
rumor of one) ignited stampedes of gold seekers. As soon as word got
out, hundreds of prospectors were scouring the Kantishna Hills, staking
claims on every drainage—and even on worthless ground. To meet the
demand for food, professional shooters called market hunters combed
the piedmont plateau and mountains for Dall's sheep, caribou, and

Mount McKinley reflected in kettle lake, Denali National Park and Preserve

moose. Soon tons of wild meat were en route to markets in Kantishna and Fairbanks.

In 1906, lured by plentiful game, Henry P. Karstens, the future first superintendent of Mount McKinley National Park, guided Charles Sheldon on the first of two hunting trips into the very shadow of the mountain. Sheldon, a wealthy Easterner and a friend of Theodore Roosevelt's, spent the winter of 1907-08 in a simple cabin on the Toklat River. As later evidenced by his 1930 classic, *The Wilderness of Denali*, Sheldon fell in love with the region and its wildlife. He was almost as appalled by the imminent construction of a railroad nearby as he was by the wanton commercial slaughter of wild animals that he witnessed. With typical resolve, Sheldon dedicated himself to creating a national park that would protect the region.

Finally, on February 26, 1917, nine years after Sheldon proposed the park, his persistence paid off: President Woodrow Wilson signed the bill creating Mount McKinley National Park, named for former President William McKinley.

Expanded three times, the last time in 1980—when the original park was designated as wilderness—the park, today named Denali National Park and Preserve, protects an intact subarctic ecosystem shared by about 40 species of mammals and (in summer) some 160 species of birds. With only one 90-mile-long dead-end gravel road slicing to its center, this "accessible wilderness" offers the rare chance to view Alaska's marquee wildlife in their dance of survival amid stupendous landscapes.

Following pages: Sunset, Denali National Park and Preserve

What to See and Do

You cannot drive your own vehicle the length of the park road; only buses are allowed beyond Milepost 15. This public bus system was established in 1972 to protect the park's unique wildlife-viewing opportunities—and because the gravel road is dangerously narrow and winding. By using the park's Visitor Transportation System (VTS), you help preserve the park and its inhabitants while improving your chances of spotting wildlife. *(Buses operate 1st Sat. before Mem. Day–2nd Thurs. after Labor Day.)* More than two million visitors have rattled over the road in VTS buses since 1974.

Most visitors board the bus at the Denali Park Visitor Center. Before starting out, your driver will brief you on your journey west. At Milepost 3, just after a long uphill grade, you'll pass the historic log headquarters built in the 1920s. From here the road winds through taiga forest and over gurgling brooks. Watch for spruce grouse and snowshoe hare. Around Mile 9, the road breaks out of the forest into more open country. This ecotone, the transition between taiga and tundra, is the best place along the road to spot moose. Perhaps you'll also see your first willow ptarmigan and your first good views of **Mount McKinley.** The pavement ends at the **Savage River bridge.** In spring watch for harlequin ducks in the turbulent waters just upstream and Dall's sheep on the summits.

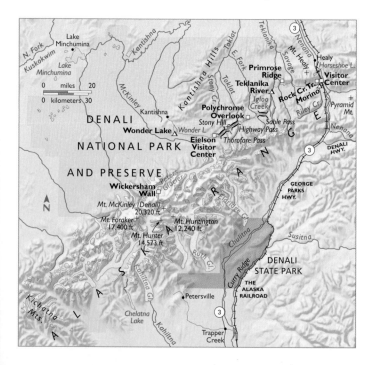

Brown bear, Denali National Park and Preserve

Where the Wild Things Lurk

In a land renowned for its wildlife, many people are both surprised and disappointed by how little they see. In truth, wild critters can be anywhere but often are not obvious due to forest or ground cover. Many animals, such as ptarmigan, sport colorations that offer excellent camouflage. You'll improve your chances considerably by looking in early morning or late evening.

If you are hoping to see a particular animal, make sure you look in the right season. Some migratory birds head south as early as August. Moose are most visible during the September rutting season. Caribou migrate spring and fall, sometimes startling visitors by crossing major highways. Bears wander salmon streams in midsummer.

Use your vehicle as a blind. Find a good vantage point, turn off the engine, and wait quietly. Many animals are not afraid of vehicles, but will fly or run if you get out. In the backcountry, sit still and scan carefully with binoculars. This strategy reveals far more wildlife than if you dash about the tundra.

Finally, look not for whole animals but for pieces of them—the flick of an ear, the tine of an antler, a color or shape that doesn't quite blend in with the rest of its surroundings. Even on the tundra, don't expect to see animals as they appear on the cover of NATIONAL GEOGRAPHIC. Some willow and alder thickets are so tall they are able to obscure even a standing moose.

Primrose turnout, at Mile 17, offers fine views of the mountain and rolling tundra. (If you don't see the mountain, remember that in summer the summit is visible only about 30 percent of the time.) Here dwarf birches, willows, and blueberry bushes predominate.

Continuing downhill from the turnout and over the Hogan Creek bridge, you'll come to the **Sanctuary River,** near the original 1917 park boundary. To the left, as you climb out of the river valley, you'll see muskeg punctuated by twisted black spruce. Until about Mile 20

View of Mount McKinley from Denali North Campground, Denali State Park

the park road lies almost directly above the **Hines Creek Fault**—a vertical break that may cut all the way through the Earth's crust.

As you near the **Teklanika Flats,** watch for caribou. Dense spruce timber grows only along the river here. (Tree line in the park is about 2,700 feet.) **Teklanika River campground,** at Mile 29, is the park's last drive-in campground *(road pass required with reservation; 907-272-7275 or 800-622-7275).* Just up the road at the Teklanika rest stop you can view braided river channels and read interpretive signs about early Athapaskans while ravens soar overhead.

Between the Teklanika bridge and **Igloo Creek,** keep a sharp lookout for wolves. As you parallel the creek beyond Igloo bridge, you may spy Dall's sheep grazing the high slopes. At Mile 37 the bus enters the **Sable Pass Critical Habitat Wildlife Closure.** From here to Mile 43, both sides of the road are closed to off-road hiking to protect the excellent grizzly habitat nearby and to ensure prime opportunities for viewing the bears.

Approaching the **East Fork Bridge,** you'll see a log cabin in a small tributary. Biologist and author Adolph Murie holed up here while conducting much of his landmark wolf study (1939-1941). Across the bridge begins the long climb to the **Polychrome Overlook.** Here golden eagles nest in the cliffs and hoary marmots scurry over rockslides. Your view of the multihued cliffs and the sweeping panorama of tundra and jagged peaks could well prove to be a trip highlight. One thing's certain: You'll never forget the winding traverse of the cliffs.

Next stop is the **Toklat River.** Scan the slopes for Dall's sheep and read the plaques honoring Charles Sheldon and Henry P.

Karstens. Downstream a few miles lies the site of their 1907-08 cabin.

The road now leads west across alpine tundra, where grizzlies often graze on roadside plants in **Highway Pass** (at 3,980 feet, the highest point on the road) and **Thorofare Pass.** Atop **Stony Hill** buses stop on crystalline days to let visitors savor the breathtaking view of Mount McKinley. Just 4 miles down the road, at Mile 66, you'll pull into the **Eielson Visitor Center**, where ranger-interpreters provide a wealth of useful and interesting information. Wildlife and geology displays, indoor and outdoor pavilions, mounted telescopes, rest rooms, and guided walks complete the picture. Ground squirrels, red foxes, and even grizzlies sometimes wander by. On clear fall days, the mountain seems close enough to touch.

It takes about four hours to reach Eielson from the main visitor center, where most buses turn around. If you've purchased tickets to go all the way to Wonder Lake, you still have some 20 miles to go. The round-trip from the main visitor center to Wonder Lake takes roughly 11 hours.

The road west from the Eielson Visitor Center traverses cliffs before dropping down to brushy tundra, where the ponds you pass are beaver impoundments. Watch for the animals' dams and their mound-shaped lodges built of sticks. Notice the small kettle lakes, formed when the ice in frozen soil melts and collapses, leaving a cavity that fills with water. You will likely see caribou as you follow this road to Wonder Lake campground.

Of Taiga and Tundra

"Tundra" derives from a Finnish word meaning "barren or treeless land." Dry or alpine tundra, found on ridges from 2,000 to 4,000 feet high, has sparse ground cover with plants that seldom grow more than a few inches tall. (Above 4,500 feet, it harbors only a few flowering plants.) Wet tundra is dominated by a low-growing plant community with a nearly continuous cover of sedges, grasses, and woody and flowering plants. Both types of tundra, usually found in the Arctic, are common in the foothills of the Alaska Range. "Taiga," a Russian word meaning "land of little sticks," refers to the boreal forest—a mosaic of thickets and muskeg. Aptly, the name for this great circumpolar forest comes from Boreas, Greek god of the north wind.

Touring and Camping

Make VTS and campground reservations at the Denali Park Visitor Center, or book them ahead of time (*March–mid-Sept. 907-272-7275 or 800-622-7275*). Fares vary according to the itinerary you choose. While at the visitor center, pick up a copy of the park newspaper, *Denali Alpenglow,* and watch the 12-minute orientation slide show given throughout the day.

The concessionaire offers two narrated, guided bus tours. The Wildlife Tour, complete with box lunch, goes to Toklat River on cloudy days, to Stony Hill on clear

Skiing Ruth Glacier, Denali National Park and Preserve

days. The Denali National History Tour provides a shorter trip. *(Denali Park Resort, 907-276-7234 or 800-276-7234)*

You may get off the VTS bus anywhere along the park road and hike, except through designated closed areas. Because the park has few established trails, hikers can look forward to an experience of personal discovery and adventure. You can go a short distance and shoot pictures, or climb to a high vantage point for a unique view. Although pathfinding is up to you, follow durable surfaces such as riverbeds and ridges wherever possible to protect the delicate tundra plants. Stay alert and make wise decisions to ensure your best possible wilderness experience.

The vast majority of park visitors never leave the bus. Those adventurous souls who do strike out into the backcountry, however, are likely to be amply rewarded: a close-up view of Mount McKinley, a glimpse of a wolverine, or the haunting sound of wolves howling in the darkness.

To curtail overuse, the park service has divided Denali's backcountry areas into 43 units and grants just a small number of permits for each unit. Backcountry permits are issued only at the visitor center in summer and at park headquarters in winter (one day in advance). Before you get your permit, you will be given an orientation in the "backcountry simulator," an excellent primer for your excursion. In peak season, high demand makes some units

unavailable on short notice, so keep an alternative in mind.

Even though you've taken a bus to your drop-off point, once you enter the wilderness you may face significant challenges: river crossings, difficult terrain, grizzly bears, weather fluctuations. Go prepared with complete and appropriate gear—summer weather typically is rainy, cool, and buggy. It can snow in any month here. To minimize encounters with bears, always cook and store food 100 yards or more downwind from your campsite. All food and garbage must be stored in special bear-resistant food canisters (BRFCs) that the park will lend you when you receive your backcountry permit at the visitor center.

Easy Loops and Lesser Trails

If you'd rather stick to less challenging hikes, six interlacing developed trails radiate from the park's entrance area. Even here, always be alert; grizzlies sometimes hunt nearby for moose calves, and bears have been seen right by the railroad depot.

The **Taiga Trail** and the **Morino Loop Trail** are easy walks. Both are relatively undemanding and only about 1.3 miles in length. For either hike, allow one hour roundtrip. Each wanders through forest where you might see grouse and red squirrels.

The **Horseshoe Lake Trail** leads to the lake's shoreline, where moose sometimes wade for food. On the peninsula in the center of the lake you'll see an old beaver

World's Tallest Mountain?

Quick—what's the tallest mountain in the world? If you answered "Mount Everest," you're correct. Yet an equally acceptable answer is "Mount McKinley." How can this be?

It's all in the way you take the measure of a mountain. Mount Everest, situated in the Himalaya on the border of Nepal and Tibet, boasts the highest absolute summit—29,035 feet above sea level—in the world. When measured from its base (which is high on the Himalayan plateau) to its peak, however, mighty Everest stands a paltry 12,000 feet tall.

Mount McKinley, by contrast, soars to 20,320 feet from a plateau of only 2,000 feet. Measured from its base to its summit, then, McKinley looms thousands of feet taller than Everest.

lodge and cuttings; at the end of the trail is a beaver dam that regulates the water level. In spring's twilight hours listen for great horned owls hooting in the timber or look for pasqueflowers growing on south-facing slopes along the upper trail. Many visitors prefer to view the lake from the overlook's log benches rather than tackle the steep trail. You can do the Horseshoe Lake hike in an hour, but on quiet mornings and evenings you'll want to linger.

For grand vistas try the strenuous **Mount Healy Overlook Trail.** This 5-mile round-trip climbs 1,700 feet and can be hiked in about four hours. From the 3,245-foot-high overlook you'll have extraordinary views south into the Nenana River and Yanert Fork Valleys, and west into the park.

Two remaining trails, the 1.8-mile-long **Roadside Trail** and the 2.3-mile **Rock Creek Trail,** can be done as separate out-and-back hikes or combined as a single loop. If you have the time, make the loop hike, a moderate trek of about 4 miles that lets you experience the boreal forest from a trail surfaced with gravel.

Pick up the Roadside Trail near the park auditorium. You'll wander through spruce and aspen forest and up an incline. Many aspens here bear scars from browsing moose, and in places the trail is littered with "moose nuggets." Twigs near the ground have been chiseled by snowshoe hare (see sidebar p. 250). Occasionally spruce grouse are seen on the trail. As it leaves the aspen forest along the edge of the park road but before it heads upward, the trail passes a black-spruce muskeg. Near the top of the slope, a log bench offers views of the forest, railroad trestle, **Mount Fellows,** and the more distant **Pyramid Mountain.** Along the way you'll see the stumps of trees that were chopped down in the 1920s and 1930s for firewood or cabins. The first road the trail crosses is the service road for C-Camp, the park's employee housing area. A short distance farther, the trail crosses a second service road. Walk 100 yards up the road until you find the Rock Creek Trail sign on the right.

If you've previously attempted cross-tundra hiking, you'll appreci-

Flight-seeing, Mount McKinley

ate the ease of this rewarding hike. Except for the initial uphill leg, most of the next 2 miles lead back downhill. Thick sphagnum moss, cranberry, and crowberry cover the forest floor under the dense canopy. Piles of reddish, shredded spruce cones (sometimes 2 feet deep) are the feeding mounds of red squirrels. Once you reach the aspen flat behind the park auditorium, take time to examine the exquisite lacings of lichens and berries.

The **Savage River Loop Trail** at Mile 15 can be accessed from the parking lot on the east bank or from behind the entrance station on the west side. A shuttle bus *($2 round-trip)* will take you to the trailhead from the park entrance. This moderate loop parallels the river to a new footbridge over the sometimes turbulent waters. Golden eagles soar high above the narrow canyon below; hikers often see collared pikas, marmots, and ptarmigan.

Rangers conduct open-air programs on topics ranging from glaciers to grizzlies at Riley, Savage, Teklanika, and Wonder Lake Campgrounds *(contact park for schedule)*. Each night in the park auditorium, a film or a slide lecture interprets the park's unique natural and cultural history. Ranger-led hikes take you to Horseshoe Lake, Mount Healy, and on an "evening stroll." Three times daily at the park kennels, rangers demonstrate the use of the park's sled dogs, a traditional mode of winter patrolling. Free buses leave the visitor center and other locations 40 minutes before each demonstration.

With only 293 camping sites available in the park's seven campgrounds, securing a campsite in peak season requires some advance

Following pages: Autumn, Denali National Park and Preserve

Moose in kettle lake, Denali National Park and Preserve

planning. If you show up at the visitor center in July without a campground or bus reservation, you'll likely be out of luck. Be prepared to camp outside the park for a couple of nights until a campsite becomes available. All campsites at Riley Creek, Savage River, Wonder Lake, and Teklanika River may be reserved in advance. Sanctuary and Igloo tent campgrounds, each with only seven sites, are available at the visitor center on a first-come first-served basis; along with Wonder Lake, they are accessible only by designated camper buses. You may drive your private vehicle to Riley, Savage, and Teklanika, but the latter campground requires a minimum three-day stay and a road pass. In addition, Morino campground near the railroad depot is set aside for backpackers without vehicles. (*For transportation to the park, contact Parks Highway Express 907-479-3065.*)

White-water Adventures

You can sign up for exciting white-water trips down the **Nenana River** or take a short trip through the rugged **Nenana Gorge** (*Denali Outdoor Center 888-303-1925 or Denali Raft Adventures 907-683-1925 or 888-683-2234*). Attempt these Class IV rapids on your own *only* if you have white-water experience.

Flight-seeing

For an unforgettable experience, on a clear day take a flight-seeing trip through the Alaska Range to Mount McKinley(*Kantishna Air Taxi 907-683-1223; Denali Air 907-683-2261*). You can also charter a flight out of Talkeetna that may include a glacier landing or a trip around McKinley (*Doug Geeting Aviation 907-733-2366; Hudson Air Service 907-733-2321 or K2 Aviation 907-733-2291*).

Climbing

Climbers attempting Mount McKinley must register with the Talkeetna Ranger Station (*P.O. Box 588, Talkeetna, AK 99676. 907-733-2231*) at least 60 days in advance. Guide services are available. ■

Nenana to Fairbanks Scenic Drive

■ 53 miles ■ Mileposts 304.5 through 358 on George Parks Memorial Highway ■ Best months for wildlife viewing June-Aug.; spectacular fall foliage ■ Contact Nenana Visitor Center, George Parks Memorial Highway and A St.; phone 907-832-9953 (Mem. Day–Labor Day) or Fairbanks Visitor Center, 550 First Ave., Suite 306, Fairbanks, AK 99701; phone 907-456-5774. www.explore fairbanks.com

To watch birch and aspen burnish the rolling hills in autumn, drive the Parks Highway (Alas. 3) 53.5 miles from Nenana to Fairbanks. Located at Milepost 304.5, the town of Nenana (population about 400) began as a railroad construction camp and a native mission school. In summer, barges loaded with supplies churn the muddy waters of the Tanana in much the same way that stern-wheelers once served the river's isolated mining camps and villages. After stopping at the Nenana Visitor Center, head to the historic **railroad depot** for its museum tour.

Just north of town, the Parks Highway crosses the Tanana River. *(Danger: Do not stop or slow down on this bridge; traffic moves very fast, and there are no shoulders.)* North of the span, on the left side of the road, is a pullout from which you can view the river, barges and tugs, the 1923 railroad trestle, and Athapaskan fish wheels set for king and chum salmon. As you travel the next half mile, look to the left for more fish wheels.

You'll see some of the best autumn colors about 4 miles north of town on the ridges above **The Alaska Railroad crossing**. Go slowly and soak it all in. Keep your eyes open for spruce grouse; they often peck for gravel next to the road.

A double-ended pullout around Mile 319 overlooks the forest and wetlands of the **Minto Flats State Game Refuge**, an important area for subsistence fishing, hunting, and trapping. This habitat nurtures mallard, shovelers, pintail, goldeneyes, and scaup as well as moose and black bears. You may also hear the cacophonous cries of migrating sandhill cranes and Canada geese.

Another pullout at **Mile 324.5** (watch for the "Purvis Lookout" sign) offers great views of rolling hills, the Tanana River, and the distant snow-capped peaks of the Alaska Range, prompting some to dub this stretch of road Skyline Drive. When the sky is clear, Mount McKinley is visible from the east end of the pullout. On road shoulders watch for wood-chucks—yes, the groundhogs familiar in the eastern United States. Woodchucks, considered marmots, are closely related to the Alaskan marmot and the hoary marmot.

An unmarked 1-mile loop road affording views of 13,300-acre **Bonanza Creek Experimental Forest** begins just shy of Mile 340. Bonanza Creek has been leased to the Forest Service for research until 2018. Studies indicate that the northern (boreal) forests soak up vast quantities of carbon dioxide, helping to reduce the "greenhouse" effect. ■

A giant cabbage: by-product of long hours of summer sunlight

Creamer's Field Migratory Waterfowl Refuge

■ 1,800 acres ■ In Fairbanks ■ Hiking, bird-watching, wildlife viewing ■ Year-round ■ Contact Alaska Department of Fish and Game, Division of Wildlife Conservation, 1300 College Rd., Fairbanks, AK 99701; phone 907-459-7307. www.state.ak.us/local/akpages/FISH.GAME/wildlife/region3/refuge3/creamers.htm

LOCATED IN THE HEART OF FAIRBANKS and originally the site of a dairy, Creamer's Field provides a sanctuary for large flocks of migratory birds in spring. Seasonal ponds and plowed fields strewn with tons of grain attract waterfowl and shorebirds. Canada geese begin arriving in mid-April each year, soon followed by sandhill cranes, pintail, mallard, shovelers, and other migrants such as American golden plover. Cranes have migrated through this area for an estimated nine million years. "Their annual return," wrote biologist Aldo Leopold in *A Sand County Almanac*, "is the ticking of the geologic clock."

Observation platforms and easy access combine to provide great viewing opportunities. After feeding and resting from their long journeys, the bulk of the waterfowl move on. The refuge's mosaic of forest and open fields, however, provides seasonal habitat for a number of songbirds—including swallows, robins, and Savannah sparrows—as well as northern harriers and some nesting ducks.

While strolling one of the refuge's three trails, you might spot a moose, a bounding snowshoe hare, or a red fox hunting voles.

The **Seasonal Wetland Trail** *(wheelchair accessible in summer)* and the **Farm Road Trail** provide access to marshes and open fields. The easy, 1-mile-long **Boreal Forest Trail** wends through open fields, along marshes, and through thick woods. At the trailhead *(beyond the visitor center)*, pick up an interpretive brochure keyed to the numbered observation points. (Carry insect repellent in early summer.) Along the path, you can see where hare and moose have nibbled plants, listen to ducks calling from the marsh, and watch swallows swooping after insects. Climb the viewing tower about midway along the trail to view the transition zone between birch forest and black spruce bog. This ecotone attracts a variety of wildlife. Look and listen for Savannah sparrows, Lincoln sparrows, alder flycatchers, and orange-crowned warblers. After the tower interlude, continue your walk though black spruce bog; here you'll see cotton grass, bearberry, blueberry, and cranberry. Wild rose and bluebells punctuate forested areas. That chattering from a spruce limb is probably a red squirrel. In one spot you'll see the dramatic revegetation of a 1950s forest fire that swept the area.

Most of the dozens of bird species here utilize the refuge for seasonal nesting and rearing of their young; only a handful reside year-round. Winter bird-watchers may view 30 resident species, including boreal chickadees, gray jays, redpolls, ravens, spruce grouse, willow ptarmigan, downy and hairy woodpeckers, and even great horned owls.

Belle and Charles Hinckley started their dairy here in the early 1900s and sold it to Anna and Charles Creamer in 1928. Suffering financially, Creamer's Dairy closed in 1966; by then its wideopen grain fields were already attracting large numbers of waterfowl, and the community purchased the farmland. The Creamers' old farmhouse now serves as the refuge visitor center.

Friends of Creamer's Field *(907-452-5162)*, a nonprofit group, provides guided nature walks and

Sandhill cranes, Creamer's Field, Fairbanks

seasonal events. Don't miss the annual **Crane Festival**, which runs from late August through early September. Also headquartered here is the **Alaska Bird Observatory** *(907-451-7059)*, which offers songbird banding demonstrations and information.

What to See and Do

Fairbanks Area

Begin your Interior adventures at the Alaska Public Lands Information Center *(250 Cushman Street, Suite 1A, Fairbanks, Alaska 99701; 907-456-0527)*, a joint project of eight state and federal agencies.

Because many forays into the Interior require air transport, you may find yourself with time to kill while waiting for a flight. If so, head just west of the rental-car parking lot to hike the short, manicured **Fairbanks International Airport Nature Trail.** The path leads to benches and picnic tables on the shore of a small lake. Feel the breezes stirring the birches and relax while watching ducks or ravens wing overhead. Away from the airport bustle, for a short while you'll be back in the "real" Alaska.

Musk ox, Large Animal Research Station

University of Alaska Museum

One of Alaska's top ten attractions, this museum *(Yukon Dr., University of Alaska, Fairbanks, AK 99775; year-round; 907-474-7505. www.uaf.edu/museum. adm. fee)* is a must-see. Here you can tour displays of Alaska native culture, mining, and the gold rush, as well as natural history. You'll get a laugh out of Alaska's first automobile, built in Skagway by pioneer Bobby Sheldon in 1904. View the aurora borealis in the museum theater and have your photo taken with Otto, the 8-foot-9-inch-tall stuffed brown bear that greets visitors at the entrance to the exhibits. Among all the fossils, dinosaur bones, and the state's largest display of gold, look for "Blue Babe," a 36,000-year-old steppe bison found preserved in permafrost near Fairbanks a few years ago.

During the summer, Northern Inua athletes perform Alaska native traditional games and dances twice daily. Outdoor exhibits include totems and a restored Russian blockhouse.

Large Animal Research Station

Known as the "musk ox farm," this university research facility *(Yankovich Rd. off Ballaine Rd.; 907-474-7207)* provides platforms for visitors to view reindeer, caribou, and musk ox. Guided tours include an overview of ongoing research projects. ∎

Chillin' at Chena Hot Springs Resort

Chena River State Recreation Area

- 250,000 acres ■ Northeast of Fairbanks on Chena Hot Springs Road
- Year-round road access ■ Camping, canoeing, cross-country skiing, dog-sledding, fishing, hiking, rafting, rock climbing ■ Camping fee ■ Contact Alaska State Parks, 3700 Airport Way, Fairbanks, AK 99709; phone 907-451-2695. www.dnr.state.ak.us/parks/units/chena/index.htm

NOT 35 MILES FROM FAIRBANKS lies the Chena River State Recreation Area, its rolling hills and domes dividing the Tanana and Yukon River drainages. The crystal waters and quiet forests of the upper Chena River contrast sharply with the river's lower reaches, a muddy meander through downtown Fairbanks. In the Chena River SRA, deep sphagnum mosses and black spruce cover north-facing slopes, while aspen, birch, and some white spruce blanket well-drained south-facing slopes. Pleasant campgrounds, waysides, river-access points, and trails lure summer visitors. At road's end try a soak at Chena Hot Springs Resort *(907-452-7881)*.

What to See and Do

If you have only a day, enjoy the 56-mile drive to the end of **Chena Hot Springs Road** *(off Alaska 6)*. The state recreation area begins at Milepost 26 and enfolds the next 25 miles of the road. In summer you'll likely see grouse and moose as you drive along; take time out for a short hike or a picnic along a river sandbar.

Campgrounds include Rosehip, Granite Tors, and Red Squirrel, each with a slightly different setting (all first-come first-served). Also available are six off-road public-use cabins *(contact Alaska State Parks 907-451-2705)*, by reservation only. Year-round Twin Bears Camp on Twin Bears Lake is a state park facility operated by a community nonprofit organization *(907-451-2753)* promoting outdoor and environmental education.

Hikes in the Chena River SRA range from leisurely to strenuous. For a short hike take the **Rosehip Campground Nature Trail.** Numbered trail markers explain vegetation types, forest succession, evidence of wildlife activity, and river erosion. You might even see a moose, beaver, or wood frog.

Two other popular hiking routes are the **Granite Tors Trail** and **Angel Rocks Trail.** Both lead to exposed pinnacles of rock, called tors. Around 80 million to 60 million years ago, pieces of magma slowly drifted to the surface through metamorphic rock. Weathering and erosion of the surrounding earth sculpted these pinnacles into the strange shapes that loom today.

Day-hikers, rock climbers, and overnight backpackers access the Granite Tors Trail at Milepost 39.5 of Chena Hot Springs Road. This 15-mile loop, considered moderate to strenuous, passes through forest of birch and aspen and out into open tundra. The trail forks after about a mile. Head east along the more developed trail. Its gradual ascent grows steeper (and the path less developed) as you continue clockwise around the loop. The middle portion of the loop traverses the **Plain of Monuments,** with grand vistas of the Alaska Range and close-ups of the tors. Rock cairns and wooden tripods mark alpine trail sections and lead to a shelter cabin about halfway around the loop.

Beginning at Mile 48.9 of Chena Hot Springs Road, the 3.5-mile Angel Rocks Trail leads to large granitic outcroppings near the north boundary of the recreation area. Though this loop trail gains 900 feet, it is considered an easy day hike, the tors being less than 2 miles from the trailhead (you can watch rock climbers scale them on summer days). For the physically fit, an 8.3-mile spur—the **Angels Rocks to Chena Hot Springs Trail**—takes you to excellent views of the Alaska Range, Granite Tors, Chena Dome, and Far Mountain.

Other less visited trails offer quiet places where you can camp in solitude. The strenuous 29-mile loop of the **Chena Dome Trail** tops out at 4,421 feet, the highest point in the area.

The **Chena River** attracts canoers, kayakers, and rafters. Alaska State Parks provides a free guide to the river *(available on park's website)*. Although the Chena is considered easy to navigate, storms often muddy the water, hiding obstacles that can capsize your boat. Logjams and sweepers—trees or logs overhanging the river—also are hazards. The narrow, upper portions of this Class II water are more challenging than the wider segments downstream. Numerous river-access points and three bridge crossings offer several trip options. An easy float from first bridge (Mile 37.8) to Rosehip Campground (Mile 27) takes 3.5 to 6 hours. Chena Hot Springs Resort rents canoes and provides shuttle service between put-in and take-out points. Interior Alaska Adventures *(907-388-4193)* stages guided trips. Fishing for Arctic grayling is strictly catch-and-release. ∎

Chatanika River

Chatanika River Recreation Site and Area

- 590 acres ■ Two units north of Fairbanks ■ Best months June-Sept.
- Camping fishing, float trips ■ Contact Alaska State Parks, 3700 Airport Way, Fairbanks, AK 99709, phone 907-451-2695; or Northern District Office, Bureau of Land Management, 1150 University Ave., Fairbanks, AK 99709, phone 907-474-2200. www.dnr.state.ak.us/parks/units/chatanik.htm

IDEAL FOR A FLOAT TRIP of one to two days, the **Chatanika River** includes enough fast water (Class I to II) to make the excursion exciting. You can put in at a number of places adjacent to the Steese Highway, but it's probably best to begin your float at the **Upper Chatanika River State Recreation Site** at Milepost 39. Amenities include 25 campsites, four picnic sites, water, and toilets. Although popular with highway travelers and weekenders from Fairbanks, this is still the best place to launch for an all-day float. The trip will take from 8 to 12 hours, depending on water levels. If you want to take two days to complete the trip and perhaps try a little fishing, good camping sites and firewood are easy to find. Grayling, whitefish, and salmon can be caught, but be sure to check state regulations beforehand for restrictions.

While hiking away from the river, watch for black bears; on the river beware of hazards such as boulders and downed trees. Take out at White-fish Campground in 570-acre **Lower Chatanika River State Recreation Area** at Milepost 11 of the Elliott Highway. (Just south of here Felix Pedro made the gold strike that led to the birth of Fairbanks.) The Lower Chatanika River SRA has a boat ramp, ten campsites, toilets, and water.

For longer trips, put in at the Cripple Creek BLM Campground at Mile 60 of the Steese Highway. (This upper stretch may be difficult to navigate at very low water.) Seven- to ten-day trips will take you to the Chatanika's confluence with the Tolovana River and on to the Tanana. ■

White Mountains National Recreation Area

■ 1 million acres ■ 25 miles north of Fairbanks, between Elliott and Steese Highways ■ Year-round ■ Camping, hiking, boating, fishing, hunting, biking, cross-country skiing, skijoring, dogsledding, wildlife viewing, gold panning ■ Camping fee; cabin-use fee ■ Contact Northern Field Office, Bureau of Land Management, 1150 University Ave., Fairbanks, AK 99709; phone 907-474-2200. aurora.ak.blm.gov/WhiteMtns

JAGGED LIMESTONE SPIRES muscle above rolling hills, ice-cold streams, forests, and alpine tundra in this "accessible wilderness," as local land managers have dubbed it. Beaver Creek National Wild and Scenic River traverses the heart of White Mountains National Recreation Area, the largest NRA in the nation.

This region springs from vastly varied geologic origins. Because of compression along low thrust faults, patches of older rock now counter-intuitively lie above younger rock. Mineral fragments of both volcanic and metamorphic character litter the surface. The White Mountains themselves are sequences of limestone deposits. Forty-foot Windy Arch, one of the many area caves and arches, was formed from the continuous

South view of Alaska Range from Wickersham Dome

freezing and thawing of the fragile and easily eroded limestone. A careful traverse of the White Mountains will turn up marine fossils from ancient reefs ten million years old. Four glacial advances spanning several hundred thousand years are evident here as well. Today, however, this vast wilderness is completely free of the glaciers that once burdened the slopes of its limestone peaks.

What to See and Do

Summer road access into White Mountains NRA begins at Milepost 57 of the Steese Highway. Here, turn onto U.S. Creek Road and drive 6 miles to Nome Creek Road. Go right, and continue 4 miles to the 13-site Mount Prindle Campground. Located near the 16-mile-long **Quartz Creek Trail**—one of more than 40 miles of summer trails in the NRA—this staging point provides ideal access to alpine meadows and views of

Mount Prindle. Return to the intersection with U.S. Creek Road and travel 12 miles west on Nome Creek Road to reach the forested Ophir Creek Campground (19 sites), near the put-in for **Beaver Creek National Wild and Scenic River.**

Nome Creek Valley, the site of mining activity in the early 1900s, provides catch-and-release fishing and recreational gold panning in specified areas. Several ridges lead north to the high country around

Wickersham Dome, White Mountains NRA

Lime Peak, offering spectacular views of alpine tundra, granite tors, and limestone cliffs. Off-trail hiking can be a challenge—so be prepared.

At the Mile 57 turnoff from Steese Highway you'll see the **Davidson Ditch**, an 83-mile series of troughs and pipes that once carried water to the gold dredges of Fox and Chatanika. Capable of channeling 56,100 gallons per minute, the Davidson Ditch was an engineering marvel in 1929. Just up the road at Mile 60 of the Steese Highway is **Cripple Creek Campground**. It has 12 campsites (2 are wheelchair-accessible) and a short hiking trail that winds through tall white spruce along the Chatanika River.

Wet and muddy trail conditions make the ten public-use cabins in the NRA accessible mostly in winter, when they are highly sought after. The 10-by-12-foot cabins sleep four, while the 12-by-16-foot cabins have a loft and sleep four to eight. Amenities are minimal, so you must provide your own firewood—as well as white gas for the lantern and cook stove. The Fred Blixt Cabin at Milepost 62.5 of the Elliott Highway, is wheelchair accessible. Reservations for all cabins *(907-474-2251 or 800-437-7021)* may be made up to 30 days in advance.

Hikers and off-road vehicles share some trails: For example, both use 16-mile **Quartz Creek Trail.** Three research natural areas are closed year-round to motorized use. You can access two popular hiking trails—the 20-mile-long **Wickersham Creek Trail** and the

20-mile **Summit Trail** *(closed to vehicles)*—from Mile 28 of the Elliott Highway. At 3,207 feet, **Wickersham Dome** provides an easy four-hour round-trip hike from the highway.

The BLM maintains more than 200 miles of winter trails groomed for both motorized and nonmotorized use. Call ahead *(907-474-2372)* for trail conditions. These trails access all the public-use cabins, spaced about a day apart for cross-country skiers, as well as the surrounding country. Special events here include skijoring races, in which dogs pull cross-country skiers. A 5-mile cross-country ski loop offering views of the Alaska Range and Mount McKinley begins and ends at the Wickersham Dome trailhead.

Beaver Creek Boating

A clear-water, Class I river, Beaver Creek National Wild and Scenic River *(BLM NFO, 1150 University Avenue, Fairbanks, AK 99709. 907-474-2200)* flows past the jagged peaks of the White Mountains and through part of **Yukon Flats National Wildlife Refuge** before joining the Yukon River. From Nome Creek Road to the Dalton Highway Bridge across the Yukon, a distance of about 360 miles, this may be the longest road-to-road float in North America. If you're not going all the way to the Yukon (a three-week trip), make arrangements to be airlifted from a gravel bar near Victoria Creek, a good 110 miles downriver.

Put-in is at the lower end of the Nome Creek Road at the Ophir Creek Campground, where a small, long-term parking area

Winter Brrrd

At about 5 inches, redpolls are among the smallest of Alaska's resident winter birds. They have distinctive red caps, small black bibs, and heavily streaked brown-and-white wings and backs. Adult males also sport reddish breasts.

Redpolls travel in groups that may exceed 100; they are common at bird feeders. The astounding insulative value of their feathers enables active redpolls to maintain a core body temperature of 105°F, even when the outside air temperature drops to -60°F.

When local seed crops fail, redpolls head south to better feeding grounds. One redpoll banded in Fairbanks was later found near Montreal—3,000 miles distant! The average life span of this tough finch is three years.

provides a place to organize and prepare. Motorboats launching in the Nome Creek Valley have a 15-horsepower limit. You'll be on Nome Creek for 3 miles before joining Beaver Creek. Be prepared to line—that is, to tow the boat from shore or while wading—through shallow water and around sweepers before the paddling improves at Mile 7. The river slows again in Yukon Flats NWR. (A small boat motor will get you through.) Gravel bars make perfect camping spots to watch for wildlife and enjoy the solitude. Fishing excels for pike, Arctic grayling, burbot, and whitefish. ∎

Steese National Conservation Area

■ 1.2 million acres ■ Northeast of Fairbanks ■ Year-round access via Steese Highway ■ Camping, hiking, fishing, hunting, winter sports, rafting, canoeing, float trips, bird-watching, wildlife viewing, gold panning ■ Contact Northern District Office, Bureau of Land Management, 1150 University Ave., Fairbanks, AK 99709; phone 907-474-2200. aurora.ak.blm.gov/Steese/SNCA.html

CRUCIAL CALVING GROUNDS and home range of the Fortymile Caribou Herd are protected by the Steese NCA, which was established by Congress through the Alaska National Interest Lands Conservation Act of 1980. Abundant wildlife—black bears, grizzly bears, Dall's sheep, moose, marmots, wolves, beavers, lynx, ptarmigan, and numerous raptors—also live here. Known for its distinctive geology, the area features patterned ground, weathered tors, and antiplanation terraces—already-flat surfaces that have eroded. Another intriguing landmark is the site's solifluction lobes (or waves), where surface materials creep downward as the underlying ground thaws and refreezes year after year. Much of the rock comes in two "flavors": a quartz-rich schist known as Yukon-Tanana Crystalline Terrane and Birch Creek schist dating back 570 million years.

Steese NCA is divided into two units. The northern portion lies adjacent to White Mountains National Recreation Area (see pp. 188-191) and contains 4,934-foot Pinnell Mountain, which shoulders its way above the surrounding alpine ridges and summits. South of Steese Highway is the drainage of the Birch Creek National Wild and Scenic River, which flows through 113 miles of terrain typical of Interior uplands. Within the south unit you'll find the magnificent 160-acre **Big Windy Hot Springs Research Natural Area**—part of a belt of geothermal springs that burble all across central Alaska. Here, an undisturbed hot spring issues water at about 141°F—way too hot for bathing. Geothermal water has weathered the local granitic bedrock, dislodging fractured boulders that are now yet another distinctive feature of the research area. Geothermal heat, meanwhile, spurs lush vegetation, which draws Dall's sheep from alpine heights to forage within the research area.

A Star in the Night

The summer solstice, the longest day of the year, generally occurs on June 21 or 22. From 3,624-foot Eagle Summit, the eastern end of the Pinnell Mountain Trail, as well as from points along the way, you can witness that quintessential phenomenon of high northern latitudes, the midnight sun. Even though it lies south of the Arctic Circle (an area 66½° north of the Equator, where the summer sun never dips below the horizon), Eagle Summit receives 24 hours of sunlight from about June 18 to 24 because of atmospheric refraction. On clear nights you can watch as the sun slowly sinks toward the horizon—but never sets.

What to See and Do

Despite its accessibility, the Steese NCA has only one recreational development: the **Pinnell Mountain National Recreation Trail.** You can hike almost anywhere you choose in the NCA, but for spectacular views of the White Mountains, the Crazy Mountains, and the Yukon River drainage, you'll want to strike out on the north unit's 27.3-mile-long Pinnell Mountain trail, which runs from Twelvemile Summit Wayside (Milepost 85.5) to Eagle Summit Wayside (Mile 107.1). You can access either end of the trail from the gravel Steese Highway.

This popular route follows a series of alpine ridgetops entirely above timberline. It is clearly marked with wooden mileposts and rock cairns. Elevations range from a low of 3,156 feet at Twelvemile Summit to 4,934 feet at Pinnell Mountain. Because the trail is quite steep and rugged in many areas, it can make for a difficult slog. More than 80 percent of the trail has a grade above 8 percent; one short section tops 35 percent! The trail varies in width from 24 inches to less than 6. Expect to encounter wet bogs, rock steps, and switchbacks on scree slopes. More than 1.5 miles of wood planking thread **Swamp Saddle** and lead the way to Twelvemile Summit.

Day hikes can begin from either trailhead. Although some hardcore hikers have trekked the entire route in a single day, most people budget three 9-mile days of backpacking. This allows plenty of time to savor sightings of wildlife, alpine birds, wildflowers, and summer's midnight sun. Two small emergency shelters are located at Mile 10.1 (Ptarmigan Creek Shelter Cabin) and Mile 17.5 (North Fork Shelter Cabin). A water catchment system is available at these first-come first-served cabins, but all water needs to be purified before drinking or cooking. Hikers regularly run into high winds and heavy rains when

Gold dredger, Chatanika River

Birch Creek and gravel bar

afternoon thunderstorms bear down. Lightning strikes are common on exposed ridges, so keep a weather eye. The trail is closed to off-road vehicles.

Birch Creek Float Trips

Wending through upland plateaus, forests, and muskeg wetlands and across private, state, and federal lands, **Birch Creek National Wild and Scenic River** travels 344 miles before emptying into the Yukon River about halfway between the villages of Fort Yukon and Beaver. The Bureau of Land Management (*1150 University Ave., Fairbanks, AK 99709; 907-474-2200*) administers the first 113 miles of Birch Creek as a wild river. Anglers cast for Arctic grayling, whitefish, and northern pike. Wildlife enthusiasts watch for black bears, caribou, falcons, and waterfowl. On a spring or fall evening you may hear the cries of migrating birds—not just honking geese but robins and thrushes and warblers, calling all night long. Motorized suction dredging for gold is prohibited, but hobbyists pan freely.

Frozen Birch Creek makes an excellent winter "highway" for cross-country skiing and dogsledding. The 1,000-mile **Yukon Quest International Sled Dog Race** from Fairbanks to Whitehorse traverses portions of Birch Creek every February.

River floaters can access Birch Creek from the Upper Birch Creek Wayside at Milepost 94.5 of Steese Highway and take out at either Lower Birch Creek Wayside (Mile 140.4) or Birch Creek Bridge (Mile 147.1). This 126-mile trip requires seven to ten days (actual float time is approximately 50 to 60 hours during normal summer flow levels). Thanks to its ready road access, this is an excellent and inexpensive choice for experienced wilderness river travelers.

Although the run features mostly Class I and Class II water, watch for a few Class III rapids, especially near Wolf Creek. Suitable for all nonmechanized watercraft, the somewhat shallow and swift Birch Creek often requires periodic lining (rope towing) over its upper 8 miles. Caution: Both aluminum and fiberglass canoes have been damaged on this upper stretch. Attractive natural campsites abound within the river corridor; camping is limited to 15 consecutive days in a calendar year.

For a pleasant six-hour float, put in at Lower Birch Creek Wayside and take out at Birch Creek Bridge. This 16-mile-long section of river meanders peacefully through forest and wetlands. In July take headnets and mosquito repellent.

By the end of August, fall colors begin to line the river and blanket the hillsides. It is then—with mosquito season over and a hint of frost in the air—that the float takes on a magical beauty. Even though this trip is popular with area residents, rarely is the river congested. Beginning in September, you may see hunters cruising the river for moose.

Some travel downstream 218 miles to the Yukon River—a sometimes tedious and noisy trip. ■

Tetlin National Wildlife Refuge

■ 730,000 acres ■ Southeast of Tok on Alaska Highway ■ Year-round access
■ Camping, hiking, hunting, fishing, bird-watching, auto tour ■ Contact the refuge, P.O. Box 779, Tok, AK 99780; phone 907-883-5312 or Alaska Public Lands Information Center (APLIC), P.O. Box 359, Milepost 1314, Alaska Hwy., Tok, AK 99780; phone 907-883-5667. www.r7.fws.gov/nwr/tetlin/tetnwr.html

THOUSANDS OF LAKES AND PONDS play host to dense concentrations of nesting waterfowl drawn to Tetlin National Wildlife Refuge. The spring thaw arrives earlier here than at sites to the north, so Tetlin is an important rest stop for migrating birds—among them sizable spring and fall migrations of sandhill cranes. The glacier-fed Chisana and Nabesna Rivers merge near the center of the refuge to create the Tanana River. Extensive stands of deciduous trees shelter wildlife, while spindly black spruce—some almost 200 years old—sprout from muskeg underlain with permafrost.

Driving into Alaska from Canada via the **Alaska Highway**, you'll see Tetlin NWR along the south (left) side of the road for the next 65 miles. With seven maintained pullouts, the highway serves as the refuge's auto-tour route; roadside exhibits explain the geology and ecology that have shaped Alaska's Interior. In summer, stop at the visitor center (Milepost 1229) and pick up an interpretive cassette to listen to en route, then drop it off at the APLIC office on Tok's main street. If you camp at Deadman Lake Campground (Mile 1249), take time to walk the quarter-mile **Taiga Trail** or fish for pike from the handicap-accessible pier. The refuge ends at Mile 1284, but the highway runs on to Tok. ■

Yukon-Charley Rivers National Preserve

Yukon-Charley Rivers National Preserve

■ 2.5 million acres ■ About 150 miles east of Fairbanks ■ Best months June-Sept. ■ Camping, hiking, boating, rafting, kayaking, canoeing, fishing, bird-watching, wildlife viewing, float trips ■ Access by boat or aircraft only ■ Contact the preserve, 201 First Ave., Fairbanks, AK 99701; phone 907-456-0281 or the preserve field office, P.O. Box 167, Eagle, AK 99738; phone 907-547-2234

SPRAWLING WESTWARD FROM the Alaska-Canada border, Yukon-Charley Rivers National Preserve guards a variety of natural, cultural, and paleontological sites within its river valleys, rolling hills, and sawtooth cliffs. This massive but subtly beautiful and unscarred wilderness protects 115 miles of the Yukon River, as well as the entire 1.1-million-acre pristine Charley River watershed, which is half the size of Yellowstone National Park. Born of spring runoff, this national wild and scenic river tumbles 108 miles before its clear waters merge with those of the murky Yukon.

In the preserve the Yukon River, silt-laden and confined, slices through a deep fault, grinding away ancient rock on its ineluctable surge to the Bering Sea. The Tintina Fault stretches east-west through the preserve and is known by geologists for its role in the Klondike gold rush. Look at a map and you'll notice that gold discoveries in Yukon-Charley have occurred only on the Yukon's south bank. Millions of years ago two crustal plates shifted along the Tintina Fault, carrying gold and silica (which later became quartz) toward the surface. Erosion then separated the gold from the quartz and washed it into mountain streams, where it gradually settled to the bottom. Since 1898, miners have used gold pans, sluice boxes, and dredges to separate this treasure from its trough.

Interior Alaska's transition from summer to winter—a long, dark season of prolonged cold snaps—is swift and sometimes sudden. Ice begins flowing in the Yukon River in October, and freeze-up comes by mid-November. As tributaries dry out and ice over, the Yukon runs clear beneath almost 6 feet of ice. In the wake of such an extreme deep-freeze, breaking up is hard to do: Ice-out does not occur until early May.

The preserve shelters wolves, moose, black bears, and lynx, as well as the calving grounds of the Fortymile caribou herd. Designated in part to protect its abundant peregrine falcons, the preserve hosts 20 percent of the state's population of those raptors. Ravaged by DDT, only 50 to 100 pairs of American peregrine falcons still nested in Alaska by the early 1970s. Their comeback well under way, 400 pairs now nest in the state.

Rocky palisades above the Charley River provide numerous nesting sites. You might also see a peregrine on Eagle Bluff near town or atop one of the 1,000-foot-high bluffs downstream, such as the Calico, Montauk, or Takoma. Although the birds summer in this remote land, they winter more than 5,000 miles to the south, in Central and South America.

Migrants in a different medium—king and chum salmon—power up the Yukon and through the preserve. Some chum travel as far as 2,000 miles to reach their Canadian spawning grounds. As they have for millennia, native Athapaskan people—the land's original inhabitants—await their coming.

Long gone are the gold seekers of yore with their dreams of sudden riches. Their decaying log cabins are now the only bits of evidence that they were once here.

What to See and Do

Yukon-Charley Rivers National Preserve has no direct road access. The 162-mile Steese Highway (Alas. 6) from Fairbanks terminates at Circle, 17 miles northwest (downstream) of the preserve, while the 161-mile Taylor Highway (Alas. 5) from Tetlin Junction ends at Eagle, 12 miles south (upstream) of the preserve. Taylor Highway is usually passable from late April to mid-October, or until snow closes the road.

Flowing from Eagle to Circle, the **Yukon River** is the principal means of access to the preserve. Free of rapids, this brawny river is ideal for rafts, canoes, and motorboats. The lower portions of the Yukon's major tributaries—the **Nation, Kandik, and Charley Rivers**—beg to be explored. Exposed geological features, historic relics, magnificent scenery, and varied wildlife are highlights of each day's travel. Most of the

Yukon River, Circle

clear-water side streams also provide excellent fishing for arctic grayling, northern pike, and whitefish. The 158-mile-long **Eagle-to-Circle float** takes paddlers five to ten days *(contact Eagle Canoe Rentals 907-547-2203)*.

Small campgrounds are located in or near both Eagle and Circle. Seven public-use cabins lie within the preserve, all of them along the Yukon River corridor. Coal Creek Cabin, Slaven's Roadhouse, and Nation Bluff Cabin were all built in the 1930s. Glenn Creek Cabin, Washington Creek Cabin, Kandik Mouth Cabin, and Slaven's Public Use Cabin followed over the next six decades. Use is on a first-come first-served basis, with a limit of 7 days per cabin in any 30-day period. The **Eagle Ranger Station** contains cultural and natural history exhibits; it also dispenses up-to-date information. Don't miss the **tour of Eagle** and nearby **Fort Egbert** staged by town residents all summer *(contact Historical Society 907-547-2325)*.

You can also access the Yukon River at Dawson City in Canada's Yukon Territory, approximately 100 miles upriver from Eagle. Even on a fast float, you'll see myriad wildlife—not to mention remnants of the Klondike gold rush and the downriver stampede to Alaska's gold. The river segment from Dawson City to Circle (allow 8 to 15 days) may be the most scenic safe river traverse in North America. To experience a part of Klondike history, take the paddle wheeler *Yukon Queen II* between Dawson City and Eagle.

For a much more rugged paddling experience *(novices should not attempt this river on their own)*, try the swift Charley River. Plunging from 4,000 feet above sea level at its source to 700 feet at its mouth, the Charley hurtles past spectacular upland cliffs, over rapids, and out onto a flat plain, where it slowly meanders to the Yukon River. Dall's sheep, usually at home on mountain slopes, often scale riverside scarps. Aircraft access necessitates the use of inflatable watercraft. Put in at the gravel airstrip located in the upper portion of the Charley just above Copper Creek. Helicopters can also drop off trekkers and floaters.

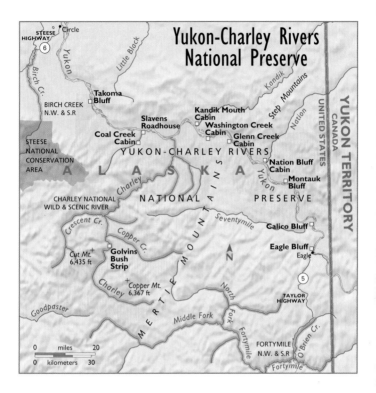

Two reputable air taxis are run by Tatonduk Flying Service *(P.O. Box 55, Eagle, AK 99738. 907-547-2221)* and 40-Mile Air *(Box 539, Tok, AK 99780; 907-883-5191).*

Boating season on this Class II-to-Class IV river usually lasts from June until water levels drop in late August. The average float time for the 75 miles from the airstrip to the Yukon River is six days. You can arrange for a powerboat or floatplane to pick you up at the mouth of the Charley—or, for that matter, anywhere along the Yukon. Plan on three or four more days to float the 70 miles to Circle.

This journey requires top-notch backcountry skills, white-water experience, and thorough preparation. Once you leave the well-traveled Yukon River corridor, you are completely on your own. Contact the rangers in Eagle for further information. Guided river trips are available through Pristine Adventures *(P.O. Box 83909, Fairbanks, AK 99707. 877-716-4366).*

There are no maintained trails here, just a few game trails and miners' paths. Open mountain ridges provide the best hiking. Explorers with good backcountry skills blaze trails through dense thickets to reach the highlands along the rivers, boldly going where few wafflestompers have gone before. Those who forge into Yukon-Charley could be sorely tested at times, but the rewards will be deep and abiding. ∎

Southwest

Floatplanes, Wood-Tikchik State Park

WE ARE WAITING FOR DEATH at any moment. A mountain has burst near here. We are covered with ashes, in some places 10 feet and 6 inches deep. All this began June 6. Night and day we light lanterns. We cannot see daylight. We have no water, the rivers are just ashes mixed with water. Here are darkness and hell, thunder and noise. I do not know whether it is day or night. The earth is trembling, it lightens every minute. It is terrible. We are praying.
—Aleut fisherman Ivan Orloff, 1912

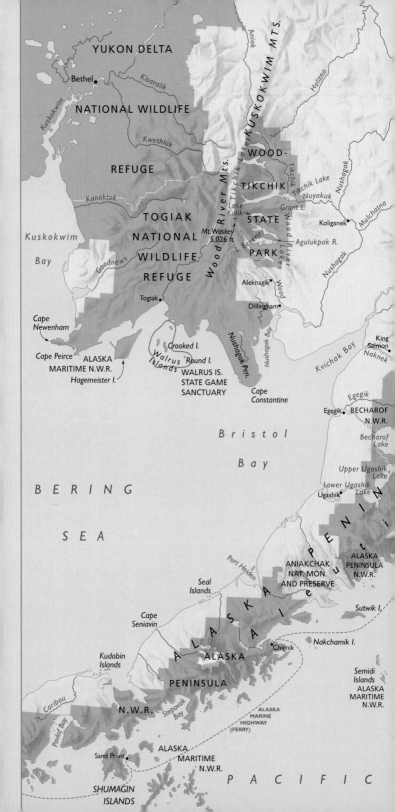

YUKON DELTA

Bethel

NATIONAL WILDLIFE

REFUGE

Kuskokwim

Kisaralik

Kwethluk

Kanektok

KUSKOKWIM MTS.

Aniak

Holitna

WOOD-

TIKCHIK

Tikchik Lakes

Tikchik Lake

Tikchik

Nuyakuk

Nushagak

STATE

Lake
Kulik

Grant L.

Koliganek

Mulchatna

Kuskokwim

Bay

TOGIAK

NATIONAL

WILDLIFE

REFUGE

Goodnews

Mt. Waskey
5,026 ft

PARK

L. Beverley

Agulukpak R.

Wood Lakes

Wood River

Nushagak

Togiak

Aleknagik

Wood

Dillingham

Wood River Mts.

Cape
Newenham

Cape Peirce

ALASKA
MARITIME N.W.R.

Hagemeister I.

Crooked I.

*Walrus
Islands*

Round I.

WALRUS IS.
STATE GAME
SANCTUARY

Nushagak Pen.

Nushagak Bay

Cape
Constantine

King
Salmon

Naknek

Kvichak Bay

Egegik

Egegik

BECHAROF
N.W.R.

*Becharof
Lake*

B r i s t o l

B a y

*Upper Ugashik
Lake*

*Lower Ugashik
Lake*

Ugashik

B E R I N G

S E A

P
E
N
I
N

A
l
e
u
t
i

Port Heiden

ANIAKCHAK
NAT. MON.
AND PRESERVE

ALASKA
PENINSULA
N.W.R.

*Seal
Islands*

Sutwik I.

Cape
Seniavin

A
L
A
S
K
A

Nakchamik I.

*Semidi
Islands*
ALASKA
MARITIME
N.W.R.

*Kudobin
Islands*

ALASKA

Chignik

P
E
N
I
N
S
U
L
A

PENINSULA

N.W.R.

*Stepovak
Bay*

Caribou

Pavlof Bay

ALASKA
MARINE
HIGHWAY
(FERRY)

Sand Point

ALASKA
MARITIME
N.W.R.

*SHUMAGIN
ISLANDS*

P A C I F I C

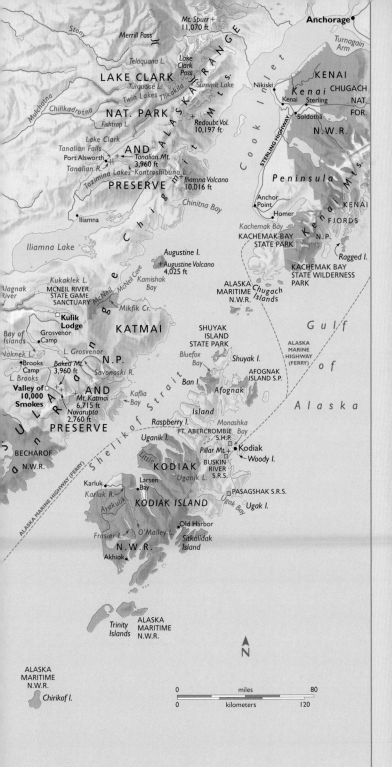

Stony

Merrill Pass

Mt. Spurr +
11,070 ft

Anchorage

Turnagain
Arm

Telaquana L.

Lake
Clark
Pass

Summit Lake

LAKE CLARK

Turquoise L.

Twin Lakes

Tlikakila

KENAI

Nikiski

CHUGACH

Mulchatna

Chilikadrotna

Kenai

Kenai

Sterling

NAT. PARK

Fishtrap L.

Redoubt Vol.
10,197 ft

Soldotna

**NAT.
FOR.**

N.W.R.

Lake Clark

Tanalian Falls

AND

Tanalian Mt.
3,960 ft

Peninsula

Port Alsworth

Tanalian R.

Tazimina Lakes

Kontrashibuna L.

Chinitna Bay

PRESERVE

Iliamna Volcano
10,016 ft

Anchor
Point

Homer

**KENAI
FJORDS**

Iliamna

Kachemak Bay

**KACHEMAK BAY
STATE PARK**

Ragged I.

N.P.

Iliamna Lake

Augustine I.

+ Augustine Volcano
4,025 ft

Kamishak
Bay

**ALASKA
MARITIME
N.W.R.**

Chugach
Islands

**KACHEMAK BAY
STATE WILDERNESS
PARK**

Kukaklek L.

**McNEIL RIVER
STATE GAME
SANCTUARY**

McNeil

McNeil Cove

Mikfik Cr.

Alagnak
River

**Kulik
Lodge**

Grosvenor
Camp

KATMAI

**SHUYAK
ISLAND
STATE PARK**

**SHUYAK
ISLAND
STATE PARK**

Gulf

Bay of
Islands

L. Grosvenor

N.P.

Bluefox
Bay

Shuyak I.

**ALASKA
MARINE
HIGHWAY
(FERRY)**

of

Naknek L.

Brooks
Camp

Baked Mt.
3,960 ft

Savonoski R.

Ban I.

**AFOGNAK
ISLAND S.P.**

L. Brooks

**Valley of
10,000
Smokes**

AND

Mt. Katmai
6,715 ft

Novarupta
2,760 ft

Kaflia
Bay

Afognak

Island

Monashka
Bay

Alaska

PRESERVE

Raspberry I.

**FT. ABERCROMBIE
S.H.P.**

Pillar Mt.+

Kodiak

Woody I.

BECHAROF

Uganik I.

**BUSKIN
RIVER
S.R.S.**

N.W.R.

Karluk

KODIAK

Uganik L.

Ugak Bay

PASAGSHAK S.R.S.

Karluk R.

Larsen
Bay

Little

Ugak I.

Ayakulik

KODIAK ISLAND

Frasier L.

O'Malley L.

Old Harbor

Akhiok

N.W.R.

Sitkalidak
Island

Trinity
Islands

**ALASKA
MARITIME
N.W.R.**

**ALASKA
MARITIME
N.W.R.**

Chirikof I.

N

miles

0   80

0   120

kilometers

O C E A N

From his fishing camp near Kaflia Bay on Shelikof Strait, Orloff wrote this note to his wife in life's darkest hour. He survived, having witnessed one of the most spectacular volcanic explosions ever recorded on Earth. Twenty-five miles west of Orloff's camp, the Novarupta vent at the base of Mount Katmai blew on June 6, 1912. (The eruption was ten times more powerful than would be the eruption of Washington State's Mount St. Helens in 1980.) When a National Geographic expedition arrived to explore the aftermath of the eruption four years later, thousands of fissures and cracks in the valley near the mountain were still shooting steam hundreds of feet into the air. Awestruck, expedition leader Robert Griggs named the site "The Valley of Ten Thousand Smokes." Today the valley forms part of Alaska's Katmai National Park and Preserve.

Here on the northern rim of the Pacific Ocean the Earth trembles with earthquakes and a sweeping arc of volcanoes spews forth fire, smoke, and ash. Alaska is the northern link in the spectacular Ring of Fire—a great chain of volcanoes girding the Pacific Ocean. More than 50 volcanoes stretch from the head of Cook Inlet down the Alaska Peninsula and out the Aleutian island chain into the Bering Sea, creating a 1,600-mile-long crescent of fireworks from Mount Spurr to Buldir Island.

Tossed up into the Bering Sea hundreds of miles from the western coast of Alaska, the four tiny volcanic islands known as the Pribilofs seem, at first blush, an unlikely tourist destination. But they are renowned for their wildlife and botanical riches, from the return each year of thousands of northern fur seals to cliffs upon cliffs of nesting seabirds to spectacular blooms of wildflowers.

More than 40 volcanoes along the Ring of Fire have erupted (some many times) since they were first recorded in the ships' logs and journals of Russian and European explorers who traveled to Alaska more than 250

Walrus, Round Island

years ago. Although Vulcan, the Roman god of fire, was known on Mount Olympus as kindly and peace loving, he appears to be violently active here in Alaska, forging Zeus's thunderbolts beneath the coastline of the state.

Volcanology, dedicated to explaining a volcano's unpredictable and explosive behavior, remains a difficult and inexact science. We know the Earth's surface is made up of a dozen or so rigid crusts, the tectonic plates. These float on a molten mantle much the same way ice floes move about the Arctic seas. Some of these constantly moving plates make up the continents; others constitute the ocean floors. Their edges grind together and sometimes collide, forcing one plate to plunge beneath another, subducted toward the mantle's intense heat. Slowly, the molten rock, called magma, finds its way back to the Earth's surface through cracks in the crust. Tremendous pressure builds up below the surface until the magma finally erupts through a volcano into the Earth's atmosphere.

Sad Face Mountain reflected in Tikchik Lake

In Alaska, the Pacific Ocean plate is slowly being subducted beneath the North American plate along a 25,000-foot-deep depression in the ocean floor known as the Aleutian Trench. The resulting stresses and strains provide the region with high drama, from earthquakes and tidal waves to tsunamis and erupting volcanoes. In 1946, an earthquake along the Aleutian Trench produced a series of 100-foot-high waves, destroying the lighthouse at Scotch Cap on isolated Unimak Island and sweeping the five men manning the light out to sea.

In the past century, three of Cook Inlet's six volcanoes (Spurr, Redoubt, and Augustine) have erupted nine times; all six have spouted off at least once in the past 15 years. Lying within 200 miles of Anchorage (and thus half the population of Alaska), the volcanoes often blanket nearby cities with ash, closing airports and disrupting flights (not to mention lives).

Though this region may seem to be a caldron of natural calamities, it is also a cascade of wilderness treasures. Spectacular numbers of wildlife—in some cases the largest populations in the world—live or travel seasonally to these shores, from salmon and trophy rainbow trout to brown bears, seabirds, and whales. A glance at the map reveals one national park tumbling over huge pristine lakes into the boundaries of another, bumping against the borders of wildlife sanctuaries, state parks, and game refuges. Wherever you land in southwest Alaska, it's bound to be an adventure. ■

Lake Clark National Park and Preserve

■ 4 million acres, including 2.6 million acres (park) and 1.4 million acres (preserve) ■ Directly west of Kenai Peninsula, across Cook Inlet ■ Best months June–mid-Sept. for summer activities and fall colors; March–early April for cross-country skiing with long daylight hours ■ Camping, hiking, backpacking, white-water rafting and kayaking, canoeing, fishing, hunting (in preserve), cross-country skiing, river trips ■ State of Alaska sportfishing or hunting license required ■ Access by small aircraft or boat only ■ Contact the park and preserve, 4230 University Dr., Suite 311, Anchorage, AK 99508; phone 907-271-3751. www.nps.gov/lacl/ home.htm

Think of all the splendors that bespeak Alaska: glaciers, volcanoes, alpine spires, wild rivers, lakes with grayling on the rise. Picture coasts feathered with countless seabirds. Imagine dense forests and far-sweeping tundra, herds of caribou, great roving bears. Now concentrate all these and more into less than one percent of the state— and behold the Lake Clark region, Alaska's epitome.

—John Kauffmann
Alaska Task Force, National Park Service

Aerial view of Lake Clark

On the western shore of Cook Inlet rises a mystical white mountain range featuring "the steaming sisters"—three active volcanoes (Mount Spurr, Redoubt, and Iliamna) that announce a chain of fire stretching more than 1,000 miles into the Bering Sea. From Anchorage, across the inlet, these 10,000-foot-high peaks are the first to catch the pink light of early morning and the last to bask in the golden-red and purple glow of the setting sun.

This panorama encompasses the raw, serrated Chigmit Mountains; with their eerie spires, arrowhead crests, and hanging glaciers, they form a sort of montane hinge joining two mighty ranges, the Alaska Range to the north and the Aleutian Range to the south. The "frenzy of peaks," as an early Park Service writer dubbed it, also constitutes the gateway to Lake Clark National Park and Preserve. Protected within the park's borders are three national wild and scenic rivers: the swift and twisting Chilika-drotna, the shallow and rocky Mulchatna, and the glacier-fed Tlikakila.

Though these jagged white pinnacles are a familiar sight to Anchorage residents, they still hold surprises. Ash floated over the city when Redoubt Volcano erupted in December 1989 and again in August 1990. And on some mornings, a glance across the inlet reveals summits seemingly twice their usual size. This is an atmospheric phenomenon known as fata mor-gana—a mirage caused when a layer of air near the Earth's surface differs drastically in temperature from the layer above it. This strange distortion

Dick Proenneke's cabin, Lake Clark National Park and Preserve

and magnification of images was named for the sorceress of Arthurian legend, Morgan le Fay, who was fond of luring sailors to their deaths by projecting images of her castle onto rocks at sea.

The illusory quality of these mountains is fitting. The park's necklace of alpine lakes descends from Telaquana to Tazimina in brilliant, otherworldly turquoise. And depending on the season, the fairy-tale picture is accented by summer's greens, the brilliant reds and yellows of fall, or the brilliant white of winter snow. No photograph or painting can do it justice. You have to be here, use all your senses, breathe it in.

Dena'ina Athapaskan Indians have called this land home for nearly a thousand years. In the last two centuries, a handful of explorers, gold miners, and trappers made their way into this mountain wilderness. In the 1970s, field researchers, young idealists, and old park hands bushwhacked their way through the area's blue-lake wilds, flew aerial surveys to count caribou, trekked over the mountains, boated the coast, ran the rivers, and walked its world-class salmon-rich streams. At the same time, they mapped the perimeters of its unusual beauty to persuade Congress to include the region in a historic piece of legislation—the Alaska National Interest Lands Act of 1980. Among other things, the act doubled the size of the National Park System in the United States. The closest national park to Alaska's largest city, Lake Clark remains one of the least visited because of the logistics and expense involved in reaching it.

Before official park designation, one man, Dick Proenneke, came to the edge of Twin Lakes, built an exquisite log cabin by hand, and lived here on his own for nearly 30 years. His daily journal, first published in the 1970s as *One Man's Wilderness*, is today an Alaska classic.

> *To see game you must move a little and look a lot. What first appears to be a branch turns into that big caribou bull up there on the benches....I wonder what he thinks about?...I wonder if he feels as I do, that this small part of the world is enough to think about?*

What to See and Do

The heart of the park, about one to two hours' flying time via small aircraft from Anchorage, Kenai, or Homer, is reached through narrow, twisting mountain passes. The trip can be heart-stoppingly beautiful and, as one pilot said, like "flying into the jaws of a shark." If the weather starts to close in, stay on the ground. The best pilots in the world fly through here, but a few are overly bold. You can see the wreckage of the unlucky, particularly in Merrill Pass.

Access to the park is primarily by air: Lake and Peninsula Air *(907-781-2228)* and Lake Clark Air *(907-781-2211)* both fly direct from Merrill Field in Anchorage to Port Alsworth on Lake Clark, where the park's field headquarters *(907-781-2218)* is located. In addition, ranger cabins are staffed seasonally at Twin Lakes, Telaquana Lake, and Chinitna Bay on Cook Inlet.

In case of emergencies, file a trip plan with the Park Service as soon as you arrive and be aware that this is strictly a wilderness park—it requires experience and equipment. If you do not possess the necessary outdoor skills, go with a guide. One outfitter, Alaska Alpine Adventures *(877-525-2577)*, arranges small custom-designed backpacking or river-running trips.

Hiking and Canoeing

This park has only one established trail—a 2.5-mile walk carved through the woods *(trailhead just past Homestead Café in Port Alsworth)* to **Tanalian Falls** and, a mile farther, **Kontrashibuna Lake.** The country it leads through exemplifies all that is grand about Lake Clark National Park. En route, you will pass a sign pointing you to **Tanalian Mountain,** which stands 3,960 feet high. The route to the summit is flagged in places, but it is not a trail. The round-trip climb should take a good hiker about seven hours.

Add on canoeing and camping down 13-mile-long Kontrashibuna Lake, and you could spend a week exploring this area. (Canoes have to be flown in, so ask your air taxi about boat-size restrictions.) Kontrashibuna means "lake in which water extends against the mountains," in the language of the Dena'ina Athapaskan people. The narrow lake jogs between steep mountains and rushing creeks.

Salmon drying at a native camp

Enjoying a hot tub near Fishtrap Lake, Lake Clark National Park and Preserve

Hiking and Kayaking

From Port Alsworth, you can charter an air taxi service to any one of the exquisite lakes in the park's northern reaches with a foldboat or kayak. The string of large lakes, including **Turquoise, Telaquana, and Twin Lakes,** makes for wonderful paddling trips and offers access to many good—though undeveloped—hiking routes. To the southwest, **Upper** and **Lower Tazimina Lakes** are also lovely (and an even shorter floatplane trip). Then, of course, there's beautiful, 40-mile **Lake Clark** itself.

These lakes can be so incredibly still that they reflect a perfect likeness of the surrounding mountains. But that can change quickly. Heed the advice from Dena'ina elder Pete Trefon about Lake Clark and apply it to any lake you paddle: "If the wind starts to blow, get the hell off the lake!"

River Trips

Only experienced river runners should consider trips on the park's three national wild rivers, reached by air taxi and floatplane from the region's populated centers.

The **Chilakadrotna** (often referred to as "The Chilly") experiences high water in June and August, when rafts and kayaks traverse Class II and III rapids through the wilderness. Begin your trip via air taxi to Twin Lakes, then fly out from any sandbar strip.

The **Mulchatna National Wild and Scenic River** flows from aptly named Turquoise Lake through the Bonanza Hills to the broader valley below. Access is by air taxi.

The small, glacier-fed **Tlikakila National Wild and Scenic River** follows a major Earth fault from Summit Lake to Lake Clark. Along the way, glaciers, sheer cliffs, waterfalls, and the craggy Chigmit peaks make this float a truly awesome experience. Rapids can reach Class IV, making the route best suited for experienced river runners. Begin the trip via floatplane to Summit Lake and end it with an air taxi from Lake Clark or Port Alsworth —a 70-mile paddle from the river's start. ■

McNeil River State Game Sanctuary

■ 114,100 acres ■ 250 miles southwest of Anchorage and 100 miles west of Homer ■ Camping, wildlife viewing ■ Lottery permit system and user fees ■ Access by aircraft June-Aug. ■ Contact the sanctuary, Alaska Department of Fish and Game, Division of Wildlife Conservation, 333 Raspberry Rd., Anchorage, AK 99518; phone 907-267-2182. www.state.ak.us/adfg

JUST WEST OF AUGUSTINE ISLAND (an active volcano), the **McNeil River** drains into the mudflats of Kamishak Bay. About a mile upstream from its mouth, boulders and fast water form a frothing falls that poses a challenge to migrating salmon. The fish leap and fight against the current and cataracts, making several attempts to navigate the falls—and dodge the waiting bears. Hundreds of salmon sometimes clog the pools below the falls. With no comparable fishing sites in the area, the **McNeil River falls** attract the world's greatest concentration of brown bears. Nowhere else can you expect to see a similar gathering. Using threats and roaring, bare-fanged assaults, thousand-pound males defend prime fishing spots from other bears. Smaller bears position themselves on exposed rocks in midstream. Juvenile bears and females with tiny spring cubs patrol back and forth. A count of bears in view is typically 20 to 30 but may climb as high as 60.

Excessive, uncontrolled public use in the early 1970s—when people sometimes outnumbered the bears at the falls—endangered this unique area. The bears abandoned the river or fished at night. But preservation of this unique ursine convocation is the sanctuary's main goal, so managers instituted a permit system limiting the number of people to ten per day. Permits are awarded by a lottery; apply by March 1 by mail to the Alaska Department of Fish and Game, Division of Wildlife Conservation (*P.O. Box 228080, Anchorage, AK 99522. Attn: McNeil River Application*).

In June, red (sockeye) salmon migrate into Mikfik Creek, which drains into McNeil Cove. From several locations along the creek you can watch bears fishing or grazing on the sedge flats, usually eight or nine at a time. When the abundant 7- to 18-pound chum salmon enter McNeil River in July, bears begin to congregate at the falls, along with bald eagles and magpies, not to mention the occasional wolf, red fox, or wolverine.

Other than a communal cook shack and pit toilets, the only campground is undeveloped; there are no concessions of any kind. You must be entirely self-sufficient and prepared for cold, wind-driven rain. Storms delay or cancel flights, so bring at least two days' additional food. From the campground, you'll hike 2 miles one way to the McNeil River falls, at times wading through knee-deep water and slogging through boot-sucking mud (backpack and hip boots are necessities). Expect mosquitoes on calm days.

Regulations prohibit solo inland jaunts; instead, visitors travel in groups led by a sanctuary employee. These stringent rules work. By always returning to the same locations, humans are viewed by the 140 bears as nonthreatening, giving site visitors close-up views of such intimate activities as mating, play-fighting, and nursing. ■

Not in Kansas Anymore

TERRIFYING ENCOUNTERS with Alaska bears make headlines, but those creatures may be the least of your outdoor concerns when traveling in the state. Due to the lack of roads, getting around Alaska involves boats and planes, both of which are subject to weather whims. Remember: It's better to pass up a flight-seeing trip or a boat ride than to come back a day or two late—or not at all. To ensure flexibility and safety, plan extra time at both ends of your trip.

Dozens of commercial flying services, called air taxis, haul passengers and freight statewide. Some offer scheduled flights; others specialize in charters. Flight-seeing trips cater to thousands of travelers, although weather-related delays and cancellations are common. Maybe you'll reach your destination but get weathered in. If so, do you have extra food?

Most flights go flawlessly, but each summer a few pilots chance the weather and planes go down. Use your own common sense. If the weather looks dicey, don't go. Also, look out for

"outlaw" bush pilots who sell their services but fly without the proper training, licensing, or insurance. Ask for proper documentation.

Sudden storms, underwater hazards, and extreme tides—tidal rips, bore tides, and fluctuations to 38 feet—can make any ocean boat trip problematic. Many charter boat operators who hold "six-pack" licenses (which limit them to six passengers or fewer) take part in a voluntary U.S. Coast Guard inspection program; visit www.uscg .mil/d17 to find out a boat's safety rating. Large tour boats face more stringent licensing and inspections. Many unlicensed charter boats ply offshore waters, so ask for credentials before paying for any trip.

Properly licensed boats occasionally experience bad weather or mechanical trouble (even giant cruise ships go aground each year), and the law requires them to carry survival gear. If you are inexperienced with Alaska tides and waters, hire a guide. Even if you are going out only for a day, follow the Coast Guard's advice: "Always file

Pilot on Bagley Icefield, with Mount St. Elias behind plane

a float plan before you go boating."

Never board a boat, canoe, raft, or kayak for even a short jaunt without a flotation device and rain gear. Once the lake gets choppy or seas start coming over the bow, it's too late to remember life jackets (nearly 40 people drown yearly in Alaska). Think of the small things; guides can do only so much. If you wear eyeglasses, for example, always secure them with a sports strap or a neck cord.

Midsummer water temperatures are cold enough to quickly immobilize even powerful swimmers. If you fall overboard without a survival suit, life expectancy can be measured in minutes. Hypothermia (often called exposure) develops when the body can no longer maintain its normal temperature. In an automatic response, blood flow to the extremities shuts down to preserve warmth in vital organs. Shivering is an early danger sign. Untreated hypothermia results in impaired judgment and coordination, eventually leading to stupor, collapse, and death.

You don't have to fall in the water or be in a snowstorm to develop hypothermia. Some experts maintain that common summer conditions—wind, rain, temperatures in the low 50s—can quickly trigger its onset. Lack of rain gear, light clothing, and exhaustion combine to create a potentially lethal situation. Experienced Alaskans carry packs stuffed with rain gear, food, and extra clothes—even on day hikes.

Take extra care when walking on tidal flats. Wet mud loses its cohesiveness, so you could sink and be trapped. People have drowned mired in muck. Also, be wary wading streams and rivers: It's easy to underestimate the depth and current, or stumble over a slippery rock. A glacial or mountain stream that's easy to ford in the morning may become uncrossable in the afternoon from increased runoff.

Keep in mind that off-trail hiking can be extremely taxing, especially under a heavy backpack. Brush, boulders, bogs, and bugs are normal parts of almost any hike. Most treks take longer than planned; 2 miles per hour is a respectable pace in Alaska. No matter what you do or where you go, always tell someone your plans. Otherwise, help can be a very long time in coming. ■

Canoeing on Naknek Lake at Brooks Camp, Katmai National Park and Preserve

Katmai National Park and Preserve

■ 4.1 million acres ■ Alaska Peninsula, 290 miles southwest of Anchorage and 30 miles east of King Salmon ■ Camping, hiking, guided hikes, climbing, kayaking, canoeing, fishing, cross-country skiing, wildlife viewing, bus tour, float trips, flight-seeing ■ Day-use fee; camping fee. Backcountry permit required ■ Access by aircraft and boat June–mid-Sept. ■ Contact the park, P.O. Box 7, King Salmon, AK 99613; phone 907-246-3305. www.nps.gov/katm

FIRST A TREMENDOUS EXPLOSION shook the Earth. Then dense clouds of choking ash began to fall, blotting out the sun. "Here are darkness and hell, thunder and noise," wrote one survivor. "I do not know whether it is day or night…God is merciful. Pray for us." The cataclysmic eruption of Mount Katmai's Novarupta vent began on June 6, 1912, and lasted 60 hours. In that time Novarupta shot skyward enough ash and rock to darken much of North America for days. People heard the blast in Juneau, 750 miles away. In Kodiak, 100 miles distant, the weight of more than a foot of ash collapsed houses. Acid rain fell on Seattle.

Word of the eruption focused world attention on the remote Alaska Peninsula. In 1916, a team of scientists funded by the National Geographic Society made their way to the area on foot from Shelikof Strait. What they found was stunning: a once lush valley of nearly 40 square miles lay buried beneath 100 to 700 feet of ash, pumice, and rock. Team leader Robert Griggs wrote of "the most amazing visions ever beheld by mortal eye…the whole valley…was full of hundreds, no thousands—literally tens of thousands—of smokes curling up from its fissured floor." Galvanized by Griggs' reports and expeditions, President Woodrow Wilson established Katmai National Monument on September 24, 1918, to preserve the geologic wonders of "The Valley of Ten Thousand Smokes."

Gone now are all but a few of those smoking fumaroles, yet it's only a matter of time before others appear in the wake of another eruption. Katmai's active volcanoes, part of the Pacific Ring of Fire, align over a subduction zone that extends southwest through the Aleutian Islands. The park's segment of the snowcapped Aleutian Range includes 15 volcanoes, some of them more than 7,000 feet high. Eruptions and frequent earthquakes signal tectonic instability.

Katmai's wilderness mosaic of rivers, lakes, broad valleys, and emergent coastlines protects wolves, caribou, moose, marten, otters, beavers, and more than 2,000 brown bears. Seals, sea lions, sea otters, gray whales, and beluga whales frolic in the tides of Shelikof Strait. In addition, a rich archaeological record attests to human occupation dating back 7,500 years. **Brooks River National Historic Landmark** protects North America's highest concentration of prehistoric human dwellings (about 900). Most visitors are drawn here today by the same thing that attracted those early occupants: an abundance of sockeye salmon.

What to See and Do

Scheduled flights from Anchorage serve King Salmon, the park's gateway community. From there several local air taxis fly the 30 miles to Brooks Camp daily in peak season *(reserve in advance)*.

In King Salmon, stop first at the **visitor center** *(907-246-4250)*, beside the King Salmon airport terminal. Here interpreters and interactive displays give insight into the region's natural, cultural, and recreational offerings.

Camping

Once you reach **Brooks Camp—** the park's main destination—you will be required to attend the "Brooks Camp School of Bear Etiquette," a 15- to 20-minute safety program held at the visitor center *(June–mid-Sept.)*. The center is located on Naknek Lake near the mouth of the Brooks River.

You may overnight in the rustic campground (0.25 mile from visitor center) or in Brooks Lodge *(June–mid-Sept.)* nearby. With a campground limit of 60 people per day, permits go fast; most July campsites are reserved within hours after the advance reservation system opens in January *(301-722-1257 or 800-365-2267. www. reservations.gov)*. Reservations (as well as day-use and campground fees) must be paid before you arrive. Contact the concessionaire, Katmailand *(907-243-5448 or 800-544-0551. www.katmailand.com)*, to reserve accommodations and meals at the lodge. A store sells limited supplies.

Each afternoon, rangers lead an hour-long, half-mile-round-trip cultural walk to a re-created archaeological site. A variety of evening programs are also on tap in the auditorium near the visitor center. Other guided hikes and activities occur throughout the season.

Tours and Hikes

Sign up at Brooks Lodge for the ranger-narrated 23-mile drive to **Three Forks Overlook,** perched

A Bear of an Appetite

Often called the largest land carnivores, brown bears (known as grizzlies if more than 100 miles from the coast) are in fact omnivores: They range from tidal flats to mountaintops in search of anything edible, be it clams or berries. In spring they graze for hours on tidal sedges and grasses. When the salmon begin to run in summer, grizzlies gorge themselves, gaining 20 percent of their body weight. (A small bear weighed by biologists on the Alaska Peninsula actually doubled its body weight.) Late season berry binges add extra pounds; by hibernation time in late October, healthy brown bears are waddling fat. Some large males approach three-quarters of a ton. Upon emerging from hibernation in late March or early April, they quickly shake off their lethargy and resume their search for food.

above the **Valley of Ten Thousand Smokes.** The bus stops for scenic views and wildlife along the way, possibly moose, fox, or bear. From the station, the steep, strenuous 1.5-mile **Ukak Falls Trail** drops 700 feet to the ash-and-pumice-covered valley floor. From here you can walk over the volcanic tuff to **Ukak Falls** or to the **Three Forks Convergence,** where the roiling Ukak River and its tributaries have cut deep gashes in the accumulated ash of the 1912 eruption.

Katmai's only other dedicated hiking route, the **Dumpling Mountain Trail,** starts at the Brooks Camp Campground, climbs 1.5

miles to an overlook, then continues another 2 miles to the 2,440-foot-high summit. Through dense forest of deciduous and conifer trees, the trail wends upward into cranberry-carpeted alpine meadows with sweeping views of Brooks Camp, Naknek Lake, and the distant volcanoes. As always, watch for bears, especially in the August berry season.

For a bird's-eye view of the park, try one of the daily flightseeing trips over Naknek Lake, the valley, Novarupta, and the Mount Katmai caldera *(contact Katmailand, 907-243-5448 or 800-544-0551. www.katmailand.com).*

Fishing

In addition to Brooks Lodge, two other locations provide access to superb fishing for grayling, rainbow trout, lake trout, and red salmon. Kulik Lodge on Novianuk Lake, with accommodations for 28 anglers, is a premier fly-in sportfishing venue in the heart of the park. Grosvenor Lake Lodge provides a more intimate experience, serving only six persons at a time from its location on **Grosvenor Lake.** Both lodges are operated by Katmailand (*907-243-5448 or 800-544-0551. www.katmailand.com).*

Brooks River is a catch-and-release fishery for trophy-size rainbow trout—use barbless hooks to prevent needless injury. For salmon, there are strict procedures: Each angler is allowed to keep one per day, and any fish caught at Brooks Camp must immediately be placed in a special bag and taken to the freezer building near the lodge (cleaning and outdoor cooking are not allowed here). Visitors 16 and older must possess a valid Alaska State Fishing License *(available at Brooks Camp Visitor Center);* check the regulations before casting your first fly.

On the Water

Katmai's lake country rewards kayakers and canoers in search of solitude. One popular destination on Naknek Lake, **Bay of Islands,** offers not only island camping and sheltered paddling but a glimpse into park history. **Fure's Cabin,** built by trapper-prospector Roy Fure at the portage to Grosvenor Lake around 1914, is listed on the National Register of Historic Places and remains in a rustic state. This portage is part of the **Savonoski Loop,** a four- to ten-day round-trip from Brooks Camp. While on the water, you'll want to keep a constant lookout for sudden winds and waves, and always stay close to shore.

Looking for a float trip? The 66-mile-long **Alagnak National Wild and Scenic River** flows out of Kukaklek Lake in Katmai preserve. The Alagnak has excellent fishing, wildlife viewing, and wilderness camping *(contact Park Service for required backcountry permit).* It is accessible by chartered floatplane from Brooks Camp or one of the lodges. After a short section of white water below the lake—including some Class III rapids, which can be portaged—the river quickly smooths out downstream. Allow five to seven days for a relaxing trip.

In the Backcountry

Backcountry camping is permitted anywhere in Katmai except

Red-breasted mergansers on Brooks River, Katmai National Park and Preserve

within 5 miles of Brooks Camp. Before venturing into Katmai's challenging backcountry, stop at the visitor center for up-to-date information and the loan of bear-resistant food canisters (BRFCs).

The Valley of Ten Thousand Smokes lures hikers who want to see 6,715-foot-high **Mount Katmai.** Also here is the 200-foot-high volcanic extrusion plug **Novarupta,** formed from a vent that sucked the magma from beneath Mount Katmai, causing its summit to collapse into a caldera. More handiwork of volcanism is visible all across this lunar-like landscape.

A valley hike presents its own challenges. Fierce dust storms can blow up in minutes, blinding hikers and literally sanding a tent to pieces. "Whiteouts" of gray ash reduce visibility to nil. And bears sometimes wander out across the valley, in which case you will be particularly exposed.

River crossings, too, can be hazardous. The swift, turbid waters of Knife Creek and River Lethe, for example, may look fordable even when they are many feet deep. Never try crossing until you've tested the depth with a walking stick. Better yet, hike upstream until you can step or hop over the braids.

If a moonscape doesn't interest you, hike out the park road and then branch off on your own. Every few years, intrepid hikers attempt to duplicate Griggs's route from the coast inland to the valley. Due to extremely dense alders and rugged terrain, many fail. To succeed takes planning, experience, and yes, luck.

Wildlife Viewing
Even though Katmai offers a bounty of wildlife, wilderness, and

geologic wonders, the park has become best known for its bear viewing. Bear-watchers jam Brooks Camp during the July peak of the sockeye salmon run, as well as during the return of the spawned out salmon in September, when 40 to 60 bears congregate along the Brooks River.

Two raised platforms along the river enable close-up—and safe—viewing. Remember, the bears, not people, always have the right-of-way. The lower platform is located a quarter mile from the visitor center, where the river debouches into Naknek Lake. Though large and often crowded, this platform does not deter bears from wandering by—some even snooze beneath it. Juvenile bears tend to cluster here, the favored fishing spots upriver being controlled by the larger, dominant bears.

During peak season, you must first check in at the lower bear viewing platform, or trailhead, before continuing to the Brooks Falls platform, where high demand may limit your stay to as little as 20 minutes. This is the place to click that iconic photo of a salmon leaping into a bear's open maw.

Except when you are on the bear-viewing platforms, you may not deliberately approach or stay within 50 yards of a single bear, or within 100 yards of a female with cubs. Carrying food of any kind on trails and paths is forbidden.

For a different experience, visit Katmai's 480-mile-long seacoast to see marine mammals, eagles, volcanoes, seabirds, and bears digging clams. Contact Katmai Wilderness Lodge *(907-486-8767 or 800-488-8767)* or Katmai Coastal Outfitters *(888-235-8492)*. ∎

Moss-draped Sitka spruce, Kodiak Island

Kodiak Island Archipelago

■ 5,000 square miles ■ 250 miles southwest of Anchorage ■ Best months
May-Oct. ■ Camping, hiking, rafting, kayaking, fishing, wildlife viewing ■ Access
by airline, state ferry, and charter boat ■ Contact Kodiak National Wildlife
Refuge, 1390 Buskin River Rd., Kodiak, AK 99615; phone 907-487-2600

ABOUT 30 BLUSTERY MILES across the Shelikof Strait from the Alaska Peninsula, which it parallels, this island group—geologically a continuation of
the Kenai Mountains—is about 180 miles long and 67 miles across. The
principal islands are Shuyak, Afognak, Raspberry, Uganik, Kodiak, Sitkalidak, and the Trinity group—as a whole, roughly the size of Connecticut. Kodiak Island, at 3,588 square miles, is the second largest island in
the United States (only the island of Hawaii is bigger). Despite its immensity, the crenellated bays and inlets mean that no point of land in
the island chain is more than 15 miles from tidewater.

Thousands of years ago, glaciers carved the archipelago's mountainous landscape into pinnacles, fjords, and wide valleys. Volcanic and
seismic forces have also contorted the landscape, while ferocious winter
storms and surf rolling in off the North Pacific continue to shape the
islands. The vegetation ranges from dense Sitka spruce forest in the north
to rolling, hummocky tundra in the south. Willows, alders, and flowering
plants 5 feet tall or more—all products of the rich soils and an average
annual precipitation of 67 inches—choke many low-lying inland areas.

All five Pacific salmon spawn here. Fourteen marine mammals, including sea otters, sea lions, humpback whales, gray whales, orcas, and
finback whales, feed offshore or migrate through. Biologists list 140
seabird colonies and estimate that 1.5 million seabirds and more than
150,000 waterfowl winter along the bays and shores.

For all its size, Kodiak Island originally supported only six native land mammals. Some species that are now well-established were transplants: Sitka black-tailed deer in 1924, mountain goat in 1952, and beaver, snowshoe hare, reindeer, and Roosevelt elk on Afognak in 1929.

Several agencies manage parts of the islands. The Fish and Wildlife Service administers **Kodiak National Wildlife Refuge,** created by President Franklin D. Roosevelt in 1941 largely to protect the famed Kodiak brown bears. In addition, the Alaska State Parks system manages several smaller sites. The city of Kodiak, population about 8,000, is the major supply and transportation hub, with an airport and access from the mainland via Homer, Seward, and Anchorage. For information, call 907-235-8449 or 800-382-9229 *(akmhs.com)*.

What to See and Do

Kodiak National Wildlife Refuge

Famed for its wildlife, the nearly two-million-acre roadless Kodiak National Wildlife Refuge encompasses the southwestern two-thirds of Kodiak Island, all of Uganik Island, and parts of Afognak. The refuge has 800 miles of coastline, 11 large lakes, and 7 major watersheds. Biologists have estimated that 2,500 to 3,000 Alaska brown bears live in Kodiak NWR. This is the world's highest known density of these giant creatures, some of which weigh in at more than 1,500 pounds.

Your best chance to see a brown bear here is in July and August, when the animals congregate along salmon streams. In other seasons, the bears often move about in dense alders, where they are harder to see—and easier to unexpectedly encounter. You'll witness bears that catch fish with each try, as well as others—usually juveniles—who are less adept. Many guides and air taxi operators specialize in bear-viewing trips, and some even guarantee success. For a list of guide services, contact the Kodiak Convention and Visitors Bureau *(907-486-4782)*.

Drop into the visitor center of the Kodiak National Wildlife Refuge to get staffers' recommendations of locations where you may glimpse a bear. (They're also happy to dispense advice on safe viewing and camping techniques.) Bear-viewing locations include south Frazer Lake, Uganik Lake, Little River, and Blue Fox Bay. Other drainages boast equally

Fishing lesson, Kodiak Island

Holy Resurrection Russian Orthodox Church, Kodiak

impressive congregations of bears but are harder to access. Though not usually seen near the road system, bears can be encountered almost anywhere in Kodiak NWR.

The refuge mainly attracts hunters and fishers, but other users are growing in number. Rafters paddle the **Ayakulik** and **Karluk Rivers;** kayakers explore large lakes. (You may need permission to access private lands within the refuge.) Although summers are wet, cool, and cloudy, nature photographers will find limitless subjects. Wildflowers, land- and seascapes, seabirds, and marine mammals are favorite subjects. Bald eagles, land otters, deer, and foxes are numerous.

Hiking and Camping

The refuge offers no developed hiking trails, but don't let that stop you: Visitors are welcome to wend their way almost anywhere. Brush and terrain make hiking difficult, except on high alpine ridges.

You can also camp wherever you want—provided you take bear-safety precautions—and the refuge maintains seven public-use cabins, available by lottery *(apply in April; 907-487-2600)*. Several lodges and private cabins dot Kodiak Island as well.

Access to the refuge is by air or sea from the city of Kodiak, or from one of four native villages adjacent to the refuge: Karluk, Larsen Bay, Akhiok, and Old Harbor. Be prepared for weather delays, especially on flights through the mountains; even if your departure location is only overcast, Kodiak may be completely fogged in.

Waterside Wildlife

If you can wait out the weather and tides, you might charter a boat and explore the refuge's coast. You'll see bears and deer, seals and sea lions, eagles and oystercatchers, murres and horned puffins. In spring look for Pacific (black) brant, one of Alaska's most impressive migrators, as they dawdle northward. In fall they make an apparently nonstop flight home to Mexico, completing the 3,500-mile journey in 60 to 120 hours. During this continental commute, the four-pound birds lose one-third of their body weight. Come fall, most of the 150,000 brant who use the Pacific flyway migrate through **Izembek Lagoon** near Cold Bay, drafting low-pressure systems that propel them to speeds of 50 miles per hour and as far south as Vancouver Island.

Alaska State Parks

Inspiring wilderness experiences are available outside the refuge, too. Alaska State Parks *(1400 Abercrombie Dr., Kodiak, AK 99615; 907-486-6339)* administers two remote parks, 47,000-acre **Shuyak Island State Park** and 48,742-acre **Afognak State Park.** Located 50 air miles north of the city of Kodiak, Shuyak Island has four public-use cabins for which demand peaks in August *(applications must be received in Feb.)*. This is a hot spot for fishing and wildlife watching. Sea kayakers can also explore numerous sheltered bays and channels around the island.

Afognak offers a public-use cabin at Pillar Lake *(7-day limit)*. Hikers climb and explore the slopes of the surrounding mountains with a chance to see roaming bear, elk, or deer. The Afognak Wilderness Lodge *(907-486-6442)*, the only lodge or residence within the state park, is one of Alaska's best places to see marine mammals.

Exploring by Road

Access to Kodiak National Wildlife Refuge and the outlying state parks can be expensive. You can still get a good sense of the place, however, simply by driving the 100 miles of mostly gravel roads that radiate from the city of Kodiak. These lead from seashore to mountaintop through diverse habitats and wildlife. The downtown visitor center *(100 Marine Way, 907-486-4782)* offers a detailed road log and up-to-date reports on road conditions. Rent a car at the airport or bring your own vehicle over on the state ferry M/V *Tustumena* from Homer.

The Kodiak Audubon Society has developed a guide to the trails and hikes that are accessible from Kodiak's road system. The guide details the length, difficulty, and points of interest on each walk. In addition, the local Audubon chapter offers weekend hikes. Pick up a map and information at the visitor center downtown or from the refuge.

Despite the low likelihood of spotting any bears near the road system, you will see other wildlife, depending on the season and the time of day (dawn and dusk are best). Migrating gray whales pass fairly close to the island from March through early May, while deer fawns are born in June. Salmon begin running in late May and peak in July. Wildflowers are most profuse in July, berries later that month. Bald eagles congregate near town and on Pasagshak River in December. Timing matters: The annual Christmas bird count tallies 65 to 80 species, down from the summer peak of about 240.

Other Attractions

In addition to its beautiful forested setting on Monashka Bay, **Fort Abercrombie State Historical Park** (1400 Abercrombie Dr., 907-486-6339) contains the concrete bunkers of a World War II defensive position. Here trails, beach walks, and tide-pool explorations invite people of all ages. Also accessible from the 11-mile-long Monashka Bay Road are **Mill Bay Beach Park, Monashka Bay viewpoint,** and **Pillar Creek Beach**—a favorite for picnics, pink salmon fishing, and beach walks. The **Point Otmeloi trailhead** at the end of the road leads into the forest and uplands.

Located at the mouth of the Pasagshak River, **Pasagshak River State Recreation Area** is a fine destination for experienced sea kayakers. This area also offers good fishing at times, especially "the fishing bridge" at Milepost 8.5 on **Pasagshak Road.** Try your luck surf casting at about Mile 10. The park's campground, 2.5 miles farther up the road, provides beach access. There are nice trails and routes to walk from here, as well as beautiful views of the sea and Ugak Island.

Woody Island, a short skiff ride from the harbor in Kodiak, is a great place to see sea lions and harbor seals. A good trail crosses the island.

Before you leave town, visit the **Alutiiq Museum and Archaeological Repository** (215 Mission Rd. 907-486-7004) as well as the Russian-built **Baranof Museum** (101 Marine Way, 907-486-5920). Both are located downtown near the state ferry dock. The Baranof, listed as a national historic landmark under the name Erskine House, was built in 1792, making it the oldest wooden building on America's West Coast. When Russian fur hunters seeking the archipelago's abundant sea otters stepped ashore here in the late 1700s, they encountered the Alutiiq, who had occupied the islands for 7,500 years. The ensuing disease and armed conflict exacted a terrible toll on these native people. You may well leave town with new respect for those who continue to eke out a living on these harsh but remarkable islands. ■

Hiking above West Beach, Round Island

Walrus Islands State Game Sanctuary

■ 162,200 acres in Northern Bristol Bay, southwest of Dillingham and southeast of Togiak ■ Best months June-July ■ Camping, hiking, wildlife viewing ■ Day-use and camping permit required on Round Island ■ Access by boat only ■ Contact Alaska Dept. of Fish and Game, Wildlife Conservation Division, P.O. Box 230, Dillingham, AK 99576; phone 907-842-2334. www.state.ak.us/adfg

RAKED BY TUMULTUOUS STORMS from the Bering Sea, the treeless Walrus Islands appear lifeless and barren in winter. In summer, though still buffeted by winds and rain, these grass-covered islands abound with life.

Walruses must haul out of the water to rest after feeding forays (in

Following pages: Bull Walrus

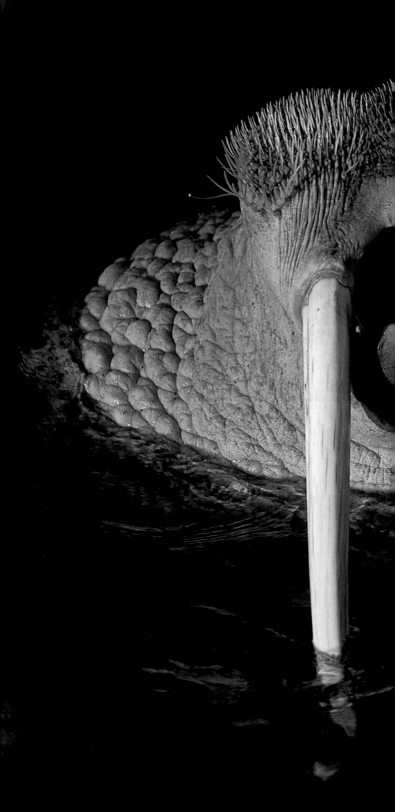

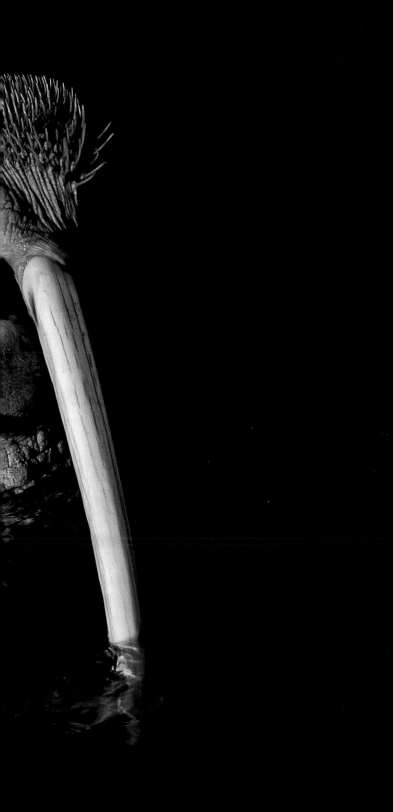

winter they congregate on ice, in summer on land). Biologists know of only four main terrestrial resting sites in Alaska: Cape Pierce, Cape Newenham, Cape Seniavin, and Round Island. Only the last lies within this sanctuary, set up in 1960 to protect the walrus from ivory hunters.

The **Walrus Islands** range in size from 6-mile-long Crooked Island to three islets that are little more than exposed, jagged rocks. In places sheer cliffs rise hundreds of feet above rocky shores, providing ideal nesting sites for more than a hundred species of birds. (No one knows the exact number of seabirds here, but estimates range from 500,000 to 1,000,000.) Seals, Steller sea lions, and walruses all feed and haul out on these stony shores.

What to See and Do

These islands aren't just off the beaten path, they're off *any* path—that's why animals congregate here. The walrus gathering on the beaches of 2-mile-long **Round Island** attracts visitors from all over the world. Each spring as the Bering Sea ice breaks up, bull walruses begin to gather. The first animals arrive in March and the last leave in October, when they migrate north to the ice pack to rejoin the females and young. Although their numbers vary, 14,000 walruses were once counted in a day. Only males come here, perhaps to avoid crushing the smaller pregnant females or their spring calves, which weigh less than 200 pounds at birth.

Walruses sport heavy tusks, some more than 3 feet long, which serve as both weapons and tools: The walruses use them for defense and to establish dominance. The tusks also prove handy as an aid when hauling out and for propulsion when feeding on the sea bottom (the animals' generic name translates as "tooth walker"). In the murky depths, walruses feel for clams with their snouts and stiff mustache whiskers, or vibrissae. They eat only the soft parts of the clams, which they suck from the

shells. When swimming, a walrus looks pink, almost whitish. When resting, though, it turns brown from increased blood circulation.

When hauled out, walruses are not exactly exciting to watch. They pack densely together and for the most part simply sleep. Every now and then one will provoke a neighbor into a brief sparring match. When the bulls come ashore, more serious fights break out as they hoist their 2,400- to 3,200-pound bodies over the rocks—and often over their comrades. Finally the newcomers settle in, sometimes draped atop adjoining animals.

When you tire of watching walruses, turn your attention to the island's other animals. Red foxes den here, living mainly off seabirds and their eggs. Common murres, black-legged kittiwakes, pelagic cormorants, parakeet auklets, pigeon guillemots, horned and tufted puffins jam cliffs and the boulder-lined beach. Some birds build nests or use burrows; others lay their eggs directly on the rock ledge. Murre eggs, for example, have a pointed shape that keeps them from plunging to the beach below.

Two charter boat operators offer regular access to Round Island from

Red fox, Round Island

the bay communities: Don's Round Island Charters *(907-493-5127)* and Johnson Maritime/Walrus Island Expeditions *(907-235-9349)*.

Hiking

Visitors must keep to a minimal trail system linking wildlife overlooks on the island's north and east sides. These muddy, primitive footpaths require rubber boots. To protect the walruses, walking off-trail or on the beaches is forbidden. The easy **south trail** provides views of small haul-outs and bird cliffs, at times passing less than 30 feet above resting walruses and surprisingly near puffins and auklets. The trail ends above a sea lion colony. For a spectacular view of bird cliffs and the main haul-out beach, head west on **Observation Point Trail.** From here, at peak times, you'll see thousands of walruses and tens of thousands of murres and kittiwakes.

The elements, tides, and rough seas all limit the accessibility of Round Island, so plan for bad weather. This is not a destination for visitors with a tight schedule, nor for those with physical limitations. From early May to mid-August, access is by permit only; only 12 camping permits and 5 day-use permits are issued at a time. (No permit is needed to visit the sanctuary's other islands.)

To minimize wildlife disruption, a special navigation corridor controls boat access to the island. You and your gear are ferried ashore in an inflatable boat—a ride of less than 100 yards made eventful by wind and surf. You then land in Boat Cove and, to avoid disturbing the walruses nearby, begin transferring your gear up a 50-foot cliff. Wear your rubber boots and be careful on the slippery rocks.

The camping area is near the top of the cliff on a relatively flat plateau on the flank of this slab-sided island. Other than an outhouse and plywood platforms on which to pitch your tent, there are no facilities of any kind. A creek 200 yards away provides fresh water, which should be boiled or treated before drinking. There is no firewood on the island. Sanctuary personnel live in a cabin nearby, but they do not guide visitors. You are essentially on your own.

Bring top-notch rain gear, warm clothes, a waterproof tent that can withstand winds over 60 miles per hour, a tent repair kit, extra line for tying down that tent, a collapsible water jug, campstove and fuel, and at least a week's extra food stored in fox-proof containers.

Once you've set up, you can watch flying birds and swimming walruses and sea lions right from your tent. At night you'll fall asleep to a wondrous wild concert of birds, wind, and walruses. ∎

Wood-Tikchik State Park

■ 1.6 million acres ■ Southwest Alaska near Dillingham and Bristol Bay ■ Best months June–early Oct. ■ Camping, canoeing, kayaking, fishing, wildlife viewing ■ Access by aircraft or boat ■ Contact the park, 550 W. 7th Ave., Anchorage, AK 99501; phone 907-269-8698. www.dnr.state.ak.us/parks/units/woodtik.htm

ALASKA'S MOST REMOTE STATE PARK and the largest state park in the United States, Wood-Tikchik was created in 1978 to protect the area's fish and wildlife habitat. Named for its two separate drainages, each connecting a series of crystalline lakes, the park contains a landscape of diverse beauty. Wood-Tikchik State Park encompasses an ecotone—a transition area between coniferous forest and tundra. Mixed stands of white spruce and birch line the lowland lakes and waterways, while black spruce pepper open tundra and muskeg. Timberline extends to 900 feet, at which point alpine tundra, rocky slopes, and meadows take over. In the east, wet tundra, marshlands, and small ponds predominate.

Bordered on the west by the Wood River Mountains—the tallest is 5,026-foot **Mount Waskey**—and on the east by the Nushagak lowlands, the park includes views of spired peaks, alpine valleys, and deep, fjordlike arms, as well as the gravel beaches and expansive tundra of the Nushagak flats. Fourteen major lakes vary in length up to 45 miles; some are 900 feet deep. The seven **Wood River Lakes** stretch about 30 miles west to east and are drained by the 21-mile-long Wood River. In the north lie the seven **Tikchik Lakes,** drained to the east by the Nuyakuk River.

Moose and brown bear can be spotted almost anywhere in the park; smaller populations of black bear and caribou roam the north and east. You'll also notice sea gulls, bald eagles, loons, spruce grouse, and myriad waterfowl. In spring and fall, large flocks of migrating birds, such as sandhill cranes and white-fronted geese, pass overhead. But this is mainly an angler's heaven: All five species of Pacific salmon—king, red, pink, silver, and chum—spawn in the park's river systems. Non-anadromous fish (those that do not migrate out to sea) include northern pike, lake trout, arctic char, Dolly Varden, whitefish, and rainbow trout.

What to See and Do

Fishing

Wood-Tikchik State Park, larger than the state of Delaware, is managed as wild and undeveloped. The waters here act as an enormous fish hatchery, which anglers rate as one of the world's premier fishing destinations. Some years more than three million red salmon return to Wood River Lakes, and over two million to Tikchik Lakes. Reds (sockeyes) support a vast commercial fishery in Bristol Bay. (Annual catches in the bay vary from 20 million to 25 million fish.)

Obviously, the salmon fishing can be extraordinary. But many dedicated fishers disdain it, instead

Hiker atop Sad Face Mountain, overlooking Tikchik Lake

Fishing guide on Grant River

seeking out the giant rainbow trout that weigh up to 12 pounds and measure 28 inches long. There's nothing like the strike of a hefty rainbow trout hitting a fly; always take two rods—and more flies or lures than you think you'll need. Some waters are catch-and-release only; check the rule book.

Camping and Lodging

Four very basic designated camping sites are scattered throughout the park.One first-come first-served cabin stands on the Agulukpak River where it flows out of Beverley Lake. In addition, five private, exclusive fishing lodges in the park cater to guests with advance reservations. Otherwise, you can camp anywhere.

On the Water

You can access the Wood River drainage by air or by chartered boat from Dillingham (which has scheduled air service from Anchorage) or from the native village of Aleknagik, 24 miles north of Dillingham. Although boat charters may be more economical, most visitors are dropped off by aircraft; they exit the park by floating or paddling the interconnected lakes and rivers to a designated pickup point. Paddlers on the Wood River system can travel from headwater lakes **Grant** or **Kulik** all the way back to Aleknagik or Dillingham, saving the expense of a charter flight or boat ride. Be prepared for travel delays due to fog, rain, or wind.

If you are interested in the Tikchik Lakes system, which is cooler and drier than the southern portion of the park, charter a flight to a headwater lake and float down to the far end of Tikchik Lake. To continue downstream from there involves a few portages and some white-water rapids on the **Nuyakuk River.** Finally you reach the Yup'ik village of Koliganek for a flight back to Dillingham.

Float trips spanning an entire lake system or just a portion can begin anywhere in the park. One of the best aspects of exploring a river teeming with wild salmon is the opportunity to see the myriad creatures that feed on the fish or their eggs—gulls, kingfishers, eagles, otters, foxes, even an occasional wolf. Brown bears are numerous, so campers and fishermen need to be alert at all times.

River trips are offered by Alaska Recreational River Guides *(907-376-8655)* and Tikchik State Park Tours *(907-243-1416)*. Be prepared for weather extremes, biting insects, and sudden winds; the latter can make travel on large lakes by canoe, kayak, or raft potentially hazardous. ■

Gravesite of Jim Heath (1864-1894), St. Paul's Island, Pribilofs

Alaska Maritime National Wildlife Refuge

■ 4.5 million acres ■ From Forrester Island near tip of southeast Alaska around coast, down Aleutian Island Chain, and up into Bering and Chukchi Seas to Cape Lisburne ■ Best months mid-May–mid-Aug. ■ Bird-watching, wildlife viewing (especially marine mammals and seabirds) ■ Be prepared for weather delays: Bring rain gear, layers of warm clothing (wool or fleece), and extra food. Temperatures in summer rarely rise above 60°F ■ Contact the refuge, 2355 Kachemak Bay Dr., Suite 101, Homer, AK 99603; phone 907-235-6546. www.fws.gov

OCEAN WAVES CRASH AGAINST lonely pinnacles of rock. Tiny bare islands, sheer cliffs, misty headlands, reefs, islets, and volcanic spires dot Alaska's coastline from its southern rain forest boundary to the ice-choked northern waters of the Chukchi Sea. More than 2,400 of these wild outposts make up the Alaska Maritime National Wildlife Refuge. Most of them lie in the northern Gulf of Alaska, out the Aleutian chain, and up into the Bering Sea. To the human eye they seem inhospitable, but their crevices, cliffs, and surf-washed ledges teem with wildlife. In spring, up to 30 million seabirds (55 species) return to nest. They swarm about the islands and stack themselves in gregarious neighborhoods all the way up the cliffs. Many of the great whales swim offshore—blue, sei, fin, sperm, bowhead, northern right, humpback, gray, minke, orca, Baird's beaked, and Cuvier's beaked.

The refuge is also host to thousands of marine mammals—seals, sea lions, walruses, and sea otters. Like curious, ghostly spirits from the deep. seals slip their large, luminescent eyes above the surface, periscope

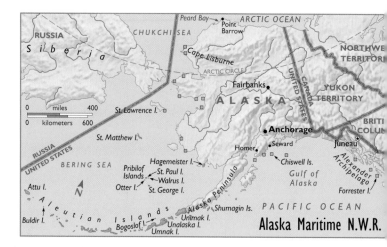

around, then silently slide back down beneath the waves.

In stark contrast, sea lions, hauled out in their rookeries, bellow and roar, defending their harems. Like their terrestrial namesakes, the lions of Africa, the bulls have a large neck and shoulders and a distinctive mane. Males weigh about 1,250 pounds on average.

The portly, tusked walruses are perhaps the most comical. Yet the male walrus can sing a love song, biologists say, "like a chorus of church bells," serenading his lady love for hours. Except when the males summer on Round Island in noisy bachelor parties (see pp. 225-229), these nearly two-ton creatures tend to follow the ice pack as it moves north and south.

The little sea otter, nicknamed "the old man of the sea" for all its whiskers, ducks and plays in the waves or floats around on its back, eating crabs and sea urchins.

Remote and pristine as these waters seem, formerly abundant populations of marine mammals in western Alaska have crashed—Steller sea lions, harbor seals, Alaska king crabs, and most recently sea otters in the Aleutians. This has raised an alarm in the scientific community. Far from being protected by their remoteness, oceans here present an intricate and vulnerable web of life. Although the exact causes of the population declines remain biological mysteries, current theories suggest a combination of stresses: warmer water temperatures, heavy commercial fishing, predators forced to seek different prey, and industrial pollution from distant lands swept up by the currents and brought to these shores.

By contrast, the return of the diminutive Aleutian Canada goose from the brink of extinction is one of Alaska's great conservation success stories. Although the geese nested on the Aleutians—among the most isolated islands in the world—they were nearly wiped out in the early 1900s when fox farmers released hundreds of foxes, which successfully preyed upon the geese and other birds.

Indeed, at one point the Aleutian Canada goose was deemed extinct—and probably would be today were it not for the dedication and courage of one man, Robert D. Jones. "Sea Otter" Jones, as he was widely known for his love of the animals (CK), was a biologist who first visited the islands with the U.S. Navy (CK) during World War II. In 1947, Jones became the first resident manager of the 1,100-mile-long Aleutian Islands National Wildlife Refuge, which has since been incorporated into the Alaska Maritime National Wildlife Refuge.

During spring forays into the refuge, Jones and his staff occasionally spotted a few migrating Aleutian Canada geese. Navigating dories and inflatable watercraft pounded by what may very well be the worst weather in the world, Jones and his crew scoured the islands until one joyful day in 1962, when they discovered a nesting population of about 200 to 300 geese on Buldir Island, the most remote outpost in the island chain. From captive flocks, Aleutian geese were then reintroduced to their former habitats (now free of foxes).

Jones died in 1998, just a few months before the Fish and Wildlife Service proposed removing the Aleutian Canada goose from the threatened species list. Jones had seen his duty, and he did it: Whereas fewer than 500 of these small but spectacular birds were still alive worldwide in 1967, the global population of Aleutian Canada geese is now estimated at more than 30,000.

On warm days, you may see a northern fur seal of either sex waving its long rear flippers in the air. Hairless and webbed with blood vessels, these flippers serve to cool off the fur seal (which is otherwise bundled up in dense fur and blubber) while it is on land.

A Prince and His Harem

Majestic if a trifle fat (up to 600 pounds), the northern fur seal strikes a singular pose at the ocean edge on tiny St. Paul Island (part of the Pribilofs), where he reigns over a noisy stretch of beach for two months in summer. Refraining from eating—and leaving his rocky perch only to deal with cocky contenders for his throne—the male fur seal spends his days defending his territory and mating with the 20 to 100 females in his harem.

Except when they haul out to mate, northern fur seals spend the bulk of their time at sea. Their shore leave begins in the middle of May, when the bulls stake out beaches for their breeding territories. Females impregnated the summer before arrive about four weeks later, at the end of their 11- to 12-month gestation period. A few days later, they give birth to a single pup—then mate again within a week. Most of the fur seals return to sea in November.

One Wet Bird

In gift shops throughout Alaska, puffin images adorn everything from T-shirts to antismoking signs ("No Puffin' Here!"). Most of this kitsch honors the horned puffin, but the tufted puffin also lives in Alaska. Distinguished by their large, colorful beaks, penguinlike coloring, and webbed orange feet, puffins of either type are nicknamed "parrots of the sea."

Wintering far out to sea, puffins are uniquely adapted for life on the ocean. In fact, they can "fly" quite well underwater. They flap half-folded wings for propulsion and use their feet as a rudder to change direction.

A puffin may emerge from the sea with as many as 15 fish in its mouth. Stiff spines inside its upper beak help hold the individual fish draped in place across the lower beak, their heads and tails poking out on either side. Puffins, not the most gifted aviators, often run along the surface of the water for some distance on takeoff, giving the impression they'll never get airborne.

What to See and Do

Birding

Inaccessible as the refuge is, many birding expeditions find their way to the island of **Attu**—so far out in the Aleutian chain that the International Date Line has to jog around it—to watch for "accidental" birds, or Asian birds on the eastern edges of their customary spring migrations north.

Closer to civilization, many people take day cruises *(907-224-8068 or 800-468-8068)* out of Seward into Resurrection Bay. Swarming **Beehive Island,** part of the **Chiswell Islands,** is a good place to view horned and tufted puffins, common and thick-billed murres, kittiwakes, and even oystercatchers, distinguished by their long, orange bills. You may also spot sea lions, porpoises, and whales on Beehive Island.

Pribilof Islands

Flung far out into the Bering Sea about 300 miles off the coast of western Alaska, the Pribilofs—nicknamed "Islands of the Seals"—are a popular summer destination for birders, botanists, and flower lovers. They are most famous, however, as seasonal territory for the world's largest population (about 800,000) of breeding northern fur seals. From observation blinds around the island, you can watch hefty "beachmasters" defending their harems from the challenges of up-and-coming young bachelors. Equally intriguing is to spy the females slithering over the rocks from one harem to the next. Pups are born on the beaches, where mating occurs about a week later.

Between the cacophony of the seals and thousands of nesting seabirds, the Pribilofs are quite lively. But they are also some of the most enchantingly peaceful islands in the world. Only a few days amongst all this beauty, serenity, and closeness with wild creatures will help restore a sense of balance to your spirit.

Four tiny volcanic islands—**St. Paul, St. George, Walrus,** and **Otter**—make up the Pribilofs. Of these, St. Paul is the largest and most visited. Blue arctic foxes bound all over the island, and reindeer—descendants of a Siberian herd imported in the 1890s—roam St. Paul's interior. Clinging to the cliffs are colony upon colony of nesting seabirds, among them parakeet and least auklets, red-faced cormorants, rare red-legged kittiwakes, horned and tufted puffins, and thick-billed murres.

Most amazing of all, in July you can sit for hours in the tundra, bent low over a rainbow of beautiful flowers: purple monkshood, chocolate lilies, pink Unalaska saxifrage, white rock jasmine, fields of blue lupine—and no mosquitoes! If you've experienced the hordes of whining, biting insects for which Alaska is famous, you will realize that you have arrived in heaven. The reason? The wind blows here.

You can travel on your own to St. Paul or St. George, but it's more fun on your first visit to be guided by the Aleut people who live here. They have great tour packages *(877-424-5637)* with local guides and knowledgeable naturalists. ∎

The Arctic

Northern lights over the Dalton Highway

ONCE THE EXCLUSIVE REALM of the Inupiat, the snowy owl, and the polar bear, Arctic Alaska—an inconceivably vast expanse that includes the state's northwest coast and all the tundra from the Brooks Range to the Arctic Ocean—has undergone immense change since commercial oil production began here in 1977. Roads, pipelines, and creeping industrialization have forged a new coastline where bears and caribou seem to be strangers in their own land. Despite this transformation, the Alaskan Arctic

remains a harsh, rugged region—a mostly unpeopled wilderness where winter winds claw the darkened land and the cold is so extreme it can split stone.

Defining Arctic Alaska is no simple task. For starters, the Arctic Circle is not some magic line where one ecoregion ends and another begins. It can be thought of, however, as a boundary between light and dark: Stand anywhere above the Arctic Circle on the summer solstice (roughly June 21) and the sun will not set. At Barrow—the northernmost community in America—the sun does not dip below the horizon from May 10 to August 2. By the same token, an observer above the Arctic Circle on the

winter solstice (December 21 or 22) will not see the sun rise that day. For residents of Barrow, this penumbral condition persists for 67 days.

Latitude aside, perhaps the truest partition between Alaska's Arctic and subarctic zones is the timberline—defined in these parts as a hazy border some 50 to 100 miles wide where the forest peters out and the treeless tundra takes over. The Arctic National Wildlife Refuge in the state's northeast corner, for example, encompasses a true ecotone—a transitional zone between two adjacent ecological communities, in this case the Arctic and the subarctic. Thus a float trip down any major river here—the Sheenjek, the Wind, the Coleen—will transport you from a true Arctic habitat to the more familiar conditions of the boreal forest.

The wild crown of the Alaskan Arctic is the Brooks Range, a jagged stone barricade that stretches 720 miles from the state's border with Canada on the east almost all the way to the Chukchi Sea on the west. This towering wall of all types of rock, topping 8,000 feet in places, is a continental and climatic divide that isolates Arctic Alaska from the state's interior. Rivers on the north side of the Brooks Range eventually flow into the Arctic Ocean; those on its south reach the Bering Sea. Jumbled peaks, remote canyons, and untrammeled rivers and lakes are just some of the natural features to visit in this "range of blue light," as pioneer forester Bob Marshall dubbed the mountain chain. Its pristine core has been protected in Gates of the Arctic National Park and Preserve since 1980.

The Brooks Range gained its craggy profile during three bouts of compression. The initial uplift occurred about 200 million to 150 million years ago, when the Arctic Ocean plate rotated into a slow but colossal collision with the North American plate. In the course of this smashup, the budding Brooks Range shed thick deposits of sandstone, shale, and conglomerates into a trough that parallels the present front. After a pause lasting millions of years, during which only a thin layer of marine shale was deposited, a second orogenic spasm convulsed the range. The third and final phase of mountain building began about 40 million years ago and continues to this day.

Four major glaciations have entombed the Brooks Range in sheets of ice. Indeed, glacial erosion and deposition sculpted the details of alpine topography, such as Mount Doonerak and the Arrigetch Peaks, that visitors to these mountains remark upon today. Although vast ice fields are no longer present in the Brooks Range, tatters of neoglacial ice, in full retreat over the last 200 years, still cling to the highest peaks.

North of the mountains, rolling foothills merge with the flat, poorly drained Arctic Coastal Plain, often referred to as the North Slope. Latticed with rivers, lakes, and ponds, this is 80,000 square miles of authentic Arctic tundra: Its permafrost, or nearly permanent frozen top soil layer, sets it apart from the alpine tundra to the south.

Permafrost, ubiquitous north of the Brooks Range, exerts strong pressure on both the topography and the ecology here. At Prudhoe Bay, for example, oil drilling has revealed a permafrost layer 2,110 feet deep. By trapping water at the Earth's surface, permafrost creates a classic Arctic paradox: The area is a desert—less than 10 inches of precipitation falls on average per year—yet standing water is a common sight.

These conditions allow certain plants—and most mosquitoes—to thrive in summer on the wet, barely thawed surface of the soil. Tussocks of cotton grass (a sedge with tufted spikes) dominate the tundra. From a distance, a tussock flat appears to be a smooth, pasturelike field. This illusion vanishes as soon as you try to walk across it. About the size and consistency of partially inflated soccer balls, tussocks are not sufficiently stable to support a human's weight. They cannot be pushed aside, nor is there room enough to step between them. Oh, and did we mention that

A tributary of the Kobuk River at Kobuk Sand Dunes, Kobuk Valley National Park

mosquitoes love to breed in the water and wet moss around each tussock?

Yet plant life is hardly blighted north of the Brooks Range. Wildflowers such as dwarf rhododendron, saxifrage, lousewort, and oxytrope abound on drier slopes and gravel bars. Lush willows crowd riverbanks inland. Birches and balsam poplars seem to shelter together in isolated thickets.

Wildlife—the state's traditional claim to wilderness immortality—is profuse as well, especially in summer. That's when some 700,000 caribou roam Alaska's Arctic, sharing it with yellow-billed loons, tundra swans, and eiders. The Arctic supports signature species such as grizzlies, wolves, and sheep, as well as musk oxen, wolverines, lemmings, arctic foxes, and (along the coast) polar bears. A variety of birds nest here; most take wing by late summer.

To survive an Arctic winter, an animal must migrate, hibernate, or endure. The arctic fox and musk oxen remain through the long, dark Arctic night. Caribou, by contrast, migrate south in fall; you can witness this movement in Noatak National Preserve or Kobuk Valley National Park.

With only the Dalton Highway running through the Brooks Range and a good chunk of the territory enshrined forever in parks and refuges, this remote stretch of Alaska may seem pristine. Yet that impression is illusory. Arctic haze—an atmospheric grunge caused by Eurasian pollutants—is now common near Toolik Lake, while chemical toxins have been deposited in circumpolar Arctic regions by sources far to the south. (Alarmingly, these contaminants often intensify as they move up the food chain.) As global warming and oil exploration on the North Slope grow more contentious, our ability to protect the Alaskan Arctic will become a litmus test of our commitment to preserving America's outdoors. ■

Driver's-eye view of the Dalton Highway

James Dalton Highway

■ 416 miles long ■ Northeast Alaska ■ Best months June–late Aug. ■ Camping, hiking, fishing bird-watching, wildlife viewing, gold panning, float trips
■ Contact Bureau of Land Management, 1150 University Ave., Fairbanks, AK 99709; phone 907-474-2250

AMERICA'S MOST UNUSUAL ROAD, the Dalton Highway—built to provide construction access to the trans-Alaska pipeline—runs 416 miles from Livengood to Deadhorse, scaling the spectacular Brooks Range en route and paralleling the pipeline the entire way. By the time the first stretch was begun in April 1974, the Dalton Highway had survived numerous legal challenges decrying the impact it would have on the area's fragile environment and native land ownership. Five months and three million man-hours later, the road stretched from the Yukon River to the Beaufort Sea. The completion of the Yukon River Bridge in 1975 connected Alaska's high Arctic to the country's continental road system for the first time.

Connected, but not cloned: This is a rough gravel road whose surface ranges from dusty to muddy, where drivers should expect broken headlights, cracked windshields, and flat tires. Travel services are extremely limited. Gas and lodging are available only at the Yukon River, Coldfoot, and Deadhorse. No emergency medical facilities are found along the way.

Obviously, then, travelers on the Dalton Highway must prepare for mishaps and delays. Carry extra gasoline, two spare tires (each mounted on a rim), extra belts and headlights, radiator coolant, common tools, and a CB radio. Towing can cost $5 per mile. Take plenty of clothing, sleeping bags, extra food, water, and insect repellent.

As you've gathered, this rugged road isn't for everyone. Still, a stiff dose of common sense should stave off most disasters: Drive slowly, with your headlights on at all times. Give trucks the right of way; they kick up rocks and dust that pose significant hazards. Pull over and stop for oncoming or passing vehicles. Finally, stay off the road in winter.

If you'd like to reach the Arctic Circle but don't want to drive there, the following companies offer single-day or multiday trips to Prudhoe Bay: Alaskan Arctic Turtle Tours *(907-457-1798)*, Northern Alaska Tour Company *(907-474-8600)*, Trans Arctic Circle Treks *(907-479-5451)*.

The Bureau of Land Management (BLM) manages the land on either side of the Dalton Highway from the Yukon River to about Milepost 300 (the state of Alaska manages the terrain from there to Prudhoe Bay). From the highway you'll find near-limitless opportunities for camping, fishing, bird-watching, wildlife viewing, photography, and hiking.

Logging six hours a day in good weather, it takes about four to five days to drive the entire Dalton Highway from its start 4 miles west of Livengood *(at Milepost 73.1 on the Elliott Hwy.)* to its end a few miles shy of Prudhoe Bay. Along the way you'll rattle over timbered ridges and pass through untouched valleys, traversing several distinct habitats (such as tundra) that give you excellent chances of spotting unique mammals and birds.

What to See and Do

As you drive north from Livengood, you'll soon enter the woods below the Yukon River. Keep your eyes open here for spruce grouse, varied thrushes, and white-winged crossbills (some birders tally more than a hundred species during this section of the drive). For guided bird-watching, contact Nature-Alaska Tours *(907-488-3746)*.

For the first 50 miles or so, you'll be driving over discontinuous permafrost. The trans-Alaska pipeline's **Pump Station Six,** at Mile 54, was installed on a refrigerated foundation to keep it from thawing out the frozen substrate.

At Mile 55.6 you rumble over the inclined 2,995-foot-long **Yukon River Bridge.** Traveler services and tours to Athapaskan fish camps—conducted by Yukon River Tours *(907-452-7162)*—are available on the northwest bank of the river. This is the last gas and tire repair for the next 120 miles. Across the highway you'll find the BLM's **Yukon Crossing Visitor**

Contact Station *(open daily in summer)*.

North of the Yukon

Near **Five-mile Camp** (confusingly, it's at Mile 60 on the Dalton Highway), look for an undeveloped campground with an artesian well and an RV dump station. The boreal forest here is good habitat for black bears, which are sometimes seen crossing the road early or late in the day.

From the pullout at Mile 70 there's a great view of the **Ray Mountains** to the west. From Mile 86.5, look south to the **Fort Hamlin Hills.** East of this point stretches the vast, roadless **Yukon Flats National Wildlife Refuge** *(800-531-0676)*. Its wetlands host about one million to two million breeding ducks and 20,000 loons.

Picturesque **Finger Mountain Wayside** (Mile 98) has an outhouse, good off-road parking, and a short nature trail. The prominent tor nearby, resembling a pointing finger, was a landmark for early aviators. To the north is **Olson Lake** and the **Kanuti River Flats.** Hikers should feel free to strike off into the surrounding uplands. On a tundra walk near the granite tors to the northeast, you'll see myriad wildflowers in season, as well as the occasional horned lark, whimbrel, or American golden plover.

Numerous thermokarst lakes pockmark the Kanuti flats near Mile 102. These bodies of water formed when the ground ice in permafrost melted. Although wildlife sightings are never guaranteed, be on the lookout for grizzlies in this area.

Just after passing 3,179-foot-high Caribou Mountain on your left, the Dalton Highway crosses the **Kanuti River** at Mile 105.8. Both greater white-fronted and Canada geese nest at **Kanuti National Wildlife Refuge** *(907-456-0329 or 800-531-0676)* downstream. More than one-third of the refuge has burned since 1990, creating a patchwork of habitats that support a variety of wildlife.

North of the Arctic Circle

The **Arctic Circle Wayside** (Mile 115.3), the only spot in Alaska where you can cross the Arctic Circle by car, marks North latitude 66° 33' N—the place where, in theory, the sun stays above the horizon for one full day at the summer solstice. In practice, however, mountains to the north block the sun as it dips to the horizon on that day; to see the midnight sun you must drive 17 miles farther north to the **Gobblers Knob pullout** at Mile 132. There, too, you'll get your first good views of the Brooks Range, Prospect Creek, and Jim River drainages.

In January 1971, at a pipeline camp on **Prospect Creek** (Mile 135), the mercury plunged to an Alaska record of minus 80°F. A rough side road leads to a pond where you can see beaver, wa-

Moose antler display, Wiseman

Alaska pipeline at Mile 146 of Dalton Highway

On a Slippery Slope

In 1968, America's largest oil reserve was discovered at Prudhoe Bay, forever changing the face of Arctic Alaska. Two years later the state leased the fields for 900 million dollars, and by 1977 oil was flowing south through the 48-inch-diameter trans-Alaska pipeline. Running 800 miles from Prudhoe Bay to the ice-free port of Valdez on the Gulf of Alaska, the pipeline crosses two mountain ranges and 350 rivers and streams en route.

Although permafrost requires more than half the pipeline to run above ground, certain segments have been buried for wildlife corridors or highway crossings. These are refrigerated to keep them from thawing out the soil (the crude is a piping-hot 120°F when it leaves Prudhoe Bay and a still tepid 85°F

by the time it reaches Valdez). For the same reason, five of the seven pump stations north of Fairbanks sit on refrigerated foundations.

Arctic Alaska's hyperactive geomorphology forced the pipeline's North Slope section to be built in a zigzag pattern. This translates the contraction and expansion caused by earthquakes and temperature extremes into lateral movement, preventing ruptures in the pipe.

All these safeguards could not keep the tanker *Exxon Valdez* from running aground in Prince William Sound in 1989, spilling 11.3 million gallons of crude oil that polluted 1,500 miles of coast and killed 390,000 birds and countless mammals. As officials debated opening the Arctic National Wildlife Refuge to oil exploration in 2001, Alaskan oil remained a combustible issue.

terfowl, and (sometimes) moose.

Jim River, Mile 140, supports grayling, burbot (a delicious freshwater cod), and that grizzly magnet, salmon. Undeveloped camp sites dot this area. Salmon fishing is not allowed on the Jim River, which also strictly limits grayling.

At Mile 156.3 you'll cross the **South Fork** of the **Koyukuk River,** entering the Arctic mountains and leaving the Interior behind. There is a slim chance you'll find placer gold—flakes and nuggets dislodged from bedrock and deposited along watercourses—within a mile of the road here. All federally managed streams south of Atigun Pass in the Brooks Range are open to recreational mining; a BLM brochure, "Dalton Highway Recreational Mineral Collection" *(907-474-2250),* details the sites and the rules governing them. Other good spots include **Nugget Creek** (Mile 196) and **Gold Creek** (Mile 197.2).

About 20 miles past the South Fork is **Coldfoot,** established in 1899 as one of Alaska's northernmost gold-mining camps but deserted in 1912 when miners rushed to the Nolan Creek strike near Wiseman. A wealth of information is on hand at the interagency **Coldfoot Visitor Center** *(907-678-5209. Late May–early Sept.).* Five miles up the road is the Marion Creek Campground *(fee).* From here to Prudhoe Bay, the elevated oil pipeline occasionally appears.

Turn left just past the **Middle Fork Koyukuk River bridge** (Mile 189) for the side road to Wiseman. From this community 60 miles north of the Arctic Circle you can hike into **Gates of the Arctic National Park** (see pp. 260-65). One such walk leads from Wiseman toward the 1912 Nolan camp along a rough dirt mining road that also furnishes access to both the Hammond and Glacier Rivers.

The marble roots of spectacular **Sukakpak Mountain** (Mile 203.5) were deposited 380 million years ago. The small spruce in this area have been canted at irregular angles by the upheaval of ice-core mounds known as palsas. From here you can set out for the base of Sukakpak, though there is no established trail. The climb to the 4,459-foot-high summit is ardu-

ous—good hikers will need five to eight hours to complete it—but rewarding: Stunning views of the Brooks Range await you at the top.

From this point on, you'll want to pull over often for the views. A stream crossing at Mile 216, for example, offers a fine panorama of the mountains and the Koyukuk and Dietrich River Valleys.

The stand of white spruce at Mile 237—some are 200 years old —marks the northern limit of tree line along the highway. The road soon begins a long climb up a 10 percent grade to the **Chandalar Shelf** (Mile 241), a large valley draining southeast into the Yukon.

At Mile 244 the highway crosses the Arctic Continental Divide through 4,732-foot-high **Atigun Pass** (actually it's a saddle in the range). On the north side begins a steep descent into a U-shaped glacial valley, scoured and deepened by successive Pleistocene glaciers. Watch for Dall's sheep, soaring golden eagles, and grizzlies.

Glittering **Galbraith Lake** lies 30 miles north of Atigun. Follow the airstrip spur road on the left 3 miles to an undeveloped campground. Look for Dall's sheep and caribou.

From Mile 280 to 288 you'll pass through a real mouthful: the **Toolik Lake Area of Critical Environmental Concern/ Research Natural Area.** Recreational camping is banned within these 82,000 acres so scientists can conduct their investigations in a near-pristine landscape. From here to the coast, look for such rara aves as Baird's sandpipers, bar-tailed godwits, wheatears, gyrfalcons, bluethroats, and Smith's longspurs.

Autumn along the Dalton Highway

Onto the North Slope

At **Slope Mountain** (Mile 302), home to Dall's sheep, raptors, and grizzlies, you enter the foothills, which then flatten into the Arctic Coastal Plain. The road picks up the **Sagavanirktok (Sag) River** and tails it all the way to Prudhoe Bay. Musk oxen and caribou may appear from here to Franklin Bluffs.

An excellent place to look for peregrine falcons and gyrfalcons is the **Ice Cut** at Mile 326. From here to the coast is a visual feast of such typical Arctic features as cotton-grass tussocks and thaw ponds.

From **Pump Station Two,** 500 feet above sea level at Mile 360, the road begins a slow descent to Prudhoe Bay, now just 70 miles to the north. This spot also marks the northern extent of dwarf birch.

Freezing of subsurface water can raise the ground into mounds, called pingos, several hundred feet high. One of these looms over the tundra flats in the west at Mile 376. Arctic foxes—known to carry rabies—commonly den on pingos.

Beyond **Franklin Bluffs,** the

Missing Lynx

A snowshoe hare—also called a varying hare for its seasonal color change from brown to white—possesses huge hind feet. Like snowshoes, these support the hare atop deep snow in which most pursuers flounder.

Although you'll spot at least a few of these fleet-footed creatures as you drive the roads of subarctic and Arctic Alaska, their abundance may occasionally astonish you. Every 8 to 11 years, the state's population of the lagomorphs explodes and then crashes. At the peak of this cycle, when their numbers reach an astounding 600 per square mile of range, snowshoe hare seem to bound from every thicket—or to lie flattened on every mile of road.

After their dramatic crash, fewer than six hare may occupy the same area. Although the cause of the cycle has yet to be determined, its effect is unmistakable: The area's population of lynx—the hare's main predator—customarily peaks precisely one year after the population crest of the snowshoe hare. Other

Lynx

predators—notably coyotes, great horned owls, and goshawks—likewise benefit from this bunny boom.

If snowshoe hare are underfoot everywhere, their main adversaries often seem to be the missing lynx. That's because these 18- to 30-pound northern wildcats hunt mainly at night. Moving slowly and stealthily, they use hunting beds—that is, shallow depressions in the snow—to ambush the hare. The oversize paws of the lynx also act as snowshoes.

So closely intertwined are the two species that both suffer when either one does. On the upswing of the hare cycle, lynx grow fat and give birth to an average litter of three to four kittens; on the downswing lynx may starve, producing only one kitten—if any.

Resourcefully adaptable as predators, lynx undertake surprisingly long journeys to reach new hunting grounds. A radio-collared lynx from southern Yukon, for example, once traveled more than 400 miles to reach more hospitable terrain near Chalkyitsik, Alaska.

Snowshoe hare

farthest inland point reached by John Franklin of the Royal Navy in 1827, shallow thaw lakes and frost polygons dominate the tundra, and oil-field facilities loom into view. Watch for Pacific and red-throated loons.

The Dalton Highway ends at Deadhorse. Oil-field roads to the Arctic Ocean are closed to the public, but tours can be arranged by calling 907-659-2449. Commercial services here are limited. Once the Last Frontier's last frontier, the North Slope is now marred by a sprawling industrial complex the size of Rhode Island. The landscape does not invite lingering, but birders should have a look around for king and spectacled eiders, tundra swans, and snow buntings.

Off the Dalton Highway: Porcupine River Float Trip

From Canada's Ogilvie Mountains, the Porcupine River flows 500 miles to join the Yukon River 2 miles north of Fort Yukon, threading a wild corner of the **Arctic National Wildlife Refuge** (see pp. 252-259). The Porcupine, safe for novice floaters with good wilderness skills, is ideal for families with older children. Canoes and kayaks are best; oxbows and upriver winds make rafts a second choice.

From the put-in at Old Crow, the only inhabited village on the river, it's a 300-mile, 10- to 14-day paddle to Fort Yukon. The banks of the upper Porcupine contain archaeological sites and Pleistocene mammal remains. Removing anything from these sites is illegal.

This normally slow-moving, Class I river picks up speed at the Alaska-Yukon border, where it

flows for about 40 miles through the colorful, steep-walled **Upper Rampart Canyon.** All along the river you will pass remnants of abandoned cabins, such as those at Burnt Paw. Gwich'in Indians still fish and hunt along the river, so you'll also see the occasional new cabin or powerboat—especially in the fall moose and caribou season.

Below defunct Canyon Village, the Porcupine meanders through low, rolling hills before reaching its confluence with the Coleen River. A few miles below this point, you'll float past the limestone cliffs of **Lower Rampart Canyon,** followed by the forested wetlands of Yukon Flats NWR. Rafting this slow portion can try the patience of even the most poised paddler. Just before the Porcupine joins the Yukon, the Sucker River enters it from the left; you can paddle up it 3 miles to a road-accessible landing or float all the way to the Yukon, where you'll wind up 2 miles downstream from Fort Yukon. Here you'll need to find the local part-time customs agent before boarding a flight to Fairbanks. ■

Mosquito glasses for fending off same

Arctic National Wildlife Refuge

■ 19.6 million acres, including 8 million acres designated wilderness ■ Northeast Alaska ■ Best months mid-June–late Aug. ■ Camping, hiking, wildlife viewing, float trips ■ Contact the refuge, 101 12th Ave., Room 236, Box 20, Fairbanks, AK 99701; phone 907-456-0250. www.r7.fws.gov/nwr/arctic

ROADLESS AND UNDEVELOPED, America's largest national wildlife refuge stretches from the subarctic forests of Interior Alaska to the frozen shores of the Beaufort Sea. The refuge encompasses a 200-mile-long east-to-west segment of the Brooks Range, which reaches its broadest sprawl—more than 110 miles north to south—within the sanctuary.

Arctic NWR's greatest claim to fame, of course, is not crags but creatures: The refuge boasts the greatest animal variety of any protected area in the circumpolar north. Six distinct habitats—marine, coastal lagoons, Arctic lowland tundra, alpine, taiga, and boreal forests—support 180 species of birds, nine marine mammals, and 37 land mammals, including all three North American bears: grizzly, black, and polar. The latter sometimes wander in off the ice to den on land.

Birds, too, take pains to reside here. The American golden plover, for example, winters on the pampas of Argentina, then flies nearly 10,000 miles to nest on the dry tundra uplands of the reserve. By protecting a vast swath of migration routes and calving grounds, the refuge provides a safe haven for Alaska's 130,000-strong Porcupine caribou herd. Finally, Arctic NWR takes pride in its musk-ox population; reintroduced in 1969,

Caribou in fog

about 250 of the shaggy animals now wander the refuge's northern plain.

Of the 18 rivers flowing through the refuge, three have received "Wild" designation: the Ivishak, the Wind, and the Sheenjek. Although the trio merits that distinction, it can seem a tad absurd in a realm where several other watercourses—among them the Hulahula, the Coleen, and the Canning—offer spectacular beauty and pristine waters amid undefiled wilderness. Although you'll find very few large lakes in the refuge, two of them—the moraine-dammed Lake Schrader and Lake Peters, the latter at the foot of 9,020-foot-high Mount Chamberlin—have a spare, austere beauty all their own.

Winters here are long and severe. Some lakes do not thaw until mid-July, only to freeze up again in early September. Snow is possible at any time in this abbreviated summer. On south-flowing rivers, fall colors appear in late August or early September. On the North Slope the change takes place even earlier, with tundra plants turning red in early August.

Invoking the goal of energy independence in 1973, oil companies, politicians, and unions called for oil extraction to begin on a 110-mile-long section of Arctic NWR's coastal plain. Conservationists opposed the move, predicting damage to the land and its occupants. "Opening this last protected area to oil and gas development," warned Interior Secretary Bruce Babbitt in 1999, will "lead to serious threats to the native wildlife, including the Porcupine caribou herd, and the native peoples who depend on the herd to live and maintain their traditional lifestyle." Breaking the government's traditional aegis over the refuge, said Babbitt, would "shatter the balance of land and life into a thousand fragments."

What to See and Do

After making a visit here in 1953, biologist Lowell Sumner wrote that "This wilderness is big enough and wild enough to make you feel like one of the old-time explorers, knowing that each camp you place, each mountain climbed, each adventure with the boats is in untouched country." Untouched this country remains today: No lodge, campground, road, or trail is to be found anywhere within the refuge. This means visitors are completely on their own—and thus not entirely free of risk.

In addition to being well equipped, you must be well prepared, both mentally and physically, for the unique challenges the refuge presents. Experience—not high-tech gear—is paramount in traveling cross-country. Before you set out, determine your tolerance for intense plagues of mosquitoes. These insects drive caribou to distraction during peak insect season in July, but they are just as content to assail a hot, sweating backpacker.

Getting There

The vast majority of Arctic National Wildlife Refuge is accessible only by costly air charter, usually from one of three villages: Kaktovik on the north coast, Arctic Village and Fort Yukon farther south. It's possible to fly directly to the refuge from Bettles, Deadhorse, or Fairbanks, but the fare may be prohibitive. In addition, the region's limited number of air taxis require you to arrange flights far in advance. Budget several days for waiting out fog and other weather (*list of authorized air-charter services available from refuge staff*).

Complicating this already difficult access is the limited number of landing areas. Many of them are nothing more than glorified gravel bars scattered about the wildlife refuge. Your visit to this little-trod corner of the world is therefore likely to begin and end in highly rough-and-ready fashion.

Morning dew on blueberries

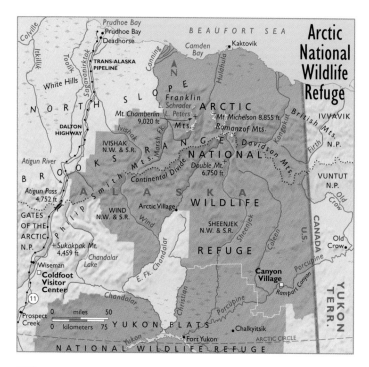

Hiking

The western boundary of Arctic National Wildlife Refuge lies 3 miles downstream from **Atigun River Crossing no. 2** (*not* no. 1!) at mile 270 on the Dalton Highway. For a challenging hike, from the road follow the north bank of the river downstream along the Atigun Gorge for 10 or 11 miles to the river's confluence with the headwater streams of the Sag River. Though tussocks make the going difficult, the cliffs may harbor falcons and the hillsides may give you a glimpse of Dall's sheep, grizzlies, or wolves.

The mountains offer the best hiking and backpacking in the refuge. Dry ridges and riverbanks provide the best routes. With the aid of your charter pilot, you may be able to get dropped off on one river and hike through a pass to a strip on another drainage. You can study maps and design your own itinerary, but it's always a good idea to check the feasibility with refuge staff and your pilot. Once you leave your drop-off site, you can go for days, even weeks, without seeing another soul. Hikers prepared for cool weather and icy winds can trek and camp on the bluffs and spare beaches along the Arctic coast. For guided backpacking trips in the refuge, contact the refuge and ask for their list called "Authorized Recreational Guiding Services."

Climbing

Climbing in Arctic NWR is just catching on. Mountaineers tackle the ice fields and spires of two peaks in the northern portion of

Fishing the Dietrich River on the western boundary of Arctic NWR (Sukakpak Mountain at right)

the refuge—9,020-foot-high **Mount Chamberlin** and 8,855-foot **Mount Michelson**—in addition to other pinnacles as yet unnamed. For guided climbing trips, check out Alaska Wildtrek (907-235-6463).

River Running

Most of the rivers in Arctic NWR —especially those on the north side—are swift, strewn with boulders, and braided—that is, split into many channels that repeatedly rejoin and redivide. Expect high, muddy water during spring breakup and after storms. Most rivers are open from mid-June through September, but you'll find the safest water levels in late June to early August (low water levels in August can require extensive lining).

Here as elsewhere in the American wilderness, river ratings are subjective; each run must be eval-

uated according to the river's current conditions. Some Kongakut River segments that are rated Class III have powerful hydraulics at higher water levels.

A hazard unique to northern rivers is thick layers of overflow ice, some more than a mile long, that persist into late summer on certain rivers. During the spring breakup, a river may carve a chute through one of these "aufeis fields," as they are known, forcing

boaters to scout the ice before floating through; if not, they may make the unpleasant (and dangerous) discovery downstream that the river suddenly flows under the ice or through a walled tunnel. These channels are usually open by late June.

To see the hidden gems of the refuge, book a guided backpacking trip, or a combination backpack and float trip. Guided trips may seem expensive, yet they include

Endless Journey

Alaska supports nearly one million caribou in about 30 separate herds. (A herd is defined by its regular and exclusive use of a calving area.) The largest group of all—some 500,000 strong—is the Western Arctic herd, which tends to roam from Barrow to the Seward Peninsula. The caribou you're likely to spot along the Dalton Highway, as well as those you may see wandering the oil fields near Prudhoe Bay, belong to the Central Arctic herd.

The Porcupine herd, which calves in Arctic National Wildlife Refuge in late May, is named for the Porcupine River, the major watercourse in the herd's range. In summer, caribou eat a wide variety of green plants; in winter they are limited to lichens, which they locate under the snow by smell.

You can't tell a caribou by its horns: These creatures are the only members of the deer family in which both sexes grow antlers. In general, however, the rack of a mature bull is much larger than that of a cow. Bulls shed their antlers in October and begin growing new ones in April. Pregnant cows keep their antlers all winter, using them to defend feeding sites from larger and stronger—but antlerless— bulls. In late May, cows give birth to a single 10- to 15-pound calf. Two-week-old calves can outrun their main predators, wolves and bears.

The survival of this species hinges on its seasonal migrations between winter and summer ranges. In June and July, large caribou herds drift north toward the cool, windswept Arctic coast and its respite from heat and mosquitoes. In August they head south again, bound for their wintering grounds on the taiga in the eastern and north-central Yukon. One radio-collared animal in the Porcupine herd made a 3,000-mile round-trip in one year—the longest measured movement of any land mammal.

the air charter fees to this refuge, which can cost hundreds of dollars for just two people. And with a guide on hand, you won't have to worry about developing ace wilderness skills on the spot *(ABEC's Alaska Adventures 907-457-8907; Wilderness Alaska 907-345-3567; Equinox Expeditions 907-274-9087).*

Many visitors access the refuge by floating one of three north-flowing rivers—the Kongakut, the Hulahula, or the Canning.

The Kongakut. The Kongakut River rises in the Davidson Mountains at the eastern extent of the Brooks Range and flows across the coastal plain to reach the Beaufort Sea. Most trips on this river end before it exits the mountains. Because a float on this river may yield sightings of caribou herds, the Kongakut is the most trafficked watercourse in the refuge. At the peak of the season in June, as many as 30 tents from several different groups may be pitched at the **Caribou Pass** pickup airstrip.

The Hulahula. From high in the Brooks Range, the Hulahula River flows north through steep-walled glacial valleys, then threads the coastal plain to the sea. Superb scenery combined with easy access makes the Hulahula the second most floated river in the refuge. Though mostly Class I and II, occasional stretches of Class III ensure a challenging descent. A narrow pass across the Continental Divide—used by hikers and pilots—connects the headwaters of the Hulahula with those of the Chandalar River.

The Canning. The longest north-flowing river in the refuge, the Canning River (as well as its tributary, the Marsh Fork) boasts good aircraft access. Whereas the Canning is relatively placid, the **Marsh Fork** offers short segments of white water. Both run through scenic valleys gouged out by glaciers thousands of years ago.

Other Runs. Marginal aircraft access and typically shallow water affect river trips on two of Arctic NWR's three wild rivers, the **Ivishak** and the **Wind.** The glacier-fed **Sheenjek River,** by contrast, ushers rafters through diverse mountain and forest habitats as it drains the south side of the highest mountains in the Brooks Range. Most of the river is Class I, with a few short sections of Class II white water *(watch for sweepers, or low-hanging branches, downstream).*

The Sheenjek can be accessed at various points, commonly Last Lake, the gravel bars below Double Mountain, or other sites as water levels and pilot experience allow. Grizzlies, moose, beavers, waterfowl, and picturesque spires may all be part of the scenery. With the refuge designed to offer visitors a true wilderness experience, the choice of good camping and hiking sites is completely up to you. The entire river is open to fishing.

A different kettle of fish—this one historical—is what truly distinguishes the Sheenjek, however. After long visits to Last Lake on the Sheenjek's upper reaches in the 1950s, conservationists Olaus and Margaret Murie lobbied to have the eastern Brooks Range set aside as a wildlife refuge. Thanks to their efforts, as well as those of Supreme Court Justice William O. Douglas, the Arctic National Wildlife Range was established in 1960. ∎

Crossing a frontier on the Dalton Highway

Gates of the Arctic National Park and Preserve

■ 8.5 million acres ■ Central Brooks Range ■ Best months June-Sept.
■ Camping, hiking, backpacking, rock climbing, white-water rafting and kayaking, wildlife viewing, float trips ■ Contact the park, 201 1st Ave., Fairbanks, AK 99701; phone 907-456-0281; www.nps.gov/gaar

JAGGED PEAKS, WILD RIVERS, DIVERSE WILDLIFE, hidden canyons, and pristine lakes all contribute to the haunting beauty of Gates of the Arctic National Park and Preserve. An untrammeled wilderness north of the Arctic Circle, the park straddles a 200-mile-long stretch of the central Brooks Range. This northernmost reach of the Rocky Mountains contains the complete spectrum of Arctic habitats, from forest to tundra. Wolves, grizzlies, wolverines, Dall's sheep, and moose roam in untouched settings, as do portions of the 500,000-strong Western Arctic caribou herd (see p. 258). All in all, Gates of the Arctic is home to 37 land mammals and 133 bird species, including nesting populations of the arctic peregrine falcon.

In this mammoth mountain kingdom the summer sun does not set for 30 straight days, creating a variegated palette of light—dark and forbidding one minute, soft and compelling the next. The long, dark, grueling winter gives way grudgingly to a short, mild summer of just 5 to 10 inches of precipitation. Continuous permafrost creates typical Arctic conditions—standing water, tussock fields, dense clouds of mosquitoes—while the Arctic's poor, thin soils produce only spare plant life.

If you know what to look for, you'll find the park's tectonic history inscribed in the land. Estimated at 470 million to 350 million years old, intrusive rock—that is, molten rock that seeped into another type of rock—indicates that compression and subduction began early in the Paleozoic period. Intense folding occurred as crustal plates collided and subduction forced up mountain peaks. Thrust faults—compressive strains in the Earth's crust—moved rocks many miles. Over eons, structures such as mountains that once ran east to west were overturned to the north.

Pleistocene valley glaciers then joined the geologic fray, eroding the land in four major glaciations that carved the central Brooks Range. These rivers of ice scoured the granitic Arrigetch Peaks and 8,510-foot-high Mount Igikpak into eerie spires and ridges. As the climate got warmer and drier, most of the glaciers disappeared.

Because today's climate does not produce enough snowfall to create large, active glaciers, Gates of the Arctic lacks the ice fields you'll find in Alaska's more southerly parks. In another contrast, the park's rivers—born of rain and melted snow—run remarkably clear of silt, rock flour (pulverized rock), and other glacial debris. Six of these have been designated Wild and Scenic Rivers.

In the heart of the park is Anaktuvuk Pass, an ancestral caribou migration route that is also home to the last band of Nunamiut (inland Eskimos). These once nomadic people settled here in the 1950s; today they still depend on natural resources for food and clothing. A handful of Athapaskan villages also skirt the southern edge of the park. Preserving both of these cultures figured prominently in the site's designation as a national park and preserve in 1980.

What to See and Do

Though the park contains no roads, developed campgrounds, or trails, two area lodges—Peace of Selby (907-672-3206) and Iniakuk (907-479-6354)—offer varied wilderness adventures.

The town of Bettles, on the Middle Fork of the Koyukuk River 35 miles above the Arctic Circle, is the main access point for the central Brooks Range. Scheduled flights from Fairbanks serve both Bettles and **Anaktuvuk Pass;** you'll need reservations, especially in the peak summer season. Strict weight allowances on these aircraft require passengers to pay dearly for every bit of gear over 40 pounds.

(contact park for up-to-date list of approved outfitters and charter services). Charter flights out of Bettles average $250 to $350 per hour.

Like other northern outposts, Bettles is known for its weather extremes. Its record low (minus 70°F) was set in 1975, 20 years after its record high of 92°F. The Koyukuk River freezes up in mid-October and ices out in early May. Starting in March, cross-country skiers, dog-mushers, and aurora-watchers avail themselves of the moderating temperatures and longer daylight before snow conditions deteriorate.

Bettles has a ranger station (907-692-5494) and services rang-

Following pages: Sunrise from atop Steele Creek Dome

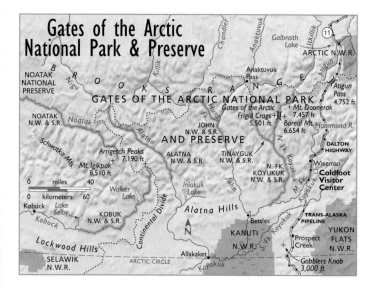

Gates of the Arctic
National Park & Preserve

NOATAK NATIONAL PRESERVE

NOATAK N.W. & S.R.

GATES OF THE ARCTIC NATIONAL PARK

Anaktuvuk Pass

Gates of the Arctic
Frigid Crags 5,501 ft

Mt. Doonerak 7,457 ft
Boreal Mt. 6,654 ft

Atigun Pass 4,752 ft

AND PRESERVE

ARCTIC N.W.R.

Schwatka Mts.

Arrigetch Peaks 7,190 ft

Mt. Igikpak 8,510 ft

ALATNA N.W. & S.R.

TINAYGUK N.W. & S.R.

N. FK. KOYUKUK N.W. & S.R.

DALTON HIGHWAY

Wiseman
Coldfoot Visitor Center

0   miles   40

0   kilometers   60

Walker Lake

Iniakuk Lake

Alatna Hills

Kobuck   Lake Selby

KOBUK N.W. & S.R.

Continental Divide

Bettles

KANUTI N.W.R.

TRANS-ALASKA PIPELINE

YUKON FLATS N.W.R.

Lockwood Hills

SELAWIK N.W.R.

ARCTIC CIRCLE

Allakaket

Prospect Creek

Gobblers Knob 3,000 ft

ing from guides *(Sourdough Outfitters 907-692-5252)* to accommodations *(Bettles Lodge 907-692-5111; Holly Hollows Cabins 907-692-5557)*.

To access the eastern part of the park, take the Dalton Highway to the village of Wiseman and hike from there into the beautiful **Hammond River** drainage, which leads to 7,457-foot-high Mount Doonerak. In summer, the nearby **Coldfoot Visitor Center** *(907-678-5209. Late May–early Sept.)* has access tips and up-to-date information.

Another entry portal is the far northern town of Anaktuvuk Pass, surrounded by some 66,000 acres of Nunamiut land. The only approved camping spot in the village is near the airstrip; camping elsewhere is considered disrespectful. Though it's permissible to cross Nunamiut lands to reach the park, check at the ranger station *(907-661-3520)* in town for detailed rules. The Nunamiut use ATVs to reach their summer hunting grounds, so expect to find a few rutted trails in the tundra.

In Anaktuvuk Pass, ask permission before taking photos. In the backcountry, respect private property—even if it looks abandoned.

Hiking

Hiking opportunities abound in Gates of the Arctic, but they are mostly of the "trek your own" variety: To prevent overuse, rangers recommend specific hikes only with reluctance. However, once you've chosen a route—near the scoured summit of Mount Igikpak, say, or through the majestic country on the North Fork Koyukuk River—the rangers will offer useful advice on how to negotiate it.

Only the well-prepared—those whose expert wilderness skills make them totally self-sufficient—should venture into the backcountry here. Use low-impact camping techniques (see pp. 6-7) and travel in a group of four to six; this number balances safety with ecological concerns. Plan for weather delays, and leave a trip plan with a responsible person. Because unattended food caches are verboten, use your own bear-resistant food canisters (BRFCs).

Paddling

You can float any or all of the park's six wild and scenic rivers. One of the most popular is the **Alatna,** which flows from glacial summits to boreal forest without leaving the park. This river also offers access to the Arrigetch Peaks. About 185 miles of mostly Class I and II water (with one segment of Class III rapids above **Ram Creek** tributary) stretch from the Alatna's headwaters to the Athapaskan village of Allakaket.

The **John River** flows from Anaktuvuk Pass through glacial valleys to join the Koyukuk below Bettles—a five- to six-day float.

Most trips begin on the **Hunt Fork** tributary, below which the John is an ideal river for a family float.

Excellent backpacking and some challenging white water (Class II; one short Class III run) await along the **North Fork Koyukuk River,** which threads Frigid Crags and Boreal Mountain—the Arctic gates themselves—in the heart of the park. Try to put in below Mount Doonerak, the "Matterhorn of the Koyukuk." If you put in at Redstar Lake, use the trail from the lake to the river, and camp only on gravel bars. Allow six to seven days to float the 60 miles from Redstar to Bettles.

On remote, north-flowing rivers, novice wilderness hikers or river runners may wish to consider a guided trip with Alaska Adventures *(907-457-8907)*, Arctic Treks *(907-455-6502)*, or Alaska Wildtrek *(907-235-6463)*. ■

Survival of the Coldest

Alaska's northern exposure has sparked some fascinating adaptations. With snow on the ground for up to seven months, five animals—ptarmigan, collared lemmings, arctic foxes, weasels, and hare—change color with the seasons.

Migratory birds are best known for fleeing the winter cold, but caribou, whales, and walruses also cope by moving south. Ptarmigan, too, occasionally change ranges, alternately flying and walking.

Some animals—most famously bears—sleep the winter away, emerging with the spring thaw. During hibernation, a black bear's body temperature drops 12 degrees (to 85°F); its heart rate slows to one beat every ten seconds.

Yellow jackets and arctic ground squirrels undergo a drop in body temperature below freezing without suffering permanent damage. During hibernation, the squirrels' heart rate falls from 200 beats per minute to just two, rendering the animals so dormant that ice crystals form in their body tissues.

The most amazing coping tactic of all belongs to the wood frog, one of Alaska's five amphibians: It freezes solid in winter, then comes to life again in spring. Scientists believe the secret to this cryogenic miracle lies in the frog's ability to convert some body fluids to sugar.

Noatak National Preserve

■ 6.3 million acres ■ Northwest Alaska ■ Access by aircraft from Bettles, Fairbanks, Kotzebue ■ Best months June-Sept. ■ Camping, hiking, backpacking, bird-watching, wildlife viewing, float trips ■ Contact the preserve, P.O. Box 1029, Kotzebue, AK 99572; phone 907-442-3890; www.nps.gov/noat

NO ONE DOUBTS THAT Noatak National Preserve is one of the finest wilderness areas left in North America—a notion seconded by UNESCO, which conferred International Biosphere Reserve status on the site when it was established in 1980. As one of the continent's largest undeveloped mountain-ringed river basins, Noatak features sweeping vistas that truly merit the label "awesome." Indeed, the preserve creates a world unto itself by virtue of its size alone—over 12,000 square miles.

Noatak embraces a mosaic of gaunt canyons, crystal rivers, undulating tundra, and coastal wetlands. The Noatak River rises from residual glaciers clinging to the flanks of Mount Igikpak, at 8,510 feet the highest point in the western Brooks Range. The Arrigetch and Noatak highlands spawn the Kobuk and Noatak Rivers, which roughly parallel each other as they run west to the sea, debouching into Hotham Inlet only a few miles apart.

As one of Alaska's least traveled areas, the Noatak is distinguished by its remoteness. There are no lodges, campgrounds, or trails, but those with well-honed backcountry skills will find untold opportunities for exploration and backpacking. You can float the Noatak or one of its ten tributaries, notably the Cutler, Kelly, or Nimiuktuk Rivers. Whether you hike, float, or fly in and camp, take time to savor the silence and solitude that are this preserve's unique gift to the visitor.

Noatak River

What to See and Do

The **Noatak National Wild and Scenic River** offers superlative wilderness trips from the Brooks Range to the Chukchi Sea. Most visitors fly in from area villages such as Kotzebue and Bettles (allow extra time for fog delays). The upper access lakes at the head of the river between **Portage Creek** and **Douglas Creek** get heavy use, so try not to camp near your put-in. Alternatively, arrange to get dropped off and picked up by floatplane *(contact the preserve for approved operators)*, or float all the way downstream to Noatak village.

If you raft the Noatak River on your own, allow ten days to float from the access lakes to the Cutler River (a common take-out point) or 21 days to Noatak. If you hire a guide, try to find an outfitter that combines backpacking and river running.

To enhance your enjoyment of this long, meandering trip, be sure to take sunscreen, insect repellent, and a head net or bug jacket. In summer, expect masses of mosquitoes; in autumn your fellow travelers will be whitesox—tiny, biting flies that leave nasty welts.

Limited access and shallow water above the put-in lakes make the Noatak's upper 25 miles largely devoid of boaters or hikers. For its first 50 miles, the river (here within Gates of the Arctic National Park) courses through a deep, U-shaped valley hemmed to the south by the Schwatka Mountains. Here the river is mostly placid and serpentine (Class I and II), yet some sections can be tricky: The whirlpool below Douglas Creek, called the Jaws, should be lined.

Arcing westward, the river enters its great basin—3,000 square miles of wildlife habitat ringed by the Baird Mountains in the south and the De Long Mountains in the north. Aside from a few balsam poplars and willows edging the river, the surrounding countryside is open; be aware, however, that grizzlies can hide in even small pockets of brush. These spare slopes and vast stretches of tundra offer excellent chances to spot wildlife. You may see caribou, gyrfalcons, whistling swans, pacific loons, and perhaps even a wolf or wolverine. Songbirds include Asian strays such as bluethroats, as well as migrants from South America.

In April and August you may be privy to a true Ice Age spectacle: the Western Arctic caribou herd migrating south through the preserve. Over the millennia, as land bridges periodically linked Siberia to North America, mammals such as lions, short-faced bears, horses, hare, caribou, musk oxen, and saber-toothed cats crossed into the New World. As you watch caribou thunder past today, a little imagination will populate the scene with camels and woolly mammoths.

Halfway to the sea, the Noatak enters 70-mile-long **Grand Canyon**—a beautiful carved valley with minimal white water. The **Nimiuktuk River,** which joins the Noatak here, is great for hiking explorations. You may encounter Inupiat hunters using powerboats. Below the Kelly River, the Noatak dissolves into braids and loses its Wild and Scenic designation.

About 70 to 80 river miles from the ocean, the river passes the only village on its 396-mile length, Noatak. As you near this Inupiat town (signaled by sounds of "civilization" such as motors and planes) always take the right-hand channel or you will miss it. Most boaters take out here and catch a scheduled flight to Kotzebue. ■

Kobuk Valley National Park

■ 1.8 million acres ■ 75 miles east of Kotzebue ■ Air access ■ Best months June–mid-Sept. ■ Camping, hiking, white-water rafting and kayaking, fishing, ■ Contact the park, P.O. Box 1029, Kotzebue, AK 99572, phone 907-442-3890. www.nps.gov/kova, or Gates of the Arctic National Park and Preserve, 201 1st Ave., Fairbanks, AK 99701; phone 907-456-0281. www.nps.gov/gaar

CORDONED OFF BY THE Baird and Waring Mountains, this undeveloped park protects the midsection of the Kobuk River, the drainage of the wild and scenic Salmon River, the Great Kobuk Sand Dunes, and myriad wildlife, including migrating caribou.

Near Onion Portage, a historic caribou crossing where the Kobuk River enters the park, archaeological sites dating back 12,500 years delineate several different cultures; each depended on caribou for survival. Continuing the tradition, modern Inupiat hunters still ambush caribou here.

Kobuk's management plan encourages traditional native subsistence practices over tourism, so no facilities or trails lie within the park. Access is via aircraft from Kotzebue or Fairbanks, or via aircraft or boat from two small local villages: Kiana west of the park, and Ambler to the east.

Great Kobuk Sand Dunes, Kobuk Valley National Park

What to See and Do

Tackling the Kobuk

Many visitors travel though the park on the 347-mile-long Kobuk River. Flowing from the Endicott Mountains within the central Brooks Range into Hotham Inlet, the Kobuk has served as a highway between Alaska's Interior and the sea for thousands of years. The river remains a key artery today; many people float from its source in **Gates of the Arctic National Park** (pp. 260-65) and then through Kobuk Valley National Park. Guided floats are led by Arctic Treks (907-455-6502), Alaska Wildtrek (907-235-6463), and Equinox Expeditions (907-274-9087).

If designing your own trip, you can take out or put in at any of the five Inupiat villages—Kobuk, Shungnak, Ambler, Kiana, or Noorvik—that perch beside the Kobuk; all have scheduled flights.

Such flexibility provides an opportunity for trips of one to four weeks. Most boaters put in near the Kobuk's headwaters at 14-mile-long **Walker Lake,** but you need not hurry off from here: Hiking this mountain-rimmed lake, where you may spy sheep, bears, or golden eagles, is excellent.

Three spots in the river's first 30 miles demand extreme caution. About two-thirds of a mile downstream from the lake, the outlet tributary blasts through a declivity. Powerful hydraulics and four major drop-offs make this segment a highly dangerous Class IV to V. Do *not* attempt to run this section; instead, follow the well-worn portage route on the left bank.

The second trouble spot comes 10 miles below the lake at **Upper Kobuk Canyon,** which boils with Class IV rapids during high water;

Fourth of July celebration, St. Paul's Island (Pribilof Islands)

Alaska Natives

Although the blanket term "Alaska natives" (or natives) is often used to describe the state's indigenous peoples, that catchall phrase actually encompasses several cultures, each with its own customs and traits. Three distinct groups—the Athapaskans, the Inupiat (including the Nunamiut), and the Yup'ik— make their home in the Arctic. The Inupiat, whom you'll encounter on Arctic rivers and along the Arctic Ocean, and the Yup'ik, who fringe the Bering Sea, are also called Eskimos—or, in other countries, Inuit. Athapaskans, frequently referred to as Indians, inhabit Interior Alaska north to the Brooks Range.

Variations in customs and dialects pop up within each large grouping. The Nunamiut, unlike the majority of Inupiat, are not maritime hunters; they live in the mountains instead, relying on caribou for subsistence. (So do the Gwich'in Athapaskans.)

Over the centuries, cultural interactions among Alaska natives have varied from friendly trading to veiled distrust and open warfare. As a way to guarantee the safe conduct of commerce, however, certain areas were apparently designated neutral trading sites.

Many contemporary natives follow lifestyles similar to those of their ancestors, yet a cultural upheaval is now tearing at many villages. To gain a better understanding of contemporary native life, take at least one cultural tour. For Nunamiut and Inupiat tours, contact Alaskan Arctic Adventures (907-852-3300), Arctic Tour Company (907-852-4512), Northern Alaska Tour Company (907-474-8600), or Tour Arctic (907-442-3301). For Athapaskan village tours, contact Arctic Village Tours (907-479-4648), Athabascan Cultural Journeys (907-829-2261), Yukon River Tours (907-452-7162), or Yukon Starr Enterprises (907-366-7251).

As a visitor to a different culture, be polite and deferential, honoring the privacy of others and obtaining permission before taking photos.

it should be lined on the right.

The third danger zone is about 20 miles farther down, where the river descends three segments rated Class III to IV as it plunges through mile-long **Lower Kobuk Canyon.** To avoid the canyon's drop-offs and boulders, line from the right. Water levels determine the danger level of these sections; lives have been lost here.

Below this canyon the river gentles to Class I and begins its sinuous odyssey to the sea. If you prefer to skip the white-water excitement just described, arrange for a plane to drop you off just west of the park at Ambler.

Powerboats ply the river below the canyons, serving the native fish camps that dot the shore. The slow water and profusion of oxbows downstream from Shungnak prompt many paddlers to take out there, about 140 miles from Walker Lake.

At times, fishing the Kobuk can be incredible. The quarry includes grayling, arctic char, and giant sheefish—an explosive fighter that is the tarpon of the North. Floaters and powerboaters have the best luck, but you can also reach choice spots by hiring a floatplane from Ambler Air *(907-445-2157)* or Bettles Air *(907-692-5655).*

For shorter descents of the river, float into the park from Kobuk, Shungnak, or Ambler village to Kiana, 100 miles below Ambler (and 10 miles west of the park).

Great Kobuk Sand Dunes

About 40 miles downstream from Ambler, a 1.5-mile hike leads to a curious sight on the south side of the river: The Great Kobuk Sand

Dunes rise 100 feet high and cover 30 to 40 square miles of land. Look to the south (toward the Waring Mountains) and you'll see dunes soaring 500 feet tall.

These dunes are remnants of much larger dunes that were engineered by glaciers in the Pleistocene period. During that time, rivers of ice ground away at the Brooks Range, filling the region's broad, braided rivers with abundant outwash. Strong winds then swept away this alluvial detritus, forming the great dune fields you see today. Subsurface sampling has fixed their age at 33,000 years old.

Though 500 square miles of once barren dunes are now lushly vegetated, a mix of topography and wind prevented revegetation in the open sand dune area. That's because the Waring Mountains to the south kept the sands from blowing away eons ago. In addition, prevailing easterly winds scoured the dunes, desiccating and defeating newly rooted plants.

At their western edge, the Great Kobuk Sand Dunes overrun sections of boreal forest. Here you'll see the tops of 150-year-old black spruce jutting above the sand, which is often crisscrossed by the tracks of caribou and bear.

Kavet Creek offers the best access to the dunes. Do *not* wade upstream or follow the creek margin —it's a dreadful willow entanglement. Instead, head a few hundred yards to the west, then hike south on the rather open, easy ridge.

There are native allotments within the park. The Park Service asks visitors not to disturb these cabins or camps, or to interfere with subsistence activities. ■

Cape Krusenstern

Cape Krusenstern National Monument

■ 444,673 acres ■ 10 air miles northwest of Kotzebue ■ Best months June-Aug. ■ Access by aircraft or boat ■ Camping, hiking, backpacking, kayaking, fishing, bird-watching, wildlife viewing ■ Contact the monument, P.O. Box 1029, Kotzebue, AK 99572; phone 907-442-3890. www.nps.gov/cakr

NAMED BY (OR POSSIBLY FOR) Capt. Johann Von Krusenstern—an Estonian-born German who led Russia's first round-the-world voyage in 1803—this treeless, undulating coastal plain on the Chukchi Sea is the site of 114 beach ridges that make up an archaeological treasure trove. Formed over thousands of years by storms, waves, and currents that deposited sand and gravel on the shore, the ridges chronicle 9,000 years of human use: Each ridge was once an oceanfront campsite for early hunters.

Eschewing trails, campgrounds, or any other Park Service "improvement," Cape Krusenstern National Monument protects Inupiat cultural heritage, past and present. During your visit here, keep in mind that it is forbidden to dig for or remove artifacts, or to interfere with the Inupiat hunters and fishermen whose tents dot the outer beach.

Coastal temperatures in summer seldom exceed 60°F, and the wind carries an icy bite reminding you that snow is never far away. Storms with winds up to 70 miles per hour create dangerous wind chills. Despite such inclemency, each summer a few hardy birders seek out migrant and vagrant species in habitats shared by musk oxen, arctic hare, and other mammals. In spring and fall, walrus and beluga and bowhead whales pass by on their annual journey to ice-free waters. The park is used even in winter, when access is via plane, boat, dogsled, or snowmobile.

A charter flight over the monument offers the best way to grasp the changes wrought by sea ice through the millennia. Early in the morning or late in the day, a flight from nearby Kotzebue *(contact Northwestern Aviation 907-442-3525)* reveals the sand ridges located along the cape's southern coast. For a fuller understanding of coastal Inupiat culture, visit the **NANA Museum of the Arctic** *(907-442-3747)* in Kotzebue.

If you camp here, you'll be treading the same shores where ancestral Inupiat cultures first emerged 5,000 years ago. In much the same manner as their ancient antecedents, modern Inupiat still hunt and fish on this precarious threshold of the planet's habitable terrain. ■

Seward Peninsula

■ 15 million acres ■ Western Alaska ■ Best months late May–early Sept.
■ Camping, hiking, fishing, bird-watching ■ Contact Nome Convention and Visitors Bureau, P.O. Box 240, Nome, AK 99762, phone 907-443-6624; or the BLM Nome Field Office, P.O. Box 925, Nome, AK 99762, phone 907-443-2177

THE WESTERN EXTREMITY of the American mainland—otherwise known as the Seward Peninsula—is one of Alaska's least known treasures. Not only does the peninsula boast a diversity of botanic, zoologic, and geologic riches, but this trove can be easily accessed because all roads lead from Nome: **The Kougarok Road, Council Road,** and **Teller Road** give you almost 300 miles of gravel roads to explore. These ribbons through the wilderness will take you to gold rush ruins, Pleistocene fossil sites, and spots where indigenous cultures vanished as recently as 125 years ago. Those pillars of the Alaska wildlife pantheon (the grizzly bear and the mosquito) are here, but so too are reindeer; introduced from Siberia at the dawn of the 20th century, they wander the surrounding hills, the staples of a cash economy that supplements the traditional native lifestyle.

On the Seward Peninsula you will encounter Inupiat and Yup'ik people involved in subsistence activities such as hunting, fishing, and berry-picking. In addition to satisfying basic nutritional needs, these pursuits constitute cultural cornerstones.

The jagged spires of the **Kigluaik Mountains** scrabble at the sky 30 miles north of Nome. To reach them by car, take the Kougarok Road to

Peopling the Americas

Did human beings migrate into the New World over the Bering Land Bridge 10,000 to 13,000 years ago? Many scientists think so. For evidence, they point to sites at Cape Krusenstern and on the Bering Land Bridge that have yielded artifacts dating back 9,000 to 10,000 years.

In the 1990s, investigations of the Mesa and Putu sites in the Brooks Range uncovered stone spearpoints 9,700 to 11,000 years old. Particularly intriguing to archaeologists is the close resemblance between these weapons and stone tools found thousands of miles to the south.

Combined with research from other Alaska sites such as Onion Portage on the Kobuk River, the evidence now suggests that several human migrations—both by land and by sea—to the New World may have taken place. As each new clue is unearthed, the puzzle of who peopled the Americas when (and how) comes closer to completion.

the north or the Teller Road to the west. Here outdoorsy types of every stripe pursue their particular passions. Photographers shoot cirques, sunsets, and **Crater Lake.** Hikers traverse **Mosquito Pass** and its spectacular canyons. Fisher folk try their luck in **Canyon Creek** and **Sinuk River.** Birders stalk wheatears, longspurs, and gyrfalcons. History buffs inspect the unfinished 1905 Wild Goose Pipeline.

On Kougarok Road, you can fish and camp at the **Salmon Lake campground** (don't miss the concentrations of red salmon massing at the lake's outlet in late July through August). Drive up **Anvil Mountain** for a great view of the Bering Strait.

At many places along Council Road, you can drive over part of the Iditarod National Historic Trail (pp. 139-143). Because this road passes through all nine habitats on the peninsula, it offers birders their best chances of seeing some of the 215 avian species that frequent the area.

Indeed, lying as it does at the crossroads of the Asiatic-North American flyway, the Seward Peninsula offers unique opportunities to spot resident birds, migrants, and Asian strays. In spring, rare bluethroats show up in the thickets along Kougarok Road, while bristle-thighed curlews (the only ones visible from a road in North America) populate the overlooking ridges.

The Fish and Wildlife Service, which administers segments of the Seward coast, teamed up with the state of Alaska in 1994 to build a parking lot and nature trail at the Safety Bridge on Council Road. From here birders scan **Safety Sound** for seabirds, waterfowl, and shorebirds, including rare strays such as red-necked stints and Mongolian plover.

Even **Nome** itself, where a walking tour may turn up yellow wagtails or threatened spectacled eiders, is a birding hot spot. Rounding out the town's attractions are small museums, visitor centers, historic buildings, and nature tours *(Nome Discovery Tours 907-642-3682; Arctic Winter Expeditions 907-443-2680).* ■

Bering Land Bridge National Preserve

■ 2.7 million acres ■ 90 miles north of Nome, 50 miles south of Kotzebue
■ Access by boat or aircraft ■ Best months June-July ■ Camping, hiking, fishing, bird-watching, wildlife viewing, hot springs ■ Contact the preserve, P.O. Box 220, Nome, AK 99762; phone 907-443-2522. www.nps.gov/bela

TO COMMEMORATE THE PEOPLING of the Western Hemisphere while highlighting the complexity of natural processes is the mandate of Bering Land Bridge National Preserve. With terms such as "greenhouse gases," "global warming," and "ozone depletion" now a part of the national idiom, this preserve offers crucial insights into the effects of climate change.

Several times in the Pleistocene Ice Ages, the now submerged continental shelf that connects Alaska and Siberia (just 55 miles distant) dried up. Beringia, the land thus formed, was covered with grasslands 1,000 miles wide, permitting people, plants, and animals to advance across it.

Stop first at the preserve's **visitor center** in Nome. Here you can pick up detailed site information; you can also view the tusk (7 feet long) and the bones (20,160 years old) of a woolly mammoth. Access to Bering Land Bridge is a challenge. No roads lead directly into the preserve, and its six public-use cabins are designed mainly for emergency use in winter. Once you move beyond the coastlines and barrier islands that form the preserve's frontier, you'll find extensive wet tundra. Treks inland (think teeming tussocks and massed mosquitoes) are the stuff of hiking nightmares. The rolling hills of the interior—where volcanic history is writ in lava flows near **Imuruk Lake** and in five large maar (crater) lakes in the **Devil Mountains-Cape Espenberg** area—are considerably more inviting.

Serpentine Hot Springs, a geothermal feature, is a popular fly-in destination. There you'll find a rustic bunkhouse that sleeps up to 20 people, as well as a wooden tub in a small bathhouse fed by the 140°F to 170°F spring water. Between soaks you can hike among the granite tors on the surrounding ridges and seek out alpine birds and large mammals. ■

Serpentine Hot Springs, Bering Land Bridge NP *Following pages: Near Serpentine Hot Springs*

Other Sites

The following is a select list of other sites of interest in Alaska.

Southeast

Point Bridget State Park

Forty miles north of Juneau, this 2,850-acre park offers several miles of scenic trails through meadows and open forests. The easy Point Bridget Trail (7 miles round-trip) has year-round access. Located at Mile 39 of the Glacier Highway, the trail starts on a boardwalk, crosses a meadow to the shore, then edges the beach to the point. Contact the Department of Natural Resources, Public Information Center, 550 W. 7th Ave., Ste. 1260, Anchorage, AK 99501; phone 907-269-8400. www.dnr.state .ak.us/parks/parks.htm

Sitka National Historical Park

Two special cultures in Alaska's history—Tlingit and Russian—are commemorated in the two units of this park. The Russian Bishop's House in downtown Sitka details the town's days as the capital of Russian America. The totem park at the eastern edge of town was the battle site between the Russians and Tlingits (see p. 35). Contact the park, 106 Metlakatla St., Sitka, AK 99835; phone 907-747-6281. www.nps.gov/sitk

South Prince of Wales Wilderness

At the southern tip of Prince of Wales Island, with a shoreline sculpted into myriad bays and inlets, this 91,000-acre wilderness area faces Dixon Entrance, Alaska's southern boundary waters with Canada. Exposed to winds and storms sweeping in off the North Pacific, the coast can be wild; it is accessible only by boat or floatplane. Salmon and Dolly Varden populate the wilderness area's streams and lakes. The intertidal zones along the rocky beaches are rich with giant barnacles, mussels, starfish, and clams. Contact Tongass National Forest, Centennial

Hall, 101 Egan Dr., Juneau, AK 99801; phone 907-586-8751. www.fs.fed.us/r10/tongass

Stikine-LeConte Wilderness

Located within Tongass National Forest, this 450,000-acre wilderness area is known for the powerful Stikine River, which flows out of the Cassiar Mountains of north central British Columbia and into the Inside Passage. A few miles from the town of Wrangell lies North America's southernmost tidewater glacier, LeConte Glacier. Popular activities include kayaking and rafting the Stikine from Telegraph Creek in B.C. to Wrangell; camping; and boat tours into the LeConte Glacier. Contact Tongass National Forest, Centennial Hall, 101 Egan Dr., Juneau, AK 99801; phone 907-586-8751. www.fs.fed.us/r10/tongass

West Chichagof-Yakobi Wilderness

Popular with kayakers and sailors, this wilderness of 265,000 acres lies in the extreme northwest of the Alexander Archipelago. With thousands of bays, islands, reefs, and water passages along the western portions of Chichagof and Yakobi Islands, the area offers endless exploring. Exposed to the storms of the North Pacific Ocean, open stretches can be very dangerous. Contact Tongass National Forest, Centennial Hall, 101 Egan Dr., Juneau, AK 99801; phone 907-586-8751. www.fs.fed .us/r10/tongass

South Central

Captain Cook Recreation Area

Splendid for camping and picnicking, this 3,500-acre park sits at the end of the North Kenai Road along Cook Inlet. It offers a variety of recreational activities: Walk the beaches, barbecue salmon high on the ocean bluff with a view of the Alaska Range, watch for beluga whales, or attend campfire talks. Contact the Department of Natural Resources, Public Information Center, 550 W. 7th Ave., Ste. 1260,

Anchorage, AK 99501; phone 907-269-8400. www.dnr.state .ak.us/parks/parks.htm

Clam Gulch State Recreation Area

If you're looking for the main ingredient for homemade clam chowder, this is the place to find it. Located 40 minutes south of Soldotna, the site invites you to dig for razor clams on the beach at low tide (fishing license required). Consult a tide book and local experts for ideal times and locations. You'll also need a bucket, a clam shovel, quick eyes, and fast reflexes. This 129-acre recreation area is near the town of Nilnilchik on the Kenai Peninsula at Mile 117 of the Sterling Highway. Contact the Department of Natural Resources, Public Information Center, 550 W. 7th Ave., Ste. 1260, Anchorage, AK 99501; phone 907-269-8400. www.dnr.state.ak .us/parks/parks.htm

Gulkana Wild and Scenic River

A popular Class I to IV white-water river, the main stem of the Gulkana can be accessed at Paxson Lake off the Richardson Highway at Mile 175 or Mile 179.5. The full 80-mile paddle is recommended for experienced paddlers only. Watch for sweepers, logjams, and Canyon Rapids, which necessitates a quarter-mile portage. Contact the Bureau of Land Management, 222 W. 7th Ave., Anchorage, AK 99501; phone 907-279-5960.

Lake Louise State Recreation Area

Lake Louise SRA, at Mile 160 of the Glenn Highway, offers easy access to its namesake lake in the Nelchina Basin. Trolling for lake trout can be excellent after ice-out. In winter, caribou migrate across the lake—even as the engines of recreational snowmachines echo in the backcountry. Contact Mat-Su State Park, HC 32 Box 6706, Wasilla, AK 99654; phone 907-745-3975. www.dnr.state .ak.us/parks/parks.htm

Palmer Hay Flats State Game Refuge

Driving north from Anchorage to Palmer, whether out the Glenn Highway toward Tok or up the George Parks Memorial Highway toward Denali National Park, you will cross the Palmer Hay Flats—prime moose country. Early mornings and late evenings are best for moose watching. Auto-moose collisions occur frequently in the area, so be alert while driving; you don't want to see those big eyes in your headlights. Caution is also advised in the backcountry, as Palmer Hay Flats is a prime waterfowl hunting area. Access to the refuge is via Fairview Loop Road off the Parks Highway. Contact the Alaska Department of Fish and Game, 333 Raspberry Rd., Anchorage, AK 99518; phone 907-267-2347. www.state.ak.us/adfg/

The Interior

Fortymile National Wild and Scenic River

Various road access points along the Taylor Highway make this Class I to IV river convenient for day- and multiday adventures. A float trip provides excellent opportunities to view gold-rush-era cabins and artifacts. Experienced anglers will find grayling fishing good. Wildlife viewing is exceptional in late autumn, with migrating caribou, moose, black bears, and the occasional grizzly. Contact the Northern District Office, Bureau of Land Management, 1150 University Ave., Fairbanks, AK 99709; phone 907-474-2300.

Big Delta State Historical Park

The historic 1909 Rika's Roadhouse, a remnant of the military telegraph line that spanned Alaska, provides a glimpse into old Alaska. Located at Mile 274.5 of the Richardson Highway, the park stands where a ferry once transported vehicles across the Tanana River. Contact the park, 3700 Airport Way, Fairbanks, AK 99709; phone 907-451-2695. www.dnr.state.ak.us/parks/parks.htm

Selawik National Wildlife Refuge

With no roads in the NWR and with air access only from Galena and Kotzebue, float trips on the Selawik National Wild River are solitary experiences. Fishing is excellent for sheefish, grayling, and northern pike. Wildlife viewing for waterfowl and caribou can be good too, giving you the opportunity to see nesting Asiatic whooper swans, a rarity in North America. Many hikes are found in the upland areas of the Waring Mountains. Be aware of local subsistence hunting in September. Contact the refuge, P.O. Box 270, Kotzebue, AK 99752; phone 907-442-3799.

Tok River State Recreation Site

After the long drive up the Alaska Highway through the Yukon Territory, this campground at Mile 1309 offers pleasant riverside camping, good fishing, and river access. Contact the Alaska Public Lands Information Center, Alaska Highway, Tok, AK 99780; phone 907-883-5667.

Walker Fork Campground

This campground, at Mile 82 of the Taylor Highway, offers good day hikes. A small gold dredge visible from the highway offers mute testimony to the "men who moiled for gold." For further historical interpretation visit the BLM's field office at Chicken (summer only), Mile 68.2 of the Taylor Highway. Contact the Northern District Office, Bureau of Land Management, 1150 University Ave., Fairbanks, AK 99709; phone 907-474-2300.

Yukon Flats National Wildlife Refuge

Larger than Maryland and Delaware combined, the refuge is pure Alaska wildlife—with the exception of seven isolated Native villages. Just 100 air miles north of Fairbanks, this is prime country for hunting, fishing, and wilderness camping. You can float through sections of the refuge via Beaver Creek, Birch Creek, and the Porcupine, Sheenjek, Chan-

dalar, and Yukon Rivers. Contact the refuge, P.O. Box 20, Fairbanks, AK 99701; phone 907-456-0440.

Southwest

Aniakchak National Monument and Preserve

The Aniakchak Caldera—among the largest on the Alaska Peninsula—lies within one of the most remote and least visited parks in the state. Its last volcanic activity occurred in 1931. The Aniakchak River has been designated wild and scenic. Remote wilderness camping, backpacking, and boating (highly experienced paddlers only) are the main attractions. Contact the Bureau of Land Management, P.O. Box 7, King Salmon, AK 99613; phone 907-246-3305. www.nps.gov/ania

Becharof National Wildlife Refuge

Becharof Lake, which dominates this 1.2-million-acre refuge on the Alaska Peninsula, serves as a nursery lake for one of the world's largest runs of salmon. Located between Katmai National Park and Alaska Peninsula National Wildlife Refuge, this refuge is home to brown bears, caribou, moose, wolves, and wolverines. Migratory whales, seals, sea lions, and sea otters may be seen along its coastline. Activities range from sport fishing and wildlife viewing to photography, camping, boating, and flight-seeing. Contact the refuge, P.O. Box 277, King Salmon, AK 99613; phone 907-246-4250. www.r7.fws.gov

Innoko National Wildlife Refuge

Traversed by a portion of the Iditarod Trail, this flat, swampy landscape supports abundant concentrations of white-fronted and Canada geese and pintail ducks. Accessed only by air and boat, the remote location assures excellent fishing for sheefish and northern pike. Be careful of moose hunters in autumn. In July the NWR boasts some of Alaska's best mosquito breeding habitat. Contact the refuge, P.O. Box 69, McGrath, AK 99627; phone 907-524-3251.

Izembek National Wildlife Refuge

This refuge averages only 12 clear days a year, but if you prepare for cold, damp weather, it can be an ornithological nirvana. In autumn—late August to October—great concentrations of migrating geese, including black

brant and emperor geese, mass here for migration. Salmon fishing in midsummer makes the limited access from Cold Bay worth the effort. Contact the refuge, P.O. Box 127, Cold Bay, AK 99571; phone 907-532-2445.

Pillar Mountain

For a photogenic view of the city of Kodiak and surrounding islands, take a drive up Pillar Mountain. If you happen to be here in late March,

stick around for the nationally renowned Pillar Mountain Golf Classic—one hole, par 70. Rules allow orange balls (for better visibility in the snow) but forbid the use of animals for retrieving lost balls or chainsaws for clearing the "fairway." Contact the Kodiak Island Convention and Visitors Bureau, 100 Marine Way, Kodiak, AK 99615; phone 907-486-4782. www.kodiak.org

---

Resources

The following is a select list of resources. Contact state and local associations for additional outfitter and lodging options.

Current information about road conditions is available at 907-586-8751.

Federal and State Agencies

Alaska Department of Fish and Game
P.O. Box 25526
Juneau, AK 99802
907-465-4100

Wildlife Information Center
333 Raspberry Rd.
Anchorage, AK 99518
907-267-2347
www.state.ak.us/adfg/
Hunting and fishing licenses, and site information.

Alaska Marine Highway System
P.O. Box 25535
Juneau, AK 99802
800-642-0066

605 W. 4th Ave.
Anchorage, AK 99501
907-272-7116
www.dot.state.ak.us
//external/amhs
Providing access to 32 Alaskan communities, the AMHS is an essential resource for exploring the inside passage. Complete schedule and fare information.

Alaska's National Parks
(See Alaska Public Lands Information Centers)

Alaska Public Lands Information Centers
605 W. 4th Ave.
Anchorage, AK 99501
907-271-2737

250 Cushman St., Ste. 1A
Fairbanks, AK 99701
907-456-0527

Southeast Alaska Discovery Center
50 Main St
Ketchikan, AK 99901
907-228-6220

Milepost 1314 Alaska Hwy.
Tok, AK 99780
907-883-5667
www.nps.gov/aplic/
These inter-agency offices allow visitors one-stop shopping for information on state and federally managed public lands. Recreation permits and reservations for backcountry cabins may also be made here. The Alaska Natural History Association has outlets in each of these locations selling natural history books, maps, and guides to all areas of Alaska. Fee for Ketchikan office during summer only.

Alaska State Parks
Department of Natural Resources
Public Information Center
550 W. 7th Ave., Ste. 1260
Anchorage, AK 99501
907-269-8400

3700 Airport Way
Fairbanks, AK 99709
907-451-2705

400 Willoughby Ave.
Juneau, AK 99801
907-465-4563

www.dnr.state.ak.us/parks
/parks.htm
Information on Alaska parks, including camping and cabin rentals.

Alaska State Office of Tourism
P.O. Box 110809
Juneau, AK 99811
907-465-2012
www.dced.state.ak.us
/tourism/
General resource for statewide travel, including accommodations.

Alaska Tourism Marketing Council
3601 C St., Ste. 700
Anchorage, AK 99503
www.travelalaska.com
General resource for travel, including accommodations, activities, and attractions.

U.S.D.A. Forest Service
Chugach National Forest
Public Information
3301 C St., Ste. 300
Anchorage, AK 99503
907-271-2500
www.fs.fed.us/r10/chugach
Source for maps, as well as recreational information in the forest, including cabins and camping.

U.S.D.A. Forest Service
Tongass National Forest
Forest Service Information Center
Centennial Hall
101 Egan Dr.
Juneau, AK 99801
907-586-8751
www.fs.fed.us/r10/tongass
Source for maps, as well as recreational information in the forest, including cabins and camping.

U.S. Fish and Wildlife Service
Public Information
Division of Refuges
1011 E. Tudor Rd.
Anchorage, AK 99503
907-786-3357
www.r7.fws.gov
Indepth information on
Alaska's national wildlife
refuges.

United States Geological
Survey
Earth Science Information
Center
4230 University Dr., Ste. 101
Anchorage, AK 99508
907-786-7011
Topographic maps to the
state of Alaska.

Lodging

See Alaska Tourism Marketing
Council (p. 280)

Bed & Breakfast Association
of Alaska
P.O. Box 202663
Anchorage, AK 99520
www.bbaa.alaska.com

Alaska Travel Adventures
888-778-7700
www.alaskarv.com
Recreational Vehicle campground information as well
as rentals.

American Youth Hostel, Inc.
700 H St.
Anchorage AK 99501
907-276-3635

Katmailand, Inc.
4125 Aircraft Dr.
Anchorage, AK 99502
907-243-5448 or
800-544-0551
Premier fishing lodges in
Katmai.

Camping

For a listing of private
campgrounds, contact the
Alaska Tourism Marketing
Council (see p. 280). Alaska
State Parks (see p. 280),
the U.S.D.A. Forest Service
(see p. 280), the National
Park Service, and the U.S.
Fish and Wildlife Service also
operate campgrounds
throughout the state. Additional information is available
through the Alaska Public
Lands Information Centers
(see p. 280) or online at
www.gorp.com.

Hotel and
Motel Chains

Best Western International
800-528-1234

Choice Hotels
800-4-CHOICE

Comfort Inns
800-228 5150

Days Inn
800-325-2525

Hilton Hotels
800-Hilton

Holiday Inns
800-HOLIDAY

Hyatt Hotels and Resorts
800-223-1234

Marriott Hotels Resorts
Suites
800-228-9290

Quality Inns
800-228-5151

Ramada Inns
800-2-RAMADA

Sheraton Hotels
800-325-3535

Westin Hotels and Resorts
800-325-3000

Outfitters
and Activities

The following is a select list.
For additional recommendations on licensed outfitters,
contact the Alaska Public
Lands Information Centers
(see p. 280).

ABEC's Alaska Adventures
1550 Alpine Vista Ct.
Fairbanks, AK 99712
907-457-8907 or
877-424-8907
www.abecalaska.com
Options include exploring
Gates of the Arctic NP, Arctic NWR, and the Brooks
Range.

Alaska Alpine Adventures
General Delivery
Port Alsworth, AK 99653
877-525-2577
www.alaskaalpineadventures
.com
AAA arranges small cus-
tom-designed backpacking
and river-running trips in
Lake Clark NP.

Alaska Backcountry
Adventures
P.O. Box 362
Kenai, AK 99611
907-835-5608 or
888-283-9354

www.alaskabackcountry.com
Ski plane or helicopter
transportation into the
Chugach range for extreme
skiing and snowboarding.

Alaska Discovery
5449 Shaune Dr.
Juneau, AK 99801
907-780-6226 or
800-586-1911
www.akdiscovery.com
Guided kayak tours of
Glacier Bay and Wrangell-
St. Elias NPs

Alaska Seaplane Service
1873 Shell Simmions Dr.
Juneau, AK 99801
907-789-3331
www.akseaplanes.com
Flight-seeing and charters
in southeast Alaska.

Alaska Troutfitters
P.O. Box 570
Cooper Landing, AK 99572
907 457-8907 or
877-424-8907
www.aktroutfitters.com
Experienced fly-fishing
service on the headwaters
of the Kenai River.

Alaskan Wilderness Sailing
and Kayaking
P.O. Box 1313
Valdez, AK 99686
907-835-5175
www.alaskan.com
/alaskanwilderness
Sailing, kayaking, and hiking
tours of Prince William
Sound.

Alaska Waters, Inc.
P.O. Box 1978
Wrangell, AK 99929
907-874-2378 or
800-347-4462
www.alaskawaters.com
Adventure tours, sportfishing charters, and guided
trips of the Inside Passage
and Tongass National Forest.

Chilkat Guides, Ltd
P.O. Box 170
Haines, AK 99827
907-766-2491
Eagle tours in the Chilkat
Valley.

Equinox Wilderness Expeditions
618 W. 14th Ave.
Anchorage, AK 99501
907-274-9087 or
877-615-9087
www.equinoxexpeditions
.com

Adventures throughout the state; specializes in custom and women-only trips.

Interior Alaska Adventures
269 Topside Rd.
Fairbanks, AK 99712
800-890-3229
www.aktours.net
Single and multi-day tours showcase the Interior's fishing, hiking, and wildlife.

Kantishna Air Taxi
P.O Box 46
Denali Park, AK 99755
907-683-1223
www2.gorp.com/katair
/index.htm
Flight-seeing tours of Denali. Custom charters to any Alaska destination. Excellent photo tours.

Ketchum Air
N. Shore Lake Hood
Anchorage, AK 99501
907-423-5525 or
800-433-9114
www.ketchumair.com
Flight-seeing and charters, as well as fishing and bear-viewing tours.

Lake Clark Air Inc.
Port Alsworth, AK 99653
907-781-2208 or
888-440-2281
www.lakeclarkair.com
Located within the national park, Lake Clark provides air services, lodging, and guiding.

Lifetime Adventures
P.O. Box 1205
Palmer, AK 99645
907-746-4644
www.lifetimeadventures.net
Tours and rentals for exploring Katmai NP and Chugach SP.

McCarthy Creek Outfitters
HC 60 Box 299C
Copper Center, AK 99573
907-822-3410
www.mccarthycreek.com
Half-day to multi-day horseback and fishing trips in Wrangell-St. Elias NP.

National Outdoor
Leadership School
288 Main St.
Lander, WY 82520
307-332-5300
www.nols.edu
With a campus in Palmer, the National Outdoor Leadership School offers

courses in canoeing, kayaking, backpacking, and mountaineering.

Osprey Expeditions
HC 60 Box 246
Copper Center, AK 99573
907-822-5422
www.ospreyexpeditions.com
Fully guided wilderness rafting in the Copper River valley.

Pangaea Adventures
P.O. Box 775
Valdez, AK 99686
www.pangaeaadventures
.com
907-835-8442 or
800-660-9637
Sailing and boat tours of Prince William Sound. Multi-activity tours combine kayaking, rafting, and backpacking.

Prince William Sound Cruises and Tours
P.O. Box 1297
Valdez, AK 99686
907-835-4731 or
800-992-1297
www.princewilliamsound
.com
Cruises and guided kayaking and sailing from Valdez and Whittier.

River Wrangellers
P.O. Box 146
Gakona, AK 99586
907 822-3967 or
888-822-3967
www.alaskariver
wrangellers.com
White-water rafting in south central Alaska.

Royal Coachman Lodge,
P.O. Box 450
Dillingham, AK 99576
907-868-6033
www.royalcoachmanlodge
.com
Fishing and accommodations in Wood-Tickchik State Park

Rust's Flying Service
P.O. Box 19035
Anchorage, AK 99510
907-243-1595 or
800-544-2299
www.flyrusts.com
Fishing and flight-seeing tours in Prince William Sound.

Sea Otter Kayak
P.O. Box 228
Gustavus, AK 99836

907-697-3007
www.he.net/~seaotter
Kayak rentals and day cruises of Glacier Bay.

Sourdough Outfitters
P.O. Box 26066
Bettles, AK 99726
907-5252
www.sourdough.com
Explore the North Slope by dog sled. Summer activities include hiking and rafting in the Brooks Range.

Spirit Walker Expeditions
P.O. Box 240
Gustavus, AK 99826
907-697-2266 or
800-529-2537
www.he.net/~kayak/
Hiking, kayaking throughout the southeast.

St. Elias Alpine Guides
P.O. Box 111241
Anchorage, AK 99511
907-277-6867 or
888-933-5427
Hiking, ice climbing, mountaineering, and rafting in Wrangell-St. Elias NP.

Stickeen Wilderness
Adventures
P.O. Box 934
Wrangell, AK, 99929
907-874-2085 or
800-874-2085
www.akgetaway.com
/wildside/
Guided bear-watching trips to Anan Wildlife Observatory.

Wilderness Alaska
P.O. Box 113063
Anchorage, AK 99511
907-345-3567
www.wildernessalaska.com
Offering 4- to 8-day hiking trips in Prince William Sound, the custom outfitter limits group sizes.

Wood River Lodge
P O Box 1369
Dillingham, Ak 99576
800-842-5205
www.woodriverlodge.com
All inclusive fishing lodge in Wood-Tickchik SP.

Wrangell Mountain Air
#25 P.O. Box MXY
McCarthy, AK 99588
800-478-1160
www.wrangellmountainair
.com/
Flight-seeing tours and charters to Wrangell-St. Elias NP.

Index

Abbreviations

NF=National Forest
NHP=National Historical Park
NM=National Monument
NP=National Park
NWR=National Wildlife Refuge
SP=State Park

A

Admiralty Island NM-
  Kootznoowoo Wilderness
  26, 38–46
Admiralty Lakes Recreational
  Area 44–46
Adolphus, Point 50–51
Aerial sightseeing 20: Denali
  National Park and Preserve
  180; Katmai National Park
  and Preserve 217; Kodiak
  NWR 221; Mendenhall
  Glacier 49
Afognak SP 223
Air travel 198–199: Arctic
  NWR 254; Cape Krusen-
  stern NM 273; helicopter
  services to ski sites 94; Kat-
  mai National Park and Pre-
  serve 215; Kayak Island 101;
  Lake Clark National Park
  and Preserve 209; safety
  212–213
Alagnak National Wild and
  Scenic River 217
Alaska Bald Eagle Festival 60
Alaska Bird Observatory 184
Alaska Chilkat Bald Eagle
  Preserve 59–60
Alaska Maritime NWR 233–237
Alaska Mountain Safety
  Center 125
Alaska National Interest Lands
  Conservation Act of 1980
  (ANILCA) 39, 192, 208
Alaska Native Heritage Center
  108–110
Alaska Pipeline 244; See also
  Trans-Alaska Oil Pipeline
Alaska Range 158, 161: affecting
  interior of Alaska 165; from
  the Tony Knowles Coastal
  Trail 111
Alaska Raptor Center 37
Alaska SeaLife Center 125–126
Alaskan husky dogs 139–140
Aleutian Trench 205
Alutiiq Museum and Archaeo-
  logical Repository 224
Alyeska, Mt. 122
Alyeska Ski Resort 115
Amphitheater Mountains 158
Anan Wildlife Observatory 32
Anchorage 79: Chigmit Moun-
  tains 207; Chugach SP
  102–108; Iditarod Trail Sled
  Dog Race 139, 142; Tony
  Knowles Coastal Trail
  110–111; Wrangell-St. Elias

National Park and
  Preserve 82
Angoon 41, 45
Anktuvuk Pass 261, 264
Archaeology: Bering Land
  Bridge 274; Cape Krusen-
  stern NM 272–273; Kobuk
  Valley NP 268; Tangle Lakes
  Archaeological District 156
Arctic Circle 246; See also
  Summer solstice
Arctic NWR 241, 247, 252–259
Ardaw, "Russian Mike" 144
Athabascan Indian tribe 270
Audubon Society 224

B

Babbitt, Bruce 253
Bagley Icefield 81
Baird Mountains 267, 268
Balto (sled dog) 143
Bananza Creek Experimental
  Forest 181
Baranof Museum 224
Barnaby Rudge (Dickens) 130
Barrow 240
Bartlett Cove 57
Bay of Islands 217
Beachcombing: Admiralty Island
  NM-Kootznoowoo Wilder-
  ness 41, 44; Kayak Island
  79, 101
Bears: safety around 42–43,
  151, 175
Beaver Creek National Wild
  River 188, 189, 191
Beehive Island 237
Beluga Point 114
Bennett Lake 66
Bering, Vitus 93, 100
Bering Glacier 79, 81
Bering Land Bridge National
  Preserve 274, 275
Bettles 261
Bicycling: Kincaid Park 112;
  Seward Highway 115;
  Thompson Pass 95;
  Wrangell-St. Elias National
  Park and Preserve 85–86, 86
Big Windy Hot Springs
  Research Natural Area 192
Billy's Hole 99
Birch Creek National Wild and
  Scenic River 192, 194–195
Bird Ridge 107, 107
Bird watching 20, 100; See also
  Wildlife viewing
Bird's Eye Peak 107
Blackstone Bay 92
Blueberry picking: Chugach NF
  96; Fox Island 128; Kenai
  NWR 132; Nabesna Road 87
Boat building 108, 110
Boating: Arctic NWR 256–257,
  259; Beaver Creek National
  Wild River 191; Chugach SP
  108; Delta Wild and Scenic
  River 158; Gates of the

Arctic National Park and
  Preserve 265; Inside Passage
  22–26; Kobuk Valley NP 269,
  271; Kodiak Island Archipel-
  ago 223; Noatak National
  Wild and Scenic River
  267–268; Porcupine River
  251; safety 212–213; Wood-
  Tikchik SP 232; Yukon-
  Charley Rivers National
  Preserve 197–199; See also
  Canoeing; Cruises; Kayaking;
  Sailing
Boca de Quadra 28
British Columbia, Canada 24
Brooks Range 161, 242, 243:
  and the Arctic NWR 259;
  from Sukakpak Mountain 248
Brooks River National Historic
  Landmark 215
Buldir Island 235
Bureau of Land Management
  (BLM) 245

C

Cabin facilities 26: Admiralty
  Lakes Recreational Area 46;
  Anan Wildlife Observatory
  32; Chugach NF 98; Denali
  SP 150–151; Eagle River
  Nature Center 105; Fox
  Island 128; Kenai Fjords NP
  121; Kodiak Island Archipel-
  ago 223; Misty Fiords NM
  31; Nancy Lake SRA 145;
  Prince William Sound 91;
  Steese National Conserva-
  tion Area 193; White Moun-
  tains NRA 190; Wrangell-St.
  Elias National Park and
  Preserve 86
Caines Head SRA 127
Camping: Chatanika River
  Recreation Site and Area
  187; Chena River SRA
  185–186; Denali Highway
  Scenic Drive 157; Denali
  National Park and Preserve
  174, 177, 180; Denali SP
  150–151; and fires 7; Katmai
  National Park and Preserve
  215, 217–218; Kodiak Island
  Archipelago 222–223; low
  impact 6–7; Nancy Lake
  SRA 145; Tetlin NWR 195;
  Walrus Islands State Game
  Sanctuary 229; White
  Mountains NRA 189; Wood-
  Tikchik SP 232
Canada: Chilkoot Trail 67;
  Dawson, Yukon Territory 66,
  198; Kluane NP, Yukon
  Territory 80
Canning River 259
Canoeing: Cross Admiralty
  Canoe Route 45–46; Birch
  Creek National Wild and
  Scenic River 194–195;
  Chatanika River Recreation

Site and Area 187; Chena River SRA 186; Denali Highway Scenic Drive 156, 157; Denali SP 152; Katmai National Park and Preserve 217; Kenai NWR 132; Lake Clark National Park and Preserve 209, 210; Nancy Lake SRA 145; *See also* Boating; Kayaking

Canyon Creek 274

Cape Krusenstern NM 272–273

Caribou Mountain 246

Carolus, Point 52

Cenotaph Island 73

Center for Alaskan Coastal Studies 138

Chamberlin, Mount 256

Chandalar Shelf 248

Charley River 196, 198

Chatanika River Recreation Site and Area 187

Chena River SRA 185–186

Chigmit Mountains 207

Chilkat Inlet 61

Chilkat River 60

Chilkat SP 61

Chilkoot Inlet 61

Chilkoot Trail 65–67

China Poot Lake 138

Chiswell Island 237

Chitistone canyon 82

Chugach NF 91, 96–100, 114

Chugach SP 79, 102–108, 114, 122

Clarence Strait 36

Climbing: Arctic NWR 255–256; Chugach SP 107–108; McKinley, Mt. 180; Wrangell-St. Elias National Park and Preserve 86

Coldfoot 248, 264

College Fjord 88, 92

Columbia Glacier 92, 100

Cook, James 56, 88, 114

Cook Inlet 111, 204, 205, 206

Copper River 85, 100

Copper River Delta Shorebird Festival 100

Crane Festival 184

Crater Lake 274

Creamer, Anna and Charles 183

Creamer's Field Migratory Waterfowl Refuge 182–184

Creek Street 33

Cross Admiralty Canoe Route 45–46

Cruises: Cross Admiralty Canoe Route 46; Glacier Bay National Park and Preserve 57; Kachemak Bay SP and State Wilderness Park 135, 138; Kenai Fjords NP 124; Misty Fords NM 31; Portage Lake 115; Prince William Sound 92; Russell Fiord Wilderness 71

Curry Ridge 151

D

Dall, William H. 117

Dalton Highway *see* James Dalton Highway

Dancing 110

Davidson Ditch 190

Davidson Glacier 61

Dawson, Yukon Territory, Canada 66, 198

Deadhorse 251

Deborah, Mt. 157

Deer Mountain Trail 36

Delta Wild and Scenic River 158

Denali 15; *See also* McKinley, Mt. (Denali)

Denali Highway Scenic Drive 154–157

Denali National Park and Preserve 148, 154, 166–180

Denali SP 78, 148–152

Dewey Lake 65

Dickens, Charles 130

Disenchantment Bay 68, 69, 72

Dog mushing 142–143

Douglas, William O. 259

Douglas Creek 267

Drum, Mount 155

E

Eagle Council Grounds 60

Eagle River 108

Eagle River Nature Center 105

Earthquakes 15 along Aleutian Trench 205; Lituya Bay 73; Prince William Sound 90, 95; Wrangell-St. Elias National Park and Preserve 81

Eickelberg Bay 99

Eklutna Glacier 107

Eklutna Lake 108

Endicott Arm 47

Exit Glacier 118, 121

Exxon Valdez (ship) 90, 125, 247

F

Fairbanks 181, 183

Fairweather, Mount 56

Fairweather Range 73

False Peak 104

Far North Bicentennial Park 112

Fata morgana (atmospheric phenomenon) 202

Ferries 26; Angoon 45; Prince William Sound 91–92

Fesler, Doug 107

Fires, camp 7

Fishing: Admiralty Lakes Recreational Area 45; Birch Creek National Wild and Scenic River 194; Chena River SRA 186; Chugach NF 98–99; Denali SP 152; Jim River 247; Katmai National Park and Preserve 217; Kenai Fjords NP 124; Kenai River 129–131; Kobuk Valley NP 271; Minto Flats State Game Sanctuary 181; Nancy Lake

SRA 145; salmon 153; Seward Peninsula 274; Tetlin NWR 195; White Mountains NRA 189; Wood-Tikchik SP 230, 232; Wrangell-St. Elias National Park and Preserve 86; Yukon-Charley Rivers National Preserve 198

Fords Terror 47

Fort Abercrombie State Historical Park 224

Fort McGilvray 127

Fox Island 128

Franklin, Benjamin 59

Franklin, John 251

Frederick Sound 26

G

Galloping glaciers 70

Gastineau Channel 50

Gates of the Arctic National Park and Preserve 260–265

Geology 78, 204–205: affecting the Trans-Alaska Oil Pipeline 247; Alaska Range 165; arctic Alaska 242; Chena River SRA 186; Coast Mountains 20; Gates of the Arctic National Park and Preserve 260–261; Kodiak Island Archipelago 220; Steese National Conservation Area 192; White Mountains NRA 188–189; Wrangell-St. Elias National Park and Preserve 81; Yukon-Charley Rivers National Preserve 196–197; *See also* Earthquakes; Glaciers/glacial activity; Volcanic activity

George Parks Highway 148

George W. Elder (ship) 88

Georgia, Strait of 24

Glacier Bay 17–18, 50

Glacier Bay National Park and Preserve 52–58

Glaciers/glacial activity 20, 58: Admiralty Island NM-Kootznoowoo Wilderness 39–40; Brooks Range 261; Chugach NF 99–100; Chugach SP 107; Denali Highway Scenic Drive 156; Glacier Bay National Park and Preserve 53, 56; Harding Icefield 120; Hubbard Glacier 68–69, 72; Kenai Fjords NP 121; Mendenhall Glacier 48–49; movement of 70; south central region 75, 78; Tracy Arm-Fords Terror Wilderness 46–47; Wrangell-St. Elias National Park and Preserve 81–82

Gold mining 90 along Tintina fault line 196–197; Chilkoot Trail 65 Hope 118; Iditarod National Historic Trail 140; Independence Mine State

Historical Park 146; Klondike Gold Rush NHP 62–63; Koyukuk River 247–248
Griggs, Robert 204, 214
Gull Island 138

H

Haines 60
Harding Icefield 119–120, 124
Harriman, Edward 88
Harriman Fiord 88, 92
Helicopter guide services ski trips 94
Heney, Michael J. 64
Hiking 122–123; Arctic NWR 255; Bering Land Bridge National Preserve 275; Chatanika River Recreation Site and Area 187; Chena River SRA 186; Chilkat SP 61; Chilkoot Trail 66–67; Chugach NF 98; Chugach SP 104–105, 107; Creamer's Field Migratory Waterfowl Refuge 183; Deer Mountain Trail 36; Denali National Park and Preserve 175–177, 180; Denali SP 151–152; Gates of the Arctic National Park and Preserve 264–265; Glacier Bay National Park and Preserve 57; Iditarod National Historic Trail 143; Independence Mine State Historical Park 146–147; Kachemak Bay SP and State Wilderness Park 138; Katmai National Park and Preserve 215–217; Kenai Fjords NP 121, 124; Kenai NWR 132; Kincaid Park 112; Klondike Gold Rush NHP 65; Kodiak Island Archipelago 222–223, 224; Lake Clark National Park and Preserve 209–210; Mendenhall Glacier 49; Misty Fiords NM 31; Nancy Lake SRA 145; Roberts, Mount 50; safety 104, 213; Walrus Islands State Game Sanctuary 229; White Mountains NRA 188–189, 190–191; Wrangell-St. Elias National Park and Preserve 84–85; Yukon-Charley Rivers National Preserve 199
Hillside Park 112
Hilltop Ski Area 112
Hinckley, Charles and Belle 183
History: Creek Street 33; Kennicott 84; Klondike Gold Rush NHP 62–63; See also Gold mining
Hope 118
Hubbard, Gardiner Greene 72
Hubbard Glacier 68, 69–70, 72, 81
Hulahula River 259

Hunting 181, 195
Husky dogs 139–140
Hypothermia 213

I

Ice worms 90
Icebergs 20; Glacier Bay National Park and Preserve 53; Tracy Arm-Fords Terror Wilderness 46–47
Ice-climbing: Mendenhall Glacier 49; Thompson Pass 94–95
Iditarod National Historic Trail 79, 139–143; Seward 118; Yakedeyak Creek 107
Iditarod Trail Sled Dog Race 79, 139–143
Independence Mine State Historical Park 146–147
Indians of North America 25, 270; Alaska Native Heritage Center 108; Alutiiq Museum and Archaeological Repository 224; Cape Krusenstern NM 272–273; Gates of the Arctic National Park and Preserve 261; totem poles 34–35; University of Alaska Museum 184
Inside Passage 18, 22–26, 100
International Biosphere Reserve 266
International Date Line 15
Interpretive activities: Alaska SeaLife Center 126; Begich, Boggs Visitor Center 117; Center for Alaskan Coastal Studies 138; Chugach NF 100; Denali National Park and Preserve 173, 177; Denali SP 150; Eagle River Nature Center 105; Independence Mine State Historical Park 146; Katmai National Park and Preserve 216; Kenai NWR 132; Tetlin NWR 195
Inupiat Indian tribe 268, 269, 270, 272–273
Island of Fear 38

J

James Dalton Highway 243, 244–251, 264
Johns Hopkins Inlet 53
Jones, Robert D. 234–235
Juneau Icefield 48

K

Kachemak Bay SP and State Wilderness Park 134–138
Kanuti NWR 246
Karstens, Henry P. 167
Katmai, Mount 204, 214
Katmai National Park and Preserve 214–219
Kauffman, John 206
Kayak Island 100–101

Kayaking: Admiralty Island NM-Kootznoowoo Wilderness 41; Birch Creek National Wild and Scenic River 194–195; Chatanika River Recreation Site and Area 187; Chena River SRA 186; Chugach NF 98; Fox Island 128; Glacier Bay National Park and Preserve 57; Katmai National Park and Preserve 217; Kenai NWR 132; Lake Clark National Park and Preserve 210; Misty Fiords NM 31; Prince William Island 92–93; Russell Fiord Wilderness 71; Tracy Arm-Fords Terror Wilderness 47; Wrangell-St. Elias National Park and Preserve 85
Kenai Canoe Trails (Quick) 132
Kenai Fjords NP 114, 118, 119–124
Kenai NWR 131–133
Kenai Pathways (Alaska Natural History Association) 132
Kenai River 129–130
Kennicott 84
Kent, Rockwell 128
Ketchikan Creek 33
Kincaid Park 110, 112
Klondike Gold Rush NHP 20, 62–65
Kluane NP, Yukon Territory, Canada 80
Knowles, Tony 110
Kobuk Valley NP 243, 268–271
Kodiak Island Archipelago 220–224
Kodiak NWR 221–222
Kongakut River 259
Kootznoowoo Wilderness 38–46
Koyukuk River 247, 265
Krusenstern, Captain Johann Von 272
Kuskulana River 84

L

La Pérouse, Jean-François 73
Lake Clark National Park and Preserve 206–210
Large Animal Reseach Station 184
Leave No Trace (educational program) 6
Leopold, Aldo 182
Lindeman Lake 66
Lituya Bay 73
Logan, Mount 69
London, Jack 164
Lower Fuller Lake 132

M

Mackey, Dick 140
Maclaren Glacier 156
Maclaren Summit 156
Malaspina, Alessandro 68

Marathon, Mount 125
Margerie Glacier 53
Married Man's Trail 33
Marshall, Bob 242
Matanuska Glacier 78
Matanuska Valley 78–79
Maurelle Islands Wilderness 18
McCarthy Road 83–84
McKinley, Mt. (Denali) 15, 20, 78:
    climbing 180; dog sledding
    140; elevation 176; geology
    165; Tony Knowles Coastal
    Trail 111; See also Denali
    National Park and Preserve
McNeil State Game
    Sanctuary 211
McPhee, John 145
Melford, Michael 12, 71
Mendenhall Glacier 48–49
Midnight sun 192, 240–241
Migrations, human 274, 275
Minto Flats State Game
    Sanctuary 181
Misty Fiords NM 18, 28–31
Mitchell Bay 41, 44–45
Mosquito Pass 274
Mosquitoes 157, 254
Mountain biking 86
Muir, John 17, 56, 88
Murie, Adolph 172
Murie, Olaus and Margaret 259

N

Nabesna Road 83, 85, 87
Nancy Lake SRA 144–145
National Geographic Society
    70: Gardiner Hubbard 72;
    Mount Katmai explosion
    204, 21
National Park Service 70
Native Americans see Indians of
    North America
Nenana River 157
Nenana to Fairbanks 181
Nenana to Fairbanks Scenic
    Drive 181
New Eddystone Rock 28
Noatak 268
Noatak National Preserve 243,
    266–268
Noatak National Wild and
    Scenic River 267
Nome 141: gold discovered in
    140; Iditarod Trail Sled Dog
    Race 139, 142
Nome Creek Valley 189
North West Mounted Police 65
Novarupta volcano 214
Nugget Creek 86, 248
Nunamiut 264
Nunataks 119

O

Oil production 239, 247, 253;
    See also Trans-Alaska Oil
    Pipeline
Oliver Inlet 41
Olson Lake 246

One Man's Wilderness
    (Proenneke) 208
Orloff, Ivan 201, 204

P

Parasailing 50
Pedro, Felix 187
Permafrost 84, 242
Peter the Great, Emperor
    (Russia) 93
Peters Glacier 166
Phelan Creek 158
Pingos 84
Pinnell Mountain 193
Plain of Monuments 186
Plants 79, 164–165, 173:
    Admiralty Island NM;
    Kootznoowoo Wilderness
    39; Chugach NF 96; Chugach
    SP 103; Kenai Fjords NP
    120; Misty Fiords NM 31;
    Sukakpak Mountain 248
Pollution 243
Poot Peak 138
Porcupine River 251
Portage Creek 267
Portage Glacier 99, 115
Portage Lake 115
Potter Marsh 113, 114
Pribilof Islands 204, 237
Price, Stan 45
Prince of Wales Island 24
Prince William Sound 78,
    88–93, 96: earthquake (1964)
    95; Kenai Fjords NP 121
Prindle, Mount 189
Proenneke, Dick 208
Prospect Creek 246
Ptarmigan Lake 123
Punchbowl Cove 31
Punchbowl Lake 31
Pyramid Mountain 176

Q

Queen Charlotte Sound 24
Quick, Daniel 132

R

Races: Iditarod Trail Sled Dog
    Race 139–143; Iditasport
    races 142; Mount Marathon
    foot race 125; Yukon Quest
    International Sled Dog
    Race 194
Rafting: Denali National Park
    and Preserve 180; Kenai
    NWR 132–133; Prince
    William Island 93; Wrangell-
    St. Elias National Park and
    Preserve 85
Railroads 64
Rainbow Glacier 61
Redington, Joe, Sr. 12, 140
Redoubt Volcano 207
Reed Lakes 147
Reid, Frank 63
Riley, Mount 61
Ring of Fire 15, 204

Ripinski, Mount 61
Roberts, Mount 50
Roosevelt, Theodore 96, 167
Round Island 228, 234
Russell, Israel 72
Russell Fiord Wilderness 68–71
Russian Lakes 122–123

S

Safety issues 212–213: Alaska
    Mountain Safety Center
    125; Arctic NWR 254;
    avalanches 147; bears
    42–43, 151, 175; glaciers
    121; hiking 104, 123; tides
    127; weather 210
Sailing 93
Saint Elias, Mount 20, 69, 86
Saint Elias Mountains 68, 72
Salmon 33, 59, 79, 153, 211
A Sand County Almanac
    (Leopold) 182
Sand dunes 271
Sawyer Glacier 46
Saxman Totem Park 34
Scenic drives: Chena Hot
    Springs Road 185; Denali
    Highway 154–157; Denali
    National Park and Preserve
    170–173; George Parks
    Highway 154; James Dalton
    Highway 244–251; Nabesna
    Road 87; Nenana to Fair-
    banks 181; Seward Highway
    114–118; Wrangell-St. Elias
    National Park and Preserve
    83–84
Seduction Point 61
Seldovia 138
Serpentine Hot Springs 275
Service, Robert W. 90
Seward 118, 125
Seward Highway 114–118
Seward Peninsula 273–274
Seymour Canal 41, 43
Seymour Canal Eagle
    Management Area 41
Sheenjek River 259
Sheldon, Bobby 184
Sheldon, Charles 167
Shrimp 138
Shuyak SP 223
Sitka NHP 35
Skagway 26, 62–64
Skiing 79: Alyeska Ski Resort
    115; Independence Mine
    State Historical Park 147;
    Kincaid Park 112; Thompson
    Pass 94
Skilak Lake 130, 131, 132
Sleeping Lady (Mount
    Susitna) 111
Smith, Soapy 63
South Fork Campbell Creek 104
South Sawyer Glacier 46
Spencer, Bill 125
Stan Price State Wildlife
    Sanctuary 41
Steele, Samuel 63

Steese National Conservation Area 192–195
Steller, Georg Wilhelm 79, 101
Stephens Passage 26
Sukakpak Mountain 248
Summer solstice 192, 240–241
Sumner, Lowell 254
Susitna River 156, 157

T

Taiga 173
Talbot, Bruce 112
Tanana Valley State Forest 181
Tangle Lakes 156, 158
Tatshenshini-Alsek Provincial Park, British Columbia, Canada 80
Tazimina Lakes 210
Teklanika flats 172
Telaquana Lake 210
Tetlin NWR 195
Thompson Pass 94–95
Thorofare Pass 173
Tidal bores 118
Tidal Inlet 53
Tides 73
Tikchik Lakes 230
Tillion, Diana 135
Timberline zone 241
Tlikakila National Wild River 210
Togo (sled dog) 143
Tongass NF 18, 26, 28–31, 39
Tony Knowles Coastal Trail 110–111, 112
Toolik Lake Area of Critical Environmental Concern/Research Natural Area 248
Totem Bight State Historical Park 34
Totem Heritage Center 34
Totem poles 34–35

Tracy Arm-Fords Terror Wilderness Area 46–47
Train rides 64
Trans-Alaska Oil Pipeline 244, 245, 247
Tsunamis 95
Tundra 173
Turnagain Arm 114
Turnagain Pass 117–118
Turquoise Lake 210
Tustumena Lake 131
Twin Bears Lake 186

U

UNESCO 266
United Nations 80
University of Alaska 70: museum 184

V

Valdez Ice Climbing Festival 95
Vancouver, George 28, 38, 56, 92
Vancouver Island, B. C., Canada 24
Variegated Glacier 70
Volcanic activity 15: Katmai, Mount 204, 214; Redoubt Volcano 207; Ring of Fire 204–205; Wrangell-St. Elias National Park and Preserve 81

W

Walker, Tom 12
Walker Cove 28
Walrus Islands State Game Sanctuary 225–229
Weather 165, 210, 212–213: animals adapting to 265; fata morgana 207–208

Wheelchair accessibility; Tetlin NWR 195
White Mountains NRA 190
White Mountains NRA 188–191
White Pass & Yukon Railroad 64, 67
Whitewater rafting 210
Wickersham, James A. 166
Wilderness: A Journal of Quiet Adventure in Alaska (Kent) 128
Wilderness Act of 1964 18
Wilderness areas definition 18
The Wilderness of Denali (Sheldon) 167
Wilson, Woodrow 167, 214
Windfall Harbor 40
Windy Arch 188
Wolverine Peak 122
Wood-Tikchik SP 230–232
World Heritage Sites
Wrangell-St. Elias National Park and Preserve 80
World War II 127
Worthington Glacier SRA 95
Wrangell-St. Elias National Park and Preserve 78, 80–86, 87

Y

Yakutat 70, 71
Yakutat Bay 68, 85
Yukon Flats NWR 245
Yukon Quest International Sled Dog Race 194
Yukon River 66
Yukon Territory, Canada 80, 198
Yukon-Charley Rivers National Preserve 196–199
Yup'ik 270, 273

About the Authors and Photographer

Nan Elliot, a writer and filmmaker who lives in Anchorage, is the editor of *Best Places Alaska.* She loves wilderness, adventure, wild creatures, humorous characters, and the high and beautiful places of the world, and has spent her career telling stories about them.

Tom Walker lives on the outskirts of Denali National Park and Preserve. He has explored and photographed most of Alaska (as well as many other wild regions around the world) for the last 35 years. Walker's latest book is *Caribou: Wanderers of the Tundra* (Graphic Arts Center Publishing, 2000).

Michael Melford is a renowned photographer whose assignments include both travel and editorial photography. His award-winning work has appeared in many major U.S. publications, including *National Geographic Traveler, Travel and Leisure, Life, Fortune,* and *Newsweek.* He lives with his family in Mystic, Connecticut.

Illustrations Credits

All images by Michael Melford except for the following:

P. 44, Barbara Brundege/Ken Graham Agency; p. 101, Barbara Brundege/Ken Graham Agency; p. 117, Rich Reid/Colors of Nature; p. 139, Ken Souders/Ken Graham Agency; p. 141, Jeff Schultz/Alaska Stock; p. 250 (up), Rich Reid/Colors of Nature; p. 250 (low), Tom Walker/Ken Graham Agency

National Geographic Guide to America's Outdoors: Alaska
by Nan Elliot and Tom Walker
Photographed by Michael Melford

Published by the National Geographic Society
John M. Fahey, Jr., *President and Chief Executive Officer*
Gilbert M. Grosvenor, *Chairman of the Board*
Nina D. Hoffman, *Executive Vice President,*
 President, Books and School Publishing

Prepared by the Book Division
Elizabeth L. Newhouse, *Director of Travel Publishing*
Allan Fallow, *Senior Editor and Series Director*
Cinda Rose, *Art Director*
Barbara Noe, *Senior Editor*
Caroline Hickey, *Senior Researcher*
Carl Mehler, *Director of Maps*

Staff for this Book
Keith R. Moore, *Book Manager*
Robin Currie, Kim Kostyal, Mary Luders, Jarelle S. Stein, *Editors*
Joan Wolbier, *Designer*
Marilyn Gibbons, *Illustrations Editor*
Victoria Garrett Jones, Sean M. Groom, Elizabeth Lenhart,
 Jane Sunderland, *Researchers*
Lise Sajewski, *Editorial Consultant*
Matt Chwastyk, Jerome N. Cookson, Sven M. Dolling, Thomas L. Gray, Joseph F. Ochlak,
 Nicholas P. Rosenbach, Gregory Ugiansky, National Geographic Maps,
 Mapping Specialists, XNR Productions, *Map Edit, Research, and Production*
Tibor G. Tóth, *Map Relief*
R. Gary Colbert, *Production Director*
Cynthia M. Combs, *Illustrations Assistant*
Julia Marshall, *Indexer*
Larry Porges, *Editorial Coordinator*
Deb Antonini, *Contributor*
John Kauffman, *Consultant*

Manufacturing and Quality Control
George V. White, *Director;* John T. Dunn, *Associate Director;* Vincent P. Ryan, *Manager;*
Phillip L. Schlosser, *Financial Analyst*

Library of Congress Cataloging-in-Publication Data

Elliot, Nan.
  Guide to America's outdoors. Alaska / by Nan Elliot and Tom Walker; photography by Michael Melford.
      p. cm. — (National Geographic guides to America's outdoors)
    Includes index.
    ISBN 0-7922-7747-3
      1. Alaska—Guidebooks. 2. National parks and reserves—Alaska—Guidebooks. 3. Outdoor recreation—
  Alaska—Guidebooks. I. Title: Alaska. II. Walker, Tom, 1945- III. Melford, Michael IV. Title.
    F902.3 .E45 2001
    917.9804'52—dc21   2001030266
                                                                          CIP